SYLVANIA SYSTEMS GROUP-MAIN LIBRARY

Pg 54
The Job

SYLVANIA SYSTEMS GROUP-MAIN LIBRARY

D1505942

The Software
Development Project

The Software Development Project

PLANNING AND MANAGEMENT

PHILLIP BRUCE

ONEF, Incorporated
Manhattan Beach, California

SAM M. PEDERSON

Space Applications Corporation
Irvine, California

A Wiley-Interscience Publication

JOHN WILEY AND SONS

New York • Chichester • Brisbane • Toronto • Singapore

Copyright © 1982 by John Wiley & Sons, Inc.

All rights reserved. Published simultaneously in Canada.

Reproduction or translation of any part of this work
beyond that permitted by Sections 107 or 108 of the
1976 United States Copyright Act without the permission
of the copyright owner is unlawful. Requests for
permission or further information should be addressed to
the Permissions Department, John Wiley & Sons, Inc.

Library of Congress Cataloging in Publication Data:

Bruce, Phillip, 1942–
  The software development project.

  "A Wiley-Interscience publication."
  Includes index.
  1. Computer programming management. I. Pederson,
Sam M., 1943–   II. Title.

QA76.6.B774   658′.05   81–10457
ISBN 0–471–06269–3   AACR2

Printed in the United States of America

10 9 8 7 6 5 4 3

To

Kate and Mary Lou

Preface

We were tempted to follow the current trend and open this book with an apt quotation from Aristotle explaining exactly what the book is about. After arduous research, however, we are convinced that Aristotle never considered the planning and management of a software development project. At times, those of us who work on such projects in the real world are convinced that no one else has either.

Software development techniques, such as structured design, design decomposition, stepwise refinement, chief programmer teams, and structured programming, have been introduced in recent years, and the field of software engineering has emerged to solve the alleged software development crisis. These techniques and the discipline of software engineering address elements of the software development process; they do not, however, consider management of the process. Similarly, there are many excellent books that describe the design process, programming techniques, documentation standards, test methods and configuration management approaches. But how should such techniques be selected, implemented, and controlled? To avoid late delivery or a cost overrun, the methods selected to meet the needs of the project must be based on the complexity of the software, the imposed schedules, and many other developmental and operational considerations.

However, careful selection of software development techniques does not completely solve the problems of the software development project. The management approach often determines success or failure. No matter how sophisticated the design and programming techniques may be, a systematic approach to project management is necessary for success—but does not guarantee it. The software project management approach described in this book provides the framework within which the project manager can maximize the chances for project success.

In this book we present the software project manager, the software analyst, the programmer, and the computer science student with a structured approach to software project management—a road map from initial planning to delivery. We provide (1) an overview of the software development process, (2) a software project planning methodology, (3) software pricing information, (4) software management checklists for various milestones in the development process, (5) software documentation guidelines, (6) project organization options, (7) review and audit guidelines, and (8) configuration management techniques.

We describe the process by which software development resources and costs may be estimated, and we present a management perspective of software development activities from project start-up to delivery. Internal project sales strategies or competitive proposal strategies are not addressed. However, the project management information, the development approach, and the graphics provided are extremely useful in preparing successful proposals.

For students we provide an overview of the software development process. For software project managers, analysts, and programmers involved in the development of deliverable software, we provide a reference manual, a series of checklists, and a project plan. The software project management approach presented is compatible with the latest software engineering concepts. It applies equally well to commercial and scientific software projects, whether in the industrial or government sector.

This book represents the product of over thirty years of software project development and management experience acquired by the authors in both development and management positions. Their experience includes small computer programs of a few hundred lines of code; multimillion-dollar command and control software systems; spacecraft on-board microprocessor software; large analysis tools; and commercial data management, inventory, and accounting software. The techniques and concepts presented have evolved from the early project experiences of the

vii

authors to a systematic, structured management approach not fundamentally different from that developed for hardware project management, but tailored to the particular problems of *the software development project.*

We are indebted to Kate Bruce for her contributions to the testing process discussion and her helpful advice on the software development process. Our sincere appreciation goes to Ann Snyder for her hours at the keyboard.

PHILLIP BRUCE
SAM PEDERSON

Manhattan Beach, California
Irvine, California
October 1981

Contents

The Software
Development Project

chapter one

Introduction

The Software Development Project: Planning and Management provides practical guidelines and procedures for planning, managing, and developing software and for controlling the configuration of the developed product and its documentation. These guidelines and procedures are structured to (1) meet the management requirements imposed on the project by the customer, ultimate user, or upper management, (2) increase the efficiency of the software development process, and (3) provide the project manager with tools for helping the product developers and for gaining insight into the true status of *cost, schedule,* and *technical validity* of the project.

1.1 WHAT SOFTWARE IS ADDRESSED IN THIS BOOK?

Much of the groundwork on which the material in this book is based was developed in large-scale government-related software development efforts. In Appendix A we have provided cross-reference material relating the documentation standards defined in this book to various military standards. Most companies developing software in this area have tended to extend the basic concepts of the phased, formal development cycle to all software development for external customers. In general, the business computing software development discipline has lagged behind in setting rigorous planning and management standards.

The central theme of this book is that *all software projects*—simple or complex, a one-person 2-week or a 200-person multi-year effort, for external customers or for internal use only, commercial or scientific, in industry or in government—*should be planned and managed along structured guidelines.* The key for adapting the concepts in this book to a particular project is the *Project Plan.* This may be a simple memorandum for an internal 2-week project or, for a large project, a formal several hundred-page document. Such basic concepts as requirements reviews, design reviews, test plan and procedures reviews, configuration control,

and interface control transcend project size or type of software application.

1.2 WHAT IS IN THE BOOK?

The major objectives in defining the guidelines and procedures for the planning and management of software development projects are:

1 Defining the process and techniques to be used by project and software managers to plan, manage, and develop software.
2 Providing guidelines for all activities essential to the software development process.
3 Providing a baseline of uniform design and management practices.
4 Providing a method for maintaining continuity between projects, between phases of the same project, and through changing personnel assignments.

To meet these objectives and structure the presentation of the material, the book has been divided into two major parts. Part I (Chapters 2–4) discusses software project management. It defines basic software management concepts and summarizes the software development process (which is defined in detail in Part II). It provides a management overview useful to project managers, corporate management, and proposal teams.

Part II (Chapters 5–9) provides detailed information to implement the methodology defined in Part I. It is oriented mainly toward the software development team, including the software manager, software engineers, programmers, and software test and quality assurance personnel. Chapters 5 through 7 describe the three phases of a software development project: the Preliminary Design Phase, the Detailed Design Phase, and the Implementation and Operation Phase. Chapter 8 describes the testing process, which is performed across the three phases of the project. Chapter 9 provides an approach to software configuration management.

Appendix A provides a correlation between the documents described in this book and two examples of military standards for the military software developer. Appendix B defines the detailed contents of the software development documents. The tear-out charts provided in Appendix C are full-size versions of selected figures from the text. These charts are cross-referenced to the text table of contents.

1.3   WHO SHOULD READ THIS BOOK?

This Book Is for Software Project Managers

This book is designed to serve as a handbook for those engaged in the development of computer software. The guidelines presented cover all phases of the software development process, from preproposal planning through implementation and testing.

The beginning software project manager should be able to read this book, discuss its contents and their relevance to his project with other project personnel, and use the book as a reference. The book provides readily available information about (1) how to structure the Project Plan, (2) what documents are needed, (3) what the documents should contain, (4) what to consider in costing the project, and (5) what to consider when setting up a configuration control system.

The tear-out charts are useful for quick reference and provide convenient material for management presentations on project organization and status.

This Book Is for Students and Beginning Programmers

Computer science curricula in major colleges and universities are preparing substantial numbers of people qualified in the techniques of programming. Only a short time ago industry and business were changing mathematics, business, psychology, engineering, and accounting majors into computer programmers through on-the-job training. Unfortunately, developing software in the university environment often differs from developing software in a business or industry project team environment. The projects are bigger and more complex. Technical interface with other developers, managers, and customers is required. Documentation standards are imposed. Testing is integrated, formalized, and structured. Presentations are required. Milestones are imposed on the development schedule. Cost is a major factor. The list goes on.

While many new graduates are able to readily integrate their basic programming and computer system skills into the software project effort, others are not.

This book is designed to acquaint new programmers with the overall problem of starting with a set of requirements for a software project and carrying the effort forward through all phases of development until the final software product is operational. It will acquaint the new programmer with the project phases and management structure within which he will work, to which he must contribute, and from which he will learn to draw support.

This Book Is for Corporate Management

A major problem facing corporate software development managers is gaining insight into the progress and problems of each software development effort. The "we're 95% done" syndrome has driven many high-level managers of software systems organizations into farming.

A corporate manager has three major uses for this book. First, if the manager does not have a background in software development, he should read this book to generate a basic understanding of the software process. He should then use the book to provide checklists that will enable him to evaluate the content and depth of the material presented at each stage of a software development effort. Third, and perhaps most important, he should be sure that his standards for doing business in the software development area include the concepts in this book. If not, he should consider reviewing his software development standards or generating new standards to cover at least the critical planning and management concepts.

This Book Is for Project Planners

For many software development projects success or failure is determined before the first project meeting is held, the first word is written, or the first line of code has been developed. Hundreds of seemingly achievable projects have been doomed to failure from the start because of unrealistic schedules, impossible cost constraints, or, most commonly, ill-defined requirements.

This book will assist the project planner in realistically evaluating the work to be done and assist him in costing all the aspects of the software development cycle. We are not promising to provide still another inaccurate formula for software costing, although we do identify the major costing considerations. The material presented provides sufficient detail to cost and schedule a software development project. It identifies the major cost impacts on the project imposed by the unique circumstances, which must be recognized before the project is begun.

The project planner should also give careful consideration to the definition of system requirements, the derivation of associated software requirements, and the traceability of requirements. An understanding of the process of developing software requirements is essential. Deriving the requirements is necessary—and a first-level attempt at allocating design requirements is desireable—for accurate software project cost and schedule planning.

part one

Software Project Management

A software development project is defined as a *planned undertaking that is to result in producing one or more computer programs with specified functional capabilities.* These programs are to be developed in accordance with a defined schedule and within the planned resource budgets: staff support; computer time; computer capacities in terms of throughput, memory, and peripheral storage; and funding constraints. It is important to note at the outset that neither the size nor the specified cost of the software should preclude its development from being subject to established, planned development procedures. The management of these procedures is the subject of Part I of this book.

chapter two
Software Development Overview

The purpose of this chapter is to lay the foundation for effective management of a software development project by providing an overview of the process. The process begins with system requirements analysis, during which system requirements are allocated to hardware, firmware, and software subsystems. The development process concludes when the subsystems have been tested, demonstrating compliance with system requirements, and installed ready for operation. Installation and operation activities follow the testing of the hardware and software and subsequent integration to form a subsegment, segment, and; finally, the complete system. An orderly and structured approach to software development accomplishes the following:

1 Improves the probability of success.
2 Promotes customer confidence by providing a planned approach to software management.
3 Provides visibility for customer and management through standard development documentation and milestones.
4 Defines organizational responsibilities.
5 Improves software design and development cost estimating.
6 Reduces the cost of software development.
7 Improves software quality.
8 Educates the non-software engineering support personnel about the software development process.
9 Provides a data source for future proposal preparation and project planning.

2.1 WHAT IS A SOFTWARE SUBSYSTEM?

We have attempted to be consistent when we speak of systems, software subsystems, computer programs, etc. Software, as part of a system, may consist of one or more software subsystems. The position or level of the software subsystems in a system hierarchy is shown in

Figure 2.1. A computer program may be a part of a deliverable software configuration item (such as a software subsystem) or it may be the deliverable configuration item. A computer program is defined as a series of instructions or statements, in a form acceptable to a computer, designed to cause the computer to execute an operation or series of operations. A subsystem may be a collection of computer programs designed to accomplish a major computing task. A software subsystem is an organization of lower-level elements. A computer program that is a contract end item is often called a computer program configuration item (CPCI). These are shown in Figure 2.2. In a complex computer program an assembly of subordinate elements, called modules, is distinguished for convenience in specifying requirements and designing. This optional level—a logical grouping of tasks or functions within the computer

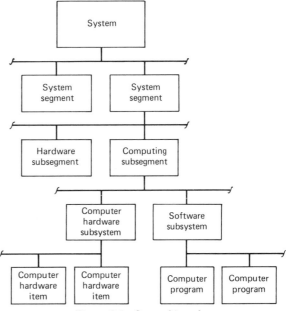

Figure 2.1 System hierarchy.

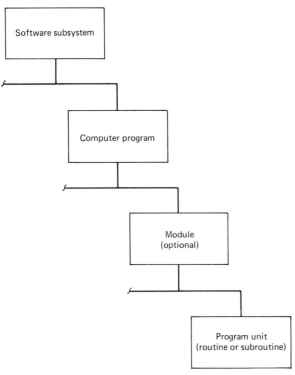

Figure 2.2 Software subsystem hierarchy.

program—may consist of one or more program units (often called routines or subroutines). The program unit is the lowest compilable element. It is the lowest level of software identification and the level at which change control is applied. The terminology defined in these figures is used throughout this book in defining the software development methodology.

2.2 DEVELOPMENT CONCEPT

Software development proceeds through three phases: Preliminary Design, Detailed Design, and Implementation and Operation. Each of these phases consists of a series of distinct steps as shown in Figure 2.3.

Historically, it has been very difficult for project management to determine the status of the development activities. Often five or six development steps are completed and three fourths of the calendar time and budget is expended before any proof of progress or quality is shown. To provide early management visibility, the software development methodology illustrated in Figure 2.3 utilizes a baseline control concept. First, during the Preliminary Design Phase, requirements analysis tasks are performed to establish a requirements baseline. This is later used to measure and validate the design products. The requirements are then analyzed and allocated to functional software areas, such as com-

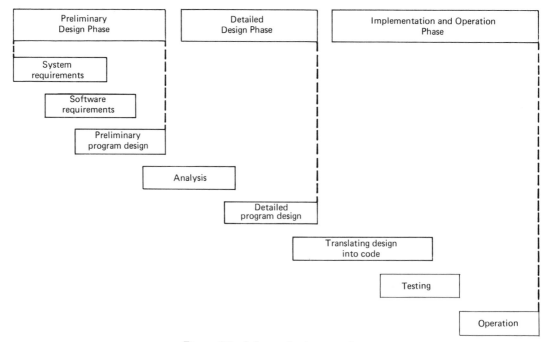

Figure 2.3 Software development phases.

puter programs and modules. This results in a preliminary design—also produced in the first phase—which reflects all the requirements and provides the baseline for the Detailed Design Phase.

Further analysis and design work on the approved preliminary design baseline results in the detailed design, which forms the baseline for the Implementation and Operation Phase. During this last phase the actual coding and testing activities occur. These activities are controlled through development and test baselines of physical code, programmer documentation, and test data and procedures. After the software is put into the operational environment the operations and maintenance activities are controlled through version baselines, consisting of specific releases of the software, formal documentation, and test procedures and results. Each baseline is documented and formally reviewed by the development personnel, other project personnel, company experts and, in most cases, customer and user personnel. These documents and reviews provide critical, measurable milestones during the entire software development process.

The software development concept incorporates configuration management elements, including configuration identification, change control, and status accounting. It also requires specific project programming standards and conventions and consideration of automated tools for development, test, and configuration management.

Each project requiring the development of deliverable computer programs should include a software development Project Plan for internal as well as customer review and approval. This plan should define at least the following:

1 Concise project summary.
2 List of discrete milestones.
3 Work breakdown structure (WBS).
4 Activity network.
5 Detailed budget and schedule.
6 Interface definition and control plan.
7 Documentation plan.
8 Cost and schedule management plan.
9 Configuration management plan.
10 Review and audit plan.
11 Identification of key personnel and responsibilities.

The above items may include brief summaries and references to sections of a company software standard for additional material. Specific information related to the project organization, system definition, and unique customer or system requirements should be explicitly included in the software development Project Plan. In addition, exceptions should be noted and approved for all items whose approach differs from the specified company standard.

2.3 CONCEPT IMPLEMENTATION

The software development concept illustrated in Figure 2.3 divides the development process into three phases. Implementation of this concept involves a further breakdown into tasks with well-defined products and reviews. Figure 2.4 identifies these products (documents) and reviews on the same task timeline as shown in Figure 2.3.

2.3.1 Documentation

The software development project must produce and maintain a minimum set of software documents in order to satisfy contract requirements and software development procedures. These documents are necessary design and planning tools for disciplined and successful software development. The following subjects must be addressed by formal software documentation:

1 Software requirements.
2 Software design.
3 Plans for test and acceptance of the software.
4 Plans for quality assurance and configuration management of the software.
5 Description of the operational use of the software.

Document content and format must satisfy contract requirements and/or applicable company software development policies; it should be appropriate to customer, user, and project needs (e.g., it is possible that a two-page interoffice memorandum may satisfy the requirements for a particular document). Documents should be organized and bound into volumes that are consistent with contract requirements and customer, user, and project needs.

The formal software documentation provides the project manager, upper management, and the customer with insight into the development status. Therefore, it is important to prepare timely documents and not to allow slippage of the formal documentation in order to develop code. The documentation and its careful review can save much time, effort, and cost during testing and validation by identifying requirements and design problems prior to coding.

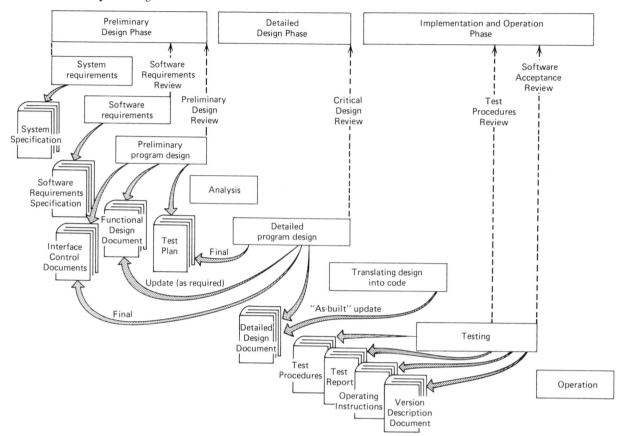

Figure 2.4 Software development products.

The following list identifies the purpose of each document in Figure 2.4:

1 Software Requirements Specification.

   (a) Provides a clear definition of the job to be done.

   (b) Allows the project manager and customer to understand what is to be done and agree on the means to do it.

   (c) Provides the customer with the option to accept or not to accept the end product(s) by means of a formal acceptance test program.

   (d) Provides the test team with the requirements that must be demonstrated.

   (e) Must be approved in writing by the customer. Ideally, once approved, the requirements do not change. If requirements changes are necessary, the impact must be evaluated and the contract changed accordingly.

2 Software Functional Design and Detailed Design Documents.

   (a) Provide the project manager and customer with the assurance that the software end products have been systematically defined and designed.

   (b) Enable the managers (and customer) to compare the code with the design and to understand project progress.

   (c) Are approved by the project manager and are the basis for customer reviews.

   (d) Are updated after completion of testing to reflect the "as-built" software product configuration. The updated documents provide the basis for delivery and subsequent software maintenance.

3 Interface Control Documents.

   (a) Provide the project manager, the customer, and other development organizations with a means to establish and control interface requirements and design.

   (b) Establish responsibility between organizations or contractors for the requirements and design of specific interfaces.

4 Software Test Plans, Procedures and Reports.

(a) Provide the project manager and customer with the assurance that the software is being tested at all levels.

(b) Enable managers of individual designers to determine that the designers understand the test requirements.

(c) Provide the basis for low-level design and test reviews. The lowest-level Software Test Plans and Procedures are usually nondeliverable; they require the approval of the work package manager and are updated as required.

(d) Provide a definition for higher-level module integration, verification, and acceptance tests.

5 Operating Instructions.

(a) Provide the project manager and customer with the assurance that the ultimate users will have the necessary instructions to operate the deliverable software system.

(b) Provide for customer commitment to the design of the man/machine interface by delivering an early version for review with the detailed software design.

6 Version Description Document.

(a) Provides a definition of each delivered software version.

(b) Provides pertinent data about the status and usage of the delivered software.

2.3.2 Reviews

Periodic reviews of various events and milestones in the software development phases are crucial to management visibility and successful product development. There are both formal and informal reviews, as required. Each review serves a different purpose. Some reviews are held to achieve written agreement with the customer, others to provide interface insight into other design and development efforts, and still others to provide the designers with supervisory experience or to enable them to review the design with other software personnel.

Reviews covering the following primary software development products must be planned and conducted:

1 *Software Requirements.* The review covering software requirements is usually referred to as the Software Requirements Review, or SRR. It is held

after the system-level requirements review for systems in which software is one element of a larger system.

2 *Software Design Approach and Interfaces.* The review of software design concepts and preliminary design for most government- or military-sponsored developments occurs at a meeting called the Preliminary Design Review (PDR) or, for some customers, the Initial Design Review (IDR). In this book PDR will be used.

3 *Software Detailed Design.* The review covering the detailed software design is usually referred to as the Critical Design Review (CDR) or, for some customers, the Detailed Design Review (DDR). In this book CDR will be used. Review of the detailed design at the program-unit level may be performed at Internal Design Reviews. These reviews are used mainly for large projects where the level of detail cannot be reviewed at CDR.

4 *Software Test Plans and Procedures.* Test plans are usually reviewed at PDR and CDR, as described in the review descriptions below. Test procedures are reviewed at the Test Procedures Review (TPR).

5 *Final Software Products.* The review of software product delivery is identified as the Software Acceptance Review (SAR).

Figures 2.5 and 2.6 summarize these reviews and documents. Reviews are the primary formal milestones that give company management and customer personnel visibility into the technical and administrative status of the project. They provide checkpoints on the progress of the primary software development products. The following paragraphs summarize the requirements for each of these checkpoints (reviews) from the project manager's perspective. Detailed descriptions of each review and the associated documents are provided in Chapters 5–8.

Software Requirements Review (SRR)

After preparation of the Software Requirements Specification and prior to the Preliminary Design Review, a Software Requirements Review (SRR) is conducted for the purpose of achieving formal concurrence with the customer on the provisions of the Software Requirements Specification. The requirements specified in this document will be the basis for software end-product acceptance. In preparation for this review project personnel must (1) analyze and evaluate the software requirements, (2) produce a Software Requirements Specification consistent with the technical and contractual constraints of the project, and (3)

Name	Purpose	Materials Reviewed
SRR (Software Requirements Review)	Verify software requirements	Software Requirements Specification
PDR (Preliminary Design Review)	Verify design approach and interfaces	Functional Design Document Interface Control Documents (requirements and preliminary design sections) Test Plan (preliminary)
CDR (Critical Design Review)	Verify detailed design and test plan	Detailed Design Document Interface Control Documents (final) Test Plan
TPR (Test Procedures Review)	Verify test procedures	Test Plan Test Procedures

SAR (Software Acceptance Review)	Verify test results and completed product (code and documentation)	Test Procedures
		 Test Report
		 Operating Instructions
		 Version Description Document
		 "As-Built" Updates
		     Functional Design Document
		     Detailed Design Document

Figure 2.5 Software development reviews.

develop a response to each problem identified in the customer specification review comments, which should be received prior to the SRR. The SRR must include both project-generated and customer-generated requirements and respond to all specification review comments.

Preliminary Design Review

After approval of the Software Requirements Specification, project personnel must perform design and planning activities to establish a preliminary software design baseline and document that baseline in a Functional (or Preliminary) Design Specification. The implementation and test plans necessary to proceed with the detailed design and development are also prepared. The preliminary design, associated plans, and any technical and/or contractual issues are reviewed at the Preliminary Design Review (PDR). Its purpose is to assess the adequacy of the designs and plans, resolve identified issues, and obtain a mutual commitment to proceed to the next (detailed) design phase. The PDR enables the customer to verify that all requirements are addressed and authorize the project to proceed with the detailed design.

At the PDR the Software Test Plan is reviewed for the purpose of achieving written agreement with the customer. The completion of the test program, as defined in the Test Plan, will result in customer acceptance of the software products. Often a subset of the formally defined tests will be identified as demonstration or acceptance tests. The customer then agrees that successful execution of these tests in a manner described in the plan will result in customer acceptance of the software. Once approved, this subset of the test cases, called the acceptance test plan, should be modified only to incorporate changes approved in writing by both the project manager and the customer.

If a set of tests is identified for acceptance, the review should assure that the Test Plan:

1 Describes how the acceptance testing relates to other project testing.
2 Defines the criteria by which the software system will be judged ready for acceptance testing.
3 Identifies the acceptance test requirements for software end products and top-level acceptance criteria.
4 Describes the data base for acceptance testing and the plan for obtaining the data values, validating them, and obtaining customer approval prior to the start of acceptance testing.
5 Identifies the support software to be used in acceptance testing and the project's plan for obtaining and validating the software prior to the start of acceptance testing.

For software projects operating under government software development standards, such as Military Stan-

Document	Purpose	Review	Control[a]	Remarks
Software Requirements Specification	Establish software requirements to provide basis for design	SRR PDR	Class II Class I	
Functional Design Document	Establish a software functional design that satisfies specified requirements	PDR CDR SAR	Class II Class II Class I	 "As-built" update
Interface Control Documents	Establish concurrence on interface requirements and design	SRR PDR CDR	Class II Class I/II Class I	{ I: Requirements { II: Design
Test Plan	Establish testing required to verify the software	PDR CDR	Project Class I	
Test Procedures	Establish procedures for test conduct	TPR SAR	Class II Class II	
Test Report	Document the test results	SAR	Class II	
Detailed Design Document	Provide complete software design	CDR SAR	Class II Class I	 "As-built" update
Operating Instructions	Describe procedures for operating the software	SAR	Class II	Update as required
Version Description Document	Describe content and capability of delivered software version	SAR	Class II	Update with each version delivery

[a]Class I changes require formal customer approval and Class II changes require project approval (see Chapter 9).

Figure 2.6   Software development documentation.

dard 483 and 490, the functions of the SRR and PDR are often combined. This is particularly common for projects in which the software development effort is not a part of a larger system. In such cases the requirements specification may be a customer-produced document or the product of an earlier study and is the document against which the software contract is written. The product reviewed at PDR is then a detailed statement of requirements and a functional definition of the software similar to that defined in this book for the Functional Design Document. The requirements are reviewed during the first part of PDR, and the preliminary design is presented during the last part of the review. The relationship between documentation required to meet military/government standards and the documents described in this book is presented in Appendix A.

Critical Design Review
After preparation of the Detailed Design Specification, a Critical Design Review (CDR) of the design, and the test plan should be conducted before proceeding to the coding phase. The detailed design, its specification, associated plans, and any critical issues are reviewed at CDR to (1) agree on the adequacy of the detailed design and plans, (2) resolve issues, (3) obtain management and customer approval to proceed to the coding phase, and (4) obtain approval of the test program supporting product acceptance. The major difference between PDR and CDR is the level of design and test information presented and reviewed.

Internal Software Design Reviews
Prior to CDR the project may periodically conduct informal software design reviews at the unit or subroutine level to facilitate the early detection of design errors. Some guidelines for these design reviews are:

1   The design review should be conducted at the unit level as the design of each unit is completed.
2   The review team should consist of from one to four people, primarily at the designer/programmer/tester level. It is desirable, but not mandatory, that

the eventual programmer(s) and tester(s) of the program unit be members of the review team.

3 The scope of the reviews should include, as a minimum, checks for responsiveness of design to requirements, completeness and consistency of design, flow of data through input/output interfaces, testability, and other appropriate criteria such as error recovery procedures, modularity, and simplicity.

4 Problems detected during the design review of a unit should be identified in a written summary and made available to the unit developer.

Test Procedures Review

The project personnel should conduct detailed development and verification Test Procedures Reviews to assure thorough testing of the software product. The purpose of these reviews is to provide formal approval for the procedures to be used in the software test program and to assure that they accomplish the intent of the Test Plan. The Test Plan is reviewed at CDR to assure that all significant design features are tested and that all specification requirements are verified.

Two series of Test Procedures Reviews should be conducted: *Development Test Procedures Reviews and Validation Test Procedures Reviews.* These should be conducted separately. Development Test Procedures Reviews should be conducted before module integration testing. Validation Test Procedures Reviews should be conducted before verification and acceptance testing.

Verification tests are conducted to ensure that the individual software elements perform as designed and that interface errors between them have been eliminated. Acceptance tests are conducted to ensure that the completed computer program or software subsystem satisfies its stated performance requirements. Thus, verification tests evaluate the software against its design documentation (Functional Design and Detailed Design Documents), while acceptance tests evaluate the software against the requirements in the Software Requirements Specification.

Software Acceptance Review

The Software Acceptance Review is a formal contractor/customer meeting held to audit the software product prior to customer acceptance. Completion of this audit signifies that the software is ready for operation and that the development phase is completed. The review normally consists of two audits, a Functional Configuration Audit (FCA) and a Physical Configuration Audit (PCA). These two audits may be conducted

incrementally as the necessary information becomes available. If they are conducted incrementally, most review items will be a matter of record at the time of the formal meetings. The SAR will then consist largely of examination of the records to ensure that all audit items have been completed.

The objective of the FCA is to *verify that the software performance complies with the software specification performance requirements.* This is accomplished by reviewing the test data accumulated during software testing.

The PCA is conducted prior to software delivery. It consists of an examination of the detailed design documentation against the "as-built" software configuration. It is conducted to *ensure the adequacy, completeness, and accuracy of the technical design documentation.* The review also includes an audit of the current change status, change records, and version description records to ensure that the "as-built" configuration is compatible with the released documents.

2.3.3 Configuration Control

The software development project manager must provide proper configuration control for the development effort. Configuration control standards are described in Chapter 9. Appropriate standards must be adopted by the project manager and the resulting configuration management implementation plan must be documented and summarized as part of the Project Plan. Each project will have some unique configuration control requirements. However, all projects should be required to meet minimum configuration control standards.

Organizational configuration management responsibilities are discussed in Section 4.2. Some configuration control functions are performed at practically every level of the development project. The project manager must ensure that these functions are properly performed. This management task is a key aid in understanding the status of the development project. In most cases the project manager will have final configuration control approval authority.

2.3.4 Standards and Conventions

At the beginning of the project the project manager must define the standards and conventions to be used. The implementation and adaptation of the standards and conventions must be documented in the Project Plan. The standards must be adhered to in the absence of conflicting customer requirements. Any deviations from company or customer standards must be documented in the Project Plan, together with a suitable justification.

The project manager's responsibility is to ensure that the standards and conventions are followed. The necessary reviews required to perform this management task help the project manager to understand the status of his development project.

chapter three

Planning the Project

The software development project can be likened to a house construction project. The probability of the project's success is directly proportional to the care taken in planning, designing, selecting contractors, monitoring construction, and reviewing the product before acceptance.

This chapter addresses the planning of the software project. It covers the tasks to be accomplished before the project's technical staff is authorized, through the standard company work authorization process, to proceed. The functions described are analogous to: (1) deciding whether a house should have three or four bedrooms, a single or double garage, a family room or a den, and deciding how large the house should be (here the budget starts to constrain the imagination); (2) preparing the design concept (modern, English Tudor, colonial, or a replica of an existing house); (3) preparing preliminary layouts, including house setback from the street and lot lines, and selection of a basic outside design consistent with initial sizing decisions and local zoning ordinances. At this point the analogy breaks down. The next steps for the house would be to prepare the detailed blueprints for customer approval, get city and county approval, then get bids from a contractor. Software is usually bid from the top-level blueprint, and the job of the developer is to prepare the detailed blueprint and build according to it. Perhaps the software industry could learn something from the construction industry.

When building a house one must first understand the process involved: the steps, regulations, required inspections, and so on. One must also understand construction cost estimating, planning, scheduling, and contracting. The same functions are involved in managing a software project; they must be well understood if the project is to succeed. We will first discuss cost estimating approaches, then outline the Project Plan (describe how the project should be planned and organized).

3.1 THE COST ESTIMATE

The most common failings of a software development effort are inconsistent and incomplete specification of system requirements and poor translation of these requirements into estimates of cost, schedule, and computer hardware required to develop and support the system. Yet, less effort is often devoted to the initial requirements definition, costing, and scheduling of a project than to any other part of the development cycle. As a result, countless software projects suffer large cost and schedule overruns, to the point that a prevailing rule of thumb is to double any initial software cost estimate.

The intent of this chapter is to provide a better understanding of the primary software cost considerations and the process by which the cost of developing software can be more precisely estimated. The multiply by 2 rule, when applied to competitive software procurements, does very poorly in the negotiating process. With the proliferation of more rigorous, planned costing activities, this crude estimating rule will be quickly replaced. The newer approaches are more precise and provide more credible support data.

In the following description of cost estimating, we will first examine the many considerations that impact the ultimate cost of developed software. Then the supporting data and tools that aid the estimating process will be discussed, followed by a summary of various costing models and their applicability to various types of software tasks. Lastly, the cost-estimating sequence will be described.

3.1.1 Cost Considerations

The process of estimating software development costs is a complex task requiring a detailed understanding of various factors that impact these costs. There is no simple approach or algorithm that will provide a cost estimate to within 10, 20, or even 40%.

Estimating software development costs involves two major problems. One problem is the high level of risk and uncertainty in the estimate. The risk and uncertainty are basically attributable to three factors: (1) requirements are subject to change, (2) innovation may be required during the development process, and (3) risks are inherent in the software development process, since errors, which may cause iteration over prior activities, are inevitable.

Each of these factors tends to increase software development costs. Good software cost estimating involves working from firm requirements, understanding the required product well, and carefully managing the development cycle to ensure that coding does not begin before the software design has been thoroughly worked out, verified, and validated.

The second major problem in estimating software development costs is the lack of accurate measures of prior costs—the lack of a *quantitative historical cost data base.* Without reference standards it is nearly impossible to accurately estimate the cost of a new project. The available information usually is not organized or disseminated at the proper level needed for estimation. This problem can be solved only by proper cost summaries archived and disseminated by the project manager of each development effort. The procedure for providing the historical record should be the final step in the overall Project Plan. This step should involve documenting and making available to the appropriate personnel the information identified in Section 4.5.

Numerous factors influence the cost of a software development project and each should be evaluated during cost estimation to ensure that proper weighting is applied to the cost estimates. The relationship between some of the key factors (divided into four categories) and software development costs is summarized in Figure 3.1. The following paragraphs define the four categories and discuss the factors within each category.

Requirement Factors

As stated earlier, one area of concern is the uncertainty in what is being estimated. How well are the software requirements defined? Two factors that can have a major impact on the ultimate cost of a software product are (1) the quality of the specifications and (2) the stability of the requirements.

Quality of Specifications.   A good definition of requirements (and their documentation in a Software Requirements Specification) is the cornerstone of a well-defined, well-understood, and well-costed software development. Incomplete requirements definition is a major cause of cost overruns. The developer interprets the vague, poorly written requirements, prices the software package on the basis of that interpretation, and proceeds to design software on the same basis. Too often it is late in the Detailed Design Phase or, worse yet, during testing or the acceptance demonstration that the customer or user realizes that the software does not have the displays, the interactive menu selection capabilities, the data base default capabilities, the

temporary override capability, and the set of control options that he had in mind (not to mention the data reduction features, formatted report writing capabilities, and generalized date base retrieval features specified in the requirements specification).

The extra effort spent firming up the requirements before the Detailed Design Phase begins is one of the keys to successful project management. It is also a key to accurate software costing. Understanding the requirements is the first step in the software costing process (described in Section 3.1.3). It is the basis for the analysis of many other costing factors, including difficulty, interfaces, size, tools, use of existing software, and data base complexity. Cost overruns are often blamed on other factors, such as poor estimates of software size or data base complexity, when the actual reason for errors in these estimates is incomplete or inadequate specification of requirements at the outset of the initial software costing.

While too little detail in the requirements specification leads to ambiguities in interpretation, too much detail usually results in specification of a design, rather than just the functional and performance requirements. This leads to unnecessary constraints on the developer and shifts greater design responsibility to the customer. If the design is later found to be inadequate, the redesign must be paid for by the customer, since the original design was specified as a requirement.

Stability of Requirements.   The availability of a good requirements specification does not assure a successful project. For many projects the well-specified requirements against which the detailed design is prepared change during the project. This is particularly true for internal company software projects and is often the source of considerable criticism of the software organization by upper management. The project was approved on the basis of an estimated cost and schedule. If the cost goals and schedule objectives are revised when requirements changes are suggested, this problem can be avoided. The responsibility of the project manager is to understand the software requirements and to point out that changes in the requirements baseline are *changes.* The project manager should then define the cost and/or schedule impact so that the change can be given a fair evaluation. If the change justifies the estimated impact on the project, a decision may be made to incorporate it. The change can then be reflected in the requirements specification and incorporated into the design; its impact is reflected in the project budget and schedule. Many changes lose their urgency when their impact on the project is known. This mechanism, properly used, helps reduce the changes to the necessary requirements and elimi-

Category	Factor	Cost Relationship	Notes
1) Requirements	a) Quality of Specs	Subjective	Rated as highest impact.
	b) Stability	Subjective	Rated as highest impact.
2) Product	a) Size	Linear, modified by other factors *Cost vs. Size graph: Management support manpower, Technical manpower*	
	b) Difficulty	*Productivity vs. Difficulty graph (decreasing line)*	Type of System: Scientific. Business. Operating System Type of Function: Real Time. I/O. Algorithms Rating: Easy, medium, hard Heritage: Adaptation, modification, new
	c) Reliability Requirements	*Test cost / Total cost vs. error criticality graph: .40, .15, Noncritical errors, Catastrophic errors*	Offers cost tradeoff. Trades testing costs for maintenance costs. Subjective parameter.
	d) External Interfaces	*Cost vs. External interface complexity graph*	Especially beware of special purpose hardware interfaces and sophisticated user interfaces (e.g., terminal user protocol).
	e) Language Requirements	Machine language > HOL	
	f) Documentation Requirements	2–5 pages per man-day or $50–150 per non-automated page or approximately 10% of total cost	Estimate total pages. Clerical support. Reproduction costs.
3) Process	a) Management Structure	Cost add-ons for higher level managers.	Direct charges for line managers—function of company policy and management organization.
	b) Management Controls	Cost add-ons for directly charged management control support.	e.g., management information processing, scheduling support, administrative support, etc.
	c) Development Methods	Systematic approaches cheaper.	Cost of unstructured programming > Cost of structured programming. Subjective.

Figure 3.1 Cost factors and relationships.

Category	Factor	Cost Relationship	Notes
3) Process (Continued)	d) Tools	Cost vs. Support software maturity	Costs sometimes significantly increased if compilers, assemblers, data base management systems, test tools and other support software must be developed.
	e) Available Software	Cheaper to modify old code . . . to a point!	Cost of new software > Cost of modifying software
	f) Data Base	Cost vs. Data base structure complexity	Cost to produce data base can be significant.
4) Resources	a) Number of People	Productivity vs. Number of people	$\dfrac{N(N-1)}{2}$ Potential paths of communication.
	b) Experience of People	No good correlation between experience level and productivity.	Specific experience in similar problem or machine or operating system is exception.
	c) Personnel Performance	Approximately 10:1 performance variability.	Flexibility of corporate personnel policies important.
	d) Availability of Computing Resources	Use of computer time vs. Elapsed time (Design, Code, Test)	Unavailability affects schedule and, hence, manpower loading. Linear relationship between turnaround time and testing costs. Consider system reliability and maintenance.
	e) Suitability of Computer Resources	Cost vs. % Utilization of speed and memory capacity	Asymptotic as approach full capacity. Consider at machine selection time to reduce software costs. 50–75% utilization = 1.5 × cost. 90% utilization = 3 × cost. Also consider representativeness of development environment with respect to installation system.

Figure 3.1 *(continued)*

Category	Factor	Cost Relationship	Notes
4) Resources (Continued)	f) Project Elapsed Time	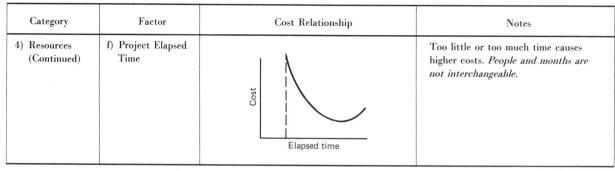	Too little or too much time causes higher costs. *People and months are not interchangeable.*

Figure 3.1   *(continued)*

nates the "desirements" of individuals in the customer organization. A Configuration Control Board is the formal mechanism by which these evaluations are made (Chapter 9).

The impact of such requirements changes need not be the concern of the cost estimator, provided the company and the selected project manager approach all changes as described above. However, the estimator must realize that there will be some changes in requirements. Consideration should be given to the level of change activity expected when determining the contract provisions necessary for initiating and processing changes and when selecting the contract type (i.e., fixed price or cost reimbursement). The cost estimator should understand the project costs associated with the contract change provisions, and the project manager must know which changes are within the scope of the contract and which are not.

Product Factors

The second category of factors that influence costing includes those factors derived from the characteristics of the software product to be developed and delivered, including both code and documentation. To evaluate these factors the software requirements must be analyzed and a functional definition of the software prepared. From this definition the data necessary to evaluate the six product factors can be derived. These factors are discussed below.

Software Size.   One of the most common methods of software costing is to estimate the number of instructions to be developed and multiply by a magic number (dollars per instruction) to get the estimated development cost. This is not a very precise estimating technique when used alone, but in conjunction with the other factors it can be very useful.

Many feel that estimating the size of the software is one of the greatest sources of error in the cost-estimat-

ing process. For this reason, our proposed costing procedure in Section 3.1.3 emphasizes software decomposition as an aid to the size-estimating process. Reduce the estimating task to a large number of more precise estimates rather than a single guess.

The significant sizing considerations are the following:

1   Care must be taken to isolate the deliverable software from the nondeliverable test software, simulations, and support software, which should be less costly to produce. The documentation requirements for nondeliverable software are less formal, and the customer may be less interested in the detailed technical aspects of these software elements.

2   Although it is generally agreed that the size of the software is linearly related to cost, other factors, such as complexity, interfaces, and the number of people involved, begin to have greater influence on cost as the size increases.

3   When trying to use size as a costing parameter, care must be taken that the cost base being used is derived from the same sizing parameter. Projects or companies may track costs by lines of code, number of object instructions, number of executable source statements (exclusive of data and comment statements), total instructions or lines of code developed, or delivered instructions or lines of code.

4   When using sizing cost factors, consideration should also be given to productivity differences between languages. For example, not all HOLs (High Order Languages) can be used with the same facility for all applications.

5   When object code sizing estimates are based on similar existing software, consideration should be given to differences in the expansion ratio from source to object instructions between different HOLs, compilers for the same HOL, or different operating systems.

6 As size increases, the number of individuals involved in the development increases and the amount of time spent in intercommunication and coordination becomes significant, driving the cost versus size from linear toward some higher multiple. In his book, *The Mythical Manmonth* (Addison Wesley Publishing Co., 1975), Brooks states that this increase is equal to $n\,(n-1)/2$, where n is the number of separate tasks to be coordinated. He points out that excessive partitioning in large systems may cause the communications effort to dominate to the extent that increasing the project staff can lengthen, not shorten, the schedule (i.e., increase the cost).

Difficulty. The relative difficulty of a software application is one of the more important factors affecting development costs. Software personnel productivity (i.e., cost) varies with the type of system being developed. Some types of applications tend to be more difficult than others. For example, operating systems tend to be two or three times as difficult as applications or utility software.

The type of software function, such as real-time, input/output, batch, or computational, also significantly influences development difficulty. Real-time applications are generally considered to cost up to five times as much as HOL nonreal-time applications.

After considering the relative difficulty of various software systems and functions, the cost estimator must consider the difficulty of the specific application and its heritage to complete the analysis of the difficulty factor. Heritage incorporates the cost difference between developing new software and modifying or adapting existing software.

Reliability Requirements. Reliability requirements determine the thoroughness of testing needed before software can be used in the intended operational environment. For software in which errors can translate into catastrophic system failures or loss of human life, much more testing is required than for a program used as a study tool (for which the impact of an error is less significant). Similarly, for software which will be difficult or impossible to modify once installed in its operating environment, a much more rigorous test program is required. Therefore, while reliability is always a desirable quality, the degree necessary for success may vary with the software application. There are four major criteria for determining the reliability of a software program. It must (1) provide continuity of operation under nonnominal conditions; (2) utilize uniform design, implementation techniques, and notation; (3)

yield the required precision in calculations and outputs; and (4) be implemented in an understandable manner. An increase in the level of requirements for handling nonnominal conditions will mean an increase in the required verification effort and, therefore, the cost.

External Interfaces. The qualitative influence of interface complexity on cost is illustrated in Figure 3.1. This influence is further affected by the experience of the developer with the interfaces. New hardware interfaces or special-purpose equipment interfaces will require more design, implementation, and integration effort and, therefore, increase costs.

Language Requirements. The cost of developing a machine language program is greater than that of the same program in HOL. Maintenance of the machine language program is also generally more costly. The use of design languages has been shown to help decrease the time required in programming and to provide well-structured and documented code.

Even though a HOL statement is more powerful and therefore accomplishes more than an assembly language instruction, experience has shown that it takes an average programmer about the same amount of effort to write a line of code in High Order Language as in an assembly language. Apparently the thought process required to write a single statement is almost independent of the language in which the statement is written. It will take a programmer significantly longer to write a program in assembly language than it would to write the same program in HOL, since a typical HOL statement expands to 5–10 assembly language statements. It should be noted that early in a project a programmer's familiarity with a language will affect the cost per statement more than the language being used.

Documentation Requirements. Just as the factors of software size, difficulty, and quality of specifications must be evaluated by the cost estimator, the cost factors associated with the preparation and acceptance of required documentation must also be evaluated. Both customer-specified documentation requirements and documentation required by the project management as part of the selected development approach must be considered.

Process Factors

The software costing factors associated with the development process, such as management structure, management controls, development methods, tools, use of available software, and data base methods, are identified in Figure 3.1 and described in the following paragraphs.

Management Structure. Management structure incorporates the effects of various company policies with respect to allocating costs for certain non-project management personnel as a direct charge to projects. For companies with matrix organizations, this project charge for line management must be considered when bidding. This charge is often incorporated as a percentage of the estimated direct technical labor cost. Government cost-accounting standards often dictate acceptable charging practices in these areas.

Management Controls. As with management structure, this factor is a function of company policy. It covers the cost of project support in such areas as management information processing, scheduling support, administrative support, and clerical support. For many companies some or all of these are considered overhead functions and therefore not separately treated by the cost estimator. For other companies these items may be considered direct costs to the project. In this case the parameters used to estimate these costs will normally be based on company experience with previous projects. The estimates will normally be provided by the support organizations. However, to appropriately question the cost estimate, the software cost estimator must realize the need for this input and have some understanding of the relative magnitude of this type of project cost.

Development Methods. This factor is subjective and difficult to incorporate because of the typical shortage of comparison data. This factor attempts to quantify the impact of various development methods. It should reflect the generally accepted concept that the more systematic, structured methods cost less than some of the older, brute-force development methods. The development methods of interest include such approaches as top-down design and testing, structured programming, use of chief programmer teams, and use of structured walk-throughs. For more information on managing projects using these methods, the reader is referred to *Managing the Structured Techniques,* by Edward Youndon (Prentice-Hall, Inc., Second Edition, 1979).

Tools. With the recent growth in the number of minicomputer- and microprocessor-based systems being developed, this factor has become increasingly important. The cost estimator must consider how the software will be developed, tested, and maintained and what tools will be needed to accomplish these tasks. For systems developed for large-scale computers, a host of compilers, data base managers, editors, display interface packages, flow chart packages, plot packages, utility routines, and test data generation tools are generally available. The cost to develop these tools for a single project would be prohibitive. In most cases they are available from the computer vendor or other sources at a minimal cost. However, this is not the situation for software development on smaller computers and microprocessors. For some projects the development of software and hardware tools is a major cost item. The cost estimator must determine whether compilers and other tools are required, available, need to be converted, or need to be developed. Test tools such as simulators, test data generators, data reduction programs, test drivers, or interpretive computer simulators may be required. It is not uncommon to develop two or three times the number of delivered lines of code to support the development and test activities. This means that special care should be taken when using cost-estimating techniques based on dollars per delivered instruction. The factor may have been derived from projects in which very little support software development was required. The total number of instructions for all developed code may need to be estimated before using the estimating factor. This is one danger of using the cost-estimating factors available in current software literature.

The costs associated with tools are a function of the tool complexity, use, features, and maturity. Experience provides the best basis for analyzing the cost impact of support software and tools on overall project cost. The cost estimator should keep in mind that developing tools requires the same steps (summarized in Chapter 2 and described in detail in Part II) as developing deliverable or product software, even though they may be informally implemented.

Available Software. A significant reduction in project costs can be achieved through the use of existing software. For many commercial applications, modestly priced packages are available and can be incorporated into developed systems. Similarly, existing packages for scientific, government, and aerospace applications are available. The adaptation of existing software as part of a system requires analysis of the software apart from the new development. The costs of modifying the existing software can then be determined subjectively. Care must be taken to include the cost of interfacing the modified software to the new software and revalidating the modified components.

Data Base. The size, complexity, and special file access requirements for the data base are extremely important parameters in deriving an accurate software development estimate. The cost estimator must review the data base requirements and subjectively analyze their cost impact. Unfortunately, no simple factor, such as cost per instruction for code, has been developed for assessing the cost impact of data base complexity.

Resource Factors

The final category of costing factors covers the unique resource factors that influence final software cost. Development costs for a given software package may vary substantially, depending on such factors as experience of available people, quality of project staff, and availability of development computer resources. Other resource factors provide insight into additional differences between projects, independent of the costing factors already described in the other three categories. These relate to the productivity difference between large and small projects and different project schedules.

Number of People. The major contributor to the reduction in productivity (increased cost) associated with projects that require larger staffs is the increase in time needed for communication between people. This factor was discussed earlier during consideration of software size (Figure 3.1).

Experience of People. Data from both large and small projects indicate that there is no direct correlation between years of experience of personnel and productivity. However, the cost estimator must consider the general level of experience and skill required for various project assignments and incorporate appropriate labor rates into the estimate. On the other hand, experience with the specific application does affect the development effort required. Generally, a programming group will require 50–100% more effort to develop a program in an unfamiliar area than they would to develop a variant of a familiar program developed previously.

Personnel Performance. One of the factors in software costing found to have sizable variations is personnel performance or productivity. Since software development is an analytical, sometimes creative activity requiring abstract reasoning, individual productivity variations are to be expected. However, experienced estimators find variations in productivity to be as high as 10:1. Productivity assessment is extremely important because cost estimation generally is reduced to deriving a productivity figure per unit of effort (hour or month) per person for a given skill category. The use of such average productivity figures for cost estimating tends to even out for large projects, but can be disastrous for small projects. If one or two of the personnel assigned to a small (four to six persons) project are on the low end of the productivity scale, an overrun is assured. Therefore, in small projects this factor should be given special consideration, possibly by subjectively analyzing the people to be assigned and deriving a productivity factor for this group.

Availability of Computing Resources. A factor often ignored in cost estimating is the availability of computing resources to support the development process. As the requirement for computer time increases during the development cycle, the impact of insufficient computing resources on schedule and cost increases. For batch development systems there is a linear relationship between turnaround time and testing costs. For interactive development systems significant development efficiencies are often realized.

In addition to the impact of availability of computing resources on staff loading and schedule (hence costs), care must be taken to properly incorporate the costs associated with providing the computing resource. The amount of computer time required for a given development effort is easily underestimated. Often the amount of computer capability required to support the development effort is more than is required for operations. Where computers are being delivered as part of a system development effort, this can mean that computers, in addition to those to be delivered, may have to be leased to support the development effort. Data from similar development efforts provide the best basis for these estimates. Suprisingly, these data are often lost. They are not properly recorded and segregated during the development and are not reported (with a breakdown that would provide a useful costing data base) at project completion. Retention and reporting of this type of data are discussed in Chapter 4 (Section 4.5).

Suitability of Computing Resources. The asymptotic effect on development costs as the hardware speed and memory size constraints are approached has been demonstrated in batch, real-time, airborne, military, and commercial systems. This effect becomes particularly crippling during the software maintenance phase, when there may be little capacity available for corrections, modifications, or test drivers required to verify changes.

Elapsed Time.   The amount of calendar time available to develop a software product is intimately related to the ultimate development cost. There appears to be a schedule threshold for each project. Below the threshold, the increased staff required to accomplish the job in a shorter period has the opposite of the desired effect. Instead of shortening the schedule, adding more people may increase (1) the complexity of the effort by breaking the effort into work elements below the natural functional breakdown, (2) the training required of the additional personnel, and (3) the project communication complexity. The net effect may be to increase the schedule as well as the cost.

The determination of the project schedule threshold is almost as difficult as cost estimating. Many development tasks are sequential and cannot be arbitrarily compressed or reorganized. Understanding these tasks and their sequential nature makes it possible to estimate minimum effective task durations for a realistic task breakdown. It is particularly important to allocate sufficient time to requirements and design analysis. Design deficiencies are much cheaper and easier to fix if discovered early (during the analysis activities) rather than during testing.

Changes in the distribution of staff effort over the project period can result in a 10–20% cost difference. An optimum staffing profile for a given development effort can be derived from a detailed definition of development tasks and their schedule relationships. Typical effort distribution ranges for development activities are: analysis/design, 30–40%; code and checkout, 10–20%; test and integration, 40–50%.

3.1.2   Cost-Estimating Models

Cost-estimating models automate cost estimation; productivity data are maintained in a data base and applied to the costing process in a procedural, automated way. The automated models reduce the estimating process to assessing a limited set of critical cost variables. The relationships of other factors to these variables are predefined within the model, thus providing an element of consistency for cost estimates. The use of such automated parametric cost models for estimating costs for large software systems

in industry and government is becoming more and more popular.

A parametric model for estimating software development cost expresses a *quantifiable relationship* between the software development cost and a number of cost variables in the form of an algorithm or set of algorithms. The algorithms are derived from analysis of historical cost data in terms of the set of cost variables. New cost estimates may then be made by estimating the values of the cost variables for the new systems and inserting them into the cost-estimating algorithms (i.e., parametric model) derived from the historical data. Cost sensitivity to uncertainties in specific cost variables can also be analyzed by producing a set of cost estimates based on variations in the given variables. Such studies are particularly easy, since parametric models are often computerized and allow relatively fast computation of the cost estimates.

The validity of a parametric model depends on a cost data base containing a large sample of comparable data. Establishing and maintaining the data base is necessary to the development of the parametric model. It requires in-depth knowledge of the software development process and an understanding of the statistical techniques used to derive the cost algorithms. The correct independent and dependent variables must be selected on the basis of analysis of data from a large number of projects. When selecting the model variables, consideration must also be given to the ease with which a variable can be measured or quantified.

The validity of a parametric model should be demonstrated by its use in several projects. Even then, models are subject to unreliable and biased results. They do, however, provide a very useful tool when used in conjunction with a detailed cost-estimation method based on detailed decomposition of the software, or when used in conjunction with other estimations based on comparable data, rules of thumb, and other techniques, as described in the next section.

A number of parametric cost models have been described in the literature and are being used experimentally to check other estimating results or as the core of the costing process. One of the more common models is the RCA PRICE model, used by a number of large corporations and government agencies to provide cost predictions or check the reasonableness of costs proposed by contractors.

3.1.3   Costing Procedure

Two major alternatives exist for developing the software development project cost. An estimate of total cost can first be derived by some means, such as comparison with a similar project, and then appropriate percentages can be allocated to each part of the software development. The percentages can be based on experience with other projects or on rules of thumb, such as those presented in Section 3.1.1. The result is a detailed cost breakdown such as might be required for a cost proposal.

The problem with this approach is that the entire process depends on one initial total cost estimate. Sufficient care can be taken to ensure that the allocation of costs is reasonable and supported by a large base of historical data. However, even if the allocation is perfect the whole cost estimate could be off by a factor or even an order of magnitude. It is extremely difficult, if not impossible, to use this method for project costing. It is, however, good for quick, "ball park" estimating to support early project and preproposal planning. A quick estimate of the number of instructions times a productivity factor (instructions per man-month) or a dollars per instruction factor can produce a useful cost estimate for planning purposes, but not for bidding.

The second costing procedure is essentially the inverse of the first. The software project is decomposed top-down until the software functional elements are sufficiently small to be estimated; that is, until they are sufficiently small for the function to be understood well enough to size, evaluate (see *Process Factors* in Section 3.1.1), and cost.

The software project cost estimate will prove to be correct and include provision for sufficient support resources only if proper preparations are made before the cost is estimated. These include:

1 Decomposing the project into manageable tasks (detailed Work Breakdown Structure).
2 Analyzing the development efforts required.
3 Identifying the risk areas and planning for risk management.
4 Anticipating typical problems and delays.
5 Identifying support resources needed.

On the basis of this information detailed schedules and cost information can be prepared, and the total project cost estimate can then be developed. This forms the basis for management of the software project and is the nucleus of the Project Plan. The results of the project definition activity should be documented in a Project Plan, which will serve as a basis for the management of the project.

Too often the required information is derived informally around the table. A cost figure is pulled out of the air. It "feels" right, and the project is proposed for completion at that price. "well, let's see . . . , a year should do it". The project thus begins without a firm plan as a foundation. Some or all of the following questions are left for the project manager to struggle with in real-time:

1 What skills and disciplines are required for which tasks?
2 Which tasks should be started first, perhaps given priority, in order not to delay other tasks that depend on their outputs?
3 What is the detailed schedule? Are there any conflicts about tasks, personnel, or computer availability?
4 What level of design should we have at the first design review, if reviews are scheduled?
5 What is the project manager's goal for each design review? Who should attend the review and what preparation is required for it?
6 How much of the budget is for computer time? What is the total monthly budget?
7 What are the risk areas? How should the most competent designers and programmers be used?
8 Which development support tools are required and by what date must they be available?
9 Which computer and interface hardware lead times will impact scheduling of various tasks?
10 What software documents will be produced? When? By which project staff? How will these documents aid the development?
11 What type of project organization is needed to effectively manage this particular development?
12 What standards will be employed?
13 What design and programming techniques will be used by all project personnel?

All of the above questions should be asked and answered during the cost-estimating process. These questions are raised as part of the decomposition and planning process. They entail a detailed analysis of the requirements and the development of a preliminary design against which the decomposition and costing process can be performed. The injection of preliminary design at the costing phase is justified in the development of high technology software, since new design features often are outside the experience of the systems analysts doing the requirements analysis and subsequent costing. For noncritical or well-understood aspects of the design, it is often possible to bridge the gap between requirements and cost without actually doing the preliminary design. This can be accomplished by finding for similar systems a set of common parameters upon which the majority of costs depend (e.g., number of instructions, rate of input data stream, percent memory utilization, processor speed, etc.). These parameters are then used to generate (by analogy) a "system size," which is compared with calibration data for other systems and appropriately modified for special considerations (inflationary factors, schedule risks, etc.).

A typical sequence for estimating software cost by decomposition is given below:

1 Define the software requirements.
2 Prepare preliminary design to the level of detail necessary to cost. Estimate module sizes (number of instructions).
3 Define detailed schedule and development policies. Identify assumptions and dependencies.
4 Identify potential development or schedule problems and higher risk elements of the development. Also, determine if the system will be stressed in terms of memory utilization or speed.
5 Define development tasks and activities to be performed in each task, including formal reviews.
6 Determine effort and experience level required for each task. Be sure to plan for extra manpower and cost for internal review of all documentation. Also, plan for support people to perform configuration control functions.
7 Estimate effort in man-hours, days, or months by development task and summarize by month.
8 Estimate informal and formal meetings, travel, installation time, off-site training support, etc.
9 Estimate computer time, graphics support, clerical support, reproduction, and other development support costs.
10 Convert estimates to dollars by task and month.
11 Make relative effort and cost checks. Compare well-understood module with other modules to see if cost and labor differences are consistent with estimated differences in difficulty. Factor in problem and risk areas. Consider all cost factors summarized in Figure 3.1 (Section 3.1.1).
12 Perform consistency checks for the module and total software development cost estimates.

   (a) Dollars per instruction.
   (b) Instructions per man-month.

Are the dollars per instruction for the total and for each module consistent with data from previous projects? Are the dollars per instruction differences be-

tween modules consistent with differences in difficulty, risk, and so on? Is the percentage of cost allocated to documentation consistent with data from previous projects? Is the percent allocation of dollars to requirements and design/code/test consistent? When using the productivity checks, care must be taken to maintain a common base (i.e., source vs. object code, new vs. existing code, written vs. delivered code, instructions vs. words with or without data base, etc.).

Figures 3.2 and 3.3 provide sample worksheets for defining activities and costing development tasks to assist in items 5 and 7 in the above list.

3.2 THE PROJECT PLAN

The Project Plan is a document that describes how the project manager plans to conduct the software development project. It must define the integrated time-phased tasks and the resources required to meet the contractual or internal company commitment. Regardless of how small a project may be, it needs a plan that clearly defines what is to be accomplished, specifies by whom and when it will be performed, and tells how much it will cost. The plan does not have to be elaborate, but it must define precisely the work for which the project manager is responsible and the methods for ensuring that the work will be performed successfully. Specifically, the Project Plan should accomplish the following:

1 Provide upper management with a high-level summary of the project.
2 Provide the project manager with a plan from start to end for monitoring progress and allocating resources.
3 Provide the customer with the same insight and progress-monitoring ability.
4 Be a customer-oriented document.
5 Be baselined with customer approval and updated as required throughout the life of the project.

3.2.1 What is in the Plan?

The essential elements that the Project Plan must include are the following:

1 A summary of the project that can be read and understood by everyone. It needs to be short and concise. It must clearly identify the deliverable end products so that, when they are produced, they can be checked off against the plan.

Description

Project Management Functions

Trips	Pages	Days	Trips	Pages	Days	Trips	Pages	Days	Trips	Pages	Days	Trips	Pages	Days	Units

□ = Deliverable document   △ = Review

Preliminary Design

Prepare Project Plan
Prepare development schedules
Audit Software Requirements Specification□
Review Software Requirements Specification (SRR△)
Audit Functional Design Document□
Audit Interface Control Document□
Audit preliminary Test Plan□
Review post-SRR documentation (PDR△)
Prepare progress reports
Perform technical management tasks

Total through PDR

Detailed Design

Update schedules
Audit Detailed Design Documents
Audit updated Test Plan
Review detailed design (CDR△)
Prepare progress reports
Perform technical management tasks

Implementation

Audit Operating Instructions Document
Audit Test Procedures
Review Module Integration Test Procedures (TPR△)
Review preliminary Version Description Document
Review Verification/Acceptance Test Procedures (TPR△)
Audit final Test Procedures□
Support Acceptance Testing
Audit Test Reports□
Audit final Version Description Document□
Audit final Operating Instructions Document□
Audit final Detailed Design Documents□
Support Software Acceptance Review (SAR△)
Perform configuration management tasks
Prepare progress reports
Perform technical management tasks

Total for detailed design and implementation

Total (preliminary design + detailed design + implementation)

Figure 3.2 Cost worksheet for project management tasks.

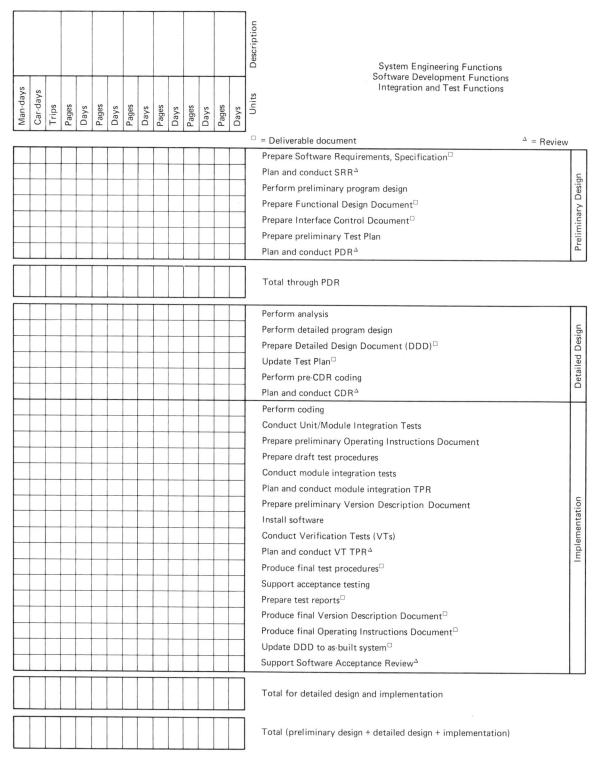

The figure contains a cost worksheet with the following column headers (rotated vertically):

	Man-days	Car-days	Trips	Pages	Days	Pages	Days	Pages	Days	Pages	Days	Pages	Days	Pages	Days	Description

Units

System Engineering Functions
Software Development Functions
Integration and Test Functions

□ = Deliverable document   △ = Review

Preliminary Design
- Prepare Software Requirements, Specification□
- Plan and conduct SRR△
- Perform preliminary program design
- Prepare Functional Design Document□
- Prepare Interface Control Dcoument□
- Prepare preliminary Test Plan
- Plan and conduct PDR△

Total through PDR

Detailed Design
- Perform analysis
- Perform detailed program design
- Prepare Detailed Design Document (DDD)□
- Update Test Plan□
- Perform pre-CDR coding
- Plan and conduct CDR△

Implementation
- Perform coding
- Conduct Unit/Module Integration Tests
- Prepare preliminary Operating Instructions Document
- Prepare draft test procedures
- Conduct module integration tests
- Plan and conduct module integration TPR
- Prepare preliminary Version Description Document
- Install software
- Conduct Verification Tests (VTs)
- Plan and conduct VT TPR△
- Produce final test procedures□
- Support acceptance testing
- Prepare test reports□
- Produce final Version Description Document□
- Produce final Operating Instructions Document□
- Update DDD to as-built system□
- Support Software Acceptance Review△

Total for detailed design and implementation

Total (preliminary design + detailed design + implementation)

Figure 3.3 Cost worksheet for technical tasks.

28

2 A list of discrete milestones identified so that there can be no doubt as to whether they were achieved.

3 A clear definition of which elements of corporate or customer software standards are applicable to the project (e.g., documents to be produced, configuration control methods, standards and conventions to be employed, etc.). This definition must include a rationale for deviating from required elements of corporate or contractually imposed standards.

4 A specification of the review process: who reviews the project, when, and for what purpose.

5 An interface plan that shows how the customer, the internal company line, and the staff organizations communicate with the project.

6 A Work Breakdown Structure (WBS) that is detailed enough to provide meaningful identification of all tasks at the lowest cost collection and reporting level plus all task groupings, such as work units or work packages, that may be defined to aid in task management.

7 A list of key project personnel and their assignments in relation to the WBS.

8 An activity network that shows the time sequence of the elements and how they are related. This network can be produced from the WBS and the list of milestones. For example, it will show which work elements can be done in parallel and which can start only when others are completed.

9 Separate budgets and schedules for all elements for which an individual is responsible.

It is essential that the final Project Plan be produced early in the contract. A preliminary Project Plan should be developed during the proposal phase, if possible. Also, and as important as producing the original plan, *the plan must be kept up to date. It is a living document.* The fact that virtually every project must deviate from its planned course requires replanning to take place, and this replanning must be documented and coordinated with upper management and the customer through the revised Project Plan. At the end of the project, the Project Plan will provide the *historical summary* of how the project was accomplished.

The objectives of each major section of a sample Project Plan are presented in Figure 3.4. A table of contents for the sample plan is provided in Figure 3.5, with each section described below.

Section 1 Introduction
The Project Plan introduction should define the scope, the intent, and use of the plan. It should summarize the project and the development philosophy. The project summary should be very brief, with the more complete description provided in a later section (Section 3 of our example). The intent of the Introduction is to inform the reader of the purpose of the plan and the basic project intent.

Section 2 Controlling Documents
This section should reference all specifications, standards, and contractual documentation applicable to the software development project.

Section 3 Project Description
The project description provides an overview of the project activities, including the statement of work, assumptions, deliverable products, and required nondeliverable support products. The statement of work describes the scope of work to be accomplished. It details all the definition and development tasks to be performed, including design review support; interface meeting support; documentation tasks; support tasks, such as simulation development, computer operations management, and configuration management; and additional tasks, such as training, operations support, and software maintenance. The assumptions inherent in the Project Plan should be explicitly documented in this section for review by management and customer personnel. Such assumptions might include:

1 Computer hardware for which the system is to be developed.

2 Languages, operating systems, and data management packages to be used in the development.

3 Location at which the major portion of the project will be performed.

4 The development facilities to be provided by the customer, including availability dates and conditions such as time-shared computer use versus prime time, batch with a specified average turnaround time versus overnight batch turnaround.

5 Responsibility for providing test data.

6 Data to be provided by the customer or other external organizations, including dates required.

7 Applicable specifications and interface design data.

8 Critical schedule milestones.

9 Throughput and memory reserve requirements.

The specific software, documentation, and services to be delivered during and at the conclusion of the project should be described. The documents should be defined in terms of contents and level of detail. The deliverable software products should be defined in

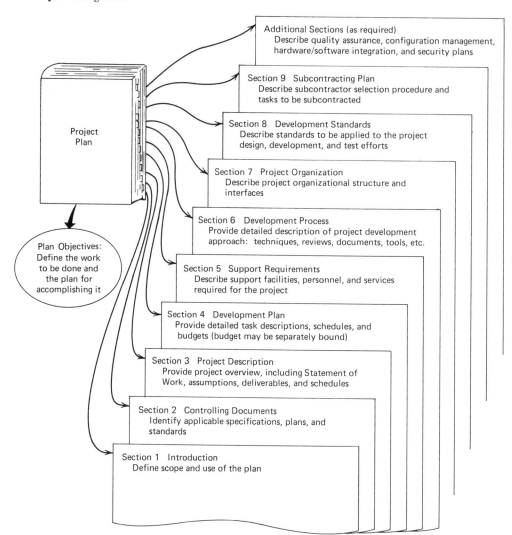

Figure 3.4 Project Plan objectives.

terms of capability by referencing an appropriate requirements specification. Services such as providing training, software maintenance, or operations support should be defined in terms of start dates, levels of support to be provided, and periods of support. Specific tasks to be performed under the services part of the project should be identified by reference to the statement of work. Acceptance criteria for *all* the deliverable products must be defined. Agreement with the customer at the outset can save a great deal of conflict between the project management and the customer during and at the conclusion of the project.

Section 4 Development Plan

This section contains the results of the task analysis and scheduling activity performed in order to cost the

project. It presents the detailed description of tasks in the form of a Work Breakdown Structure (WBS). Elements of the WBS are scheduled and costs allocated to them. The schedules and costs (i.e., budget) should also be included. The tasks presented in the WBS should define in greater detail the tasks identified in the Statement of Work (SOW) in the previous section. The SOW usually requires software requirements analysis, preliminary program design and analysis, detailed program design, coding, and so on, as identified in Figure 2.4 (Chapter 2). The WBS should define tasks that can be performed by an individual programmer or analyst or by a small group of programmers or analysts in a short period (a few weeks to a few months) with a measurable start and completion point.

In addition to the task definition, this section of the

SOFTWARE DEVELOPMENT PROJECT PLAN: CONTENTS

Section 1   Introduction

1.1   Scope
1.2   Purpose
1.3   Project Summary
1.4   Development Philosophy

Section 2   Controlling Documents

2.1   Contractual Management Documents
2.2   Contractual Specifications
2.3   Applicable Supporting Documents

Section 3   Project Description

3.1   Statement of Work
3.2   Assumptions
3.3   Deliverable Products
3.3.1   Software
3.3.2   Documentation
3.3.3   Services
3.3.4   Acceptance Criteria
3.4   Nondeliverable Products
3.5   Special Contract Provisions

Section 4   Development Plan

4.1   Work Breakdown Structure
4.2   Schedule and Activity Network
4.3   Budget
4.4   Critical Items

Section 5   Support Requirements

5.1   Computer System Support
5.2   External Company Engineering Support
5.3   Required Customer Actions
5.4   Required External Company Actions
5.5   Required Associate Contractor Actions

Section 6   Development Process

6.1   Development Phases
6.2   Documents
6.3   Reviews
6.4   Test Philosophy

Section 7   Project Organization

7.1   Customer Interface
7.2   Company Organization Interface
7.3   Key Personnel
7.4   Development Organization by Project Phase

Section 8   Development Standards

8.1   Configuration Control
8.2   Programming Standards and Conventions
8.3   Automated Aids
8.4   Project Deviations From Company Standards

Section 9   Subcontracting Plan

9.1   Summary and Justification
9.2   Consultants
9.3   Subcontract Acceptance Procedures
9.4   Subcontract A Description
9.5   Subcontract B Description

. . .

Appendix   Subcontract A
Project Plan

Appendix   Subcontract B
Project Plan

. . .

Figure 3.5   Table of contents for a sample Project Plan.

plan should identify the skill level required for each task and an estimate of the effort to complete the tasks in hours or man-months. The schedule and interrelationship of the tasks and the order in which they must be completed should be included in the form of task schedules, networks, and/or critical path charts. Schedules should also include the need dates (or periods) for all the required external resources. These resources may include interface hardware, customer-furnished data or computer time, customer approval of specifications, test data from an external source, and use of test facilities controlled by the customer or an external organization.

The development plan should also include manpower plans and budget information against which the project can be periodically reviewed. The manpower data can be presented in chart form showing assignment of tasks to individuals and the dates on which these tasks are to be completed. The budget information should include estimated costs by month and by major task. The budget should incorporate labor, clerical, travel, computer time, document production, communications, special equipment and services, and any other costs normally allocated directly to projects. The budget information may be presented in a separately bound appendix if there is a desire to provide wider distribution and use of the Project Plan than might be allowed by company policy if the financial data were included.

A final topic of the development plan section is identification of the critical items or development risks. The significant risks or problems that might delay or jeopardize the project should be enumerated. This should not be an exhaustive list of every possible problem that could occur, but should highlight specific potential problems for management and customer consideration.

Section 5 Support Requirements
This section should define all support facilities, personnel and activities required to complete the project. Software development facilities, including computers, simulations, compilers, assemblers, operating systems, data management systems, data storage capabilities, data reduction capabilities, and test support capabilities should be identified, described and scheduled. Necessary support from company personnel outside the project and from customer or associate contractor personnel should be described in as much detail as possible.

Section 6 Development Process
This section should describe the development approach to be used in the project. The description can include information on task sequencing, document preparation, reviews and audits, and development and test techniques similar to that presented in Part 2 of this book. Alternatively, it could summarize such information in the manner presented in Chapter 2 and include a reference to a company development standard that contains information at the level presented in Part 2. In the latter case, any deviations from the referenced company standard should be presented and justified in this section of the Project Plan.

Section 7 Project Organization
The plan should define: (1) the organizational structure to be used to manage the project; (2) the interface of the project organization with the company organization; (3) the interface of the project organization with company staff and administrative functions, such as contracts, accounting, configuration management, and quality assurance; (4) the interface of project personnel with customer and associate-contractor personnel; (5) the responsibility and authority of the project manager with respect to technical and contractual matters; and (6) the responsibility and authority of key project personnel. Any organizational changes planned for different project phases should also be described.

Section 8 Development Standards
This section should summarize the development standards to be applied to the project. Some of the standards may be specified by reference to available company or customer standards. Where interpretation is required, a notation should be included in this section.

Section 9 Subcontracting Plan
If subcontractors or consultants will be used, this section should describe the tasks to be subcontracted and the selection procedure to be used. Where subcontractors have already been selected, subcontractor Project Plans patterned after this plan should be included as appendixes, separately bound if appropriate.

Additional Sections
Additional sections should be included in the Project Plan covering such topics as quality assurance, configuration management, maintenance, hardware and software integration, and security required for the particular development effort.

3.2.2 Use and Update of the Plan

For many competitive software procurements a preliminary version of the Project Plan is required as part of the development proposal. For other projects the plan is one of the first deliverable items, usually due within the first few weeks. Proper cost estimating includes preparation of most of the detailed task and schedule information required for the Project Plan, so that delivery of the plan within the first few weeks is not unreasonable. Often the customer will request that the initial delivery include detailed plans for the first phase of the contract, perhaps up to the Preliminary Design Review. Then additional deliveries are scheduled prior to the start of each subsequent phase. This approach forces the project manager to review the plan and update it periodically as new software definition and development details become available.

Whatever the delivery requirements for the Project Plan, it should be the basis for management and review of project activities.

3.3 THE PLANNING STEPS

The three major steps in preparing for a successful software development project are the generation of a complete and accurate Work Breakdown Structure (WBS), schedule, and budget. In addition to providing project monitoring and control mechanisms for the software project manager, the WBS, schedule, and budget provide upper management and the customer with visibility into project progress and trouble areas. These three elements should be documented in the Project Plan to a sufficient level of detail to provide unambiguous insight into the project task structure and status at any point in the development cycle.

Special care should be taken to highlight, not mask, the items that are critical to project success. Critical items may occur in each of the three elements (i.e., a particular task that is difficult or poorly defined and is crucial to project success; a particularly crucial schedule milestone that is on the critical path for project completion; or a budget consideration with uncertain parameters, which could cause a project overrun if invalid assumptions were made). These critical items should be spelled out in the Project Plan together with an assessment of the risk, a justification of the acceptance of the risk, and special emphasis on the plans for monitoring these key portions of the development effort.

3.3.1 Work Breakdown Structure Definition

A Work Breakdown Structure is a product-oriented organized task plan formulated by the project manager and then carefully documented. It is a hierarchical definition of all tasks to be performed and accounted for in the course of the project development. Major task areas are defined, and each major area is further identified by defining subtasks. Each subtask may be further broken down so that at the lowest level of task definition each item becomes the basic unit for costing. Whether simple or complex, after the WBS is documented it should be reviewed by those who have an interest in the project and their criticisms should be considered by the project manager for incorporation into the Project Plan.

Some of the major elements and constraints in planning the WBS are given below:

1 The customer's internal budgeting procedures may constrain the content of work packages.
2 The customer may constrain the WBS to make the project structure correlate with customer management structure.
3 Generally, the WBS should segregate recurring costs from nonrecurring costs.
4 It may be desirable for the WBS to reflect certain types of activities (analysis, coding, testing, etc.).
5 It may be desirable to collect costs by tasks relative to end items or deliverable products.

6 The size of a work package may reflect an individual's capabilities and involve the project manager's desire to monitor work elements more or less closely.
7 The elements of the WBS must be related to people; someone must be in charge of each element above the lowest level at which costs are collected.

The *WBS provides the basis for cost estimation, project organization, task scheduling, and cost reporting.* The WBS is the result of task segmentation designed to identify stand-alone activities that can be scheduled and costed. The task-segmentation process provides additional understanding of the tasks and increased costing accuracy. These task segments are structured as WBS elements. The complete WBS and supporting explanation are provided by the project manager in the Project Plan and must be updated as changes occur in the task structure. Figure 3.6 provides a sample software project WBS.

The WBS should also correlate with the lowest-level organizational or management structure for the project. It is important to identify the organization responsible for a task. This provides a high traceability of resource requirements associated with each task and results in allocation of estimated resource requirements within the organization.

Similarly, there is a definite interrelationship between the WBS and project schedules. Each activity, or WBS element, has a definite time-phasing relative to other WBS elements and, since each element has its own resource requirements, a resulting distribution of cost. The WBS definition, resource estimates, and schedule therefore combine to yield the project resource or cost distribution.

The definition (and scheduling) of activities is an interactive process that provides the framework for cost estimating and the basis for the Project Plan. The depth or level of the WBS will vary depending on the complexity and size of the project. The WBS should be defined to a sufficiently low level to establish adequate visibility and confidence for cost estimating, project planning, and project control.

3.3.2 Schedule Planning

Each element of the project should have its own schedule showing milestones and delivery dates. The Project Plan includes these schedules and the master milestone schedule for the overall project.

The schedule has two main functions. First, it shows the time-phasing of the different tasks to be performed,

34

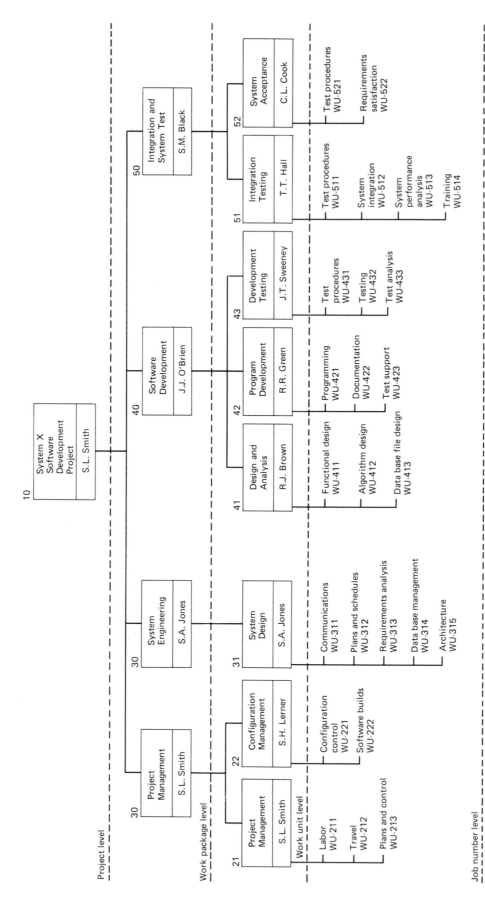

Figure 3.6 Sample software project work breakdown structure.

indicating which can be done in parallel and which must be done serially. Second, it is the basic management tool for monitoring progress.

The exercise of producing the master schedule is valuable in itself. It forces the project manager to decide what should be done first, which items must wait until other elements of the project are completed, and which can be started early to avoid problems late in the project. This exercise is usually done as an aid to developing good cost estimates. It is then refined and detailed to provide the schedule tools needed to monitor project status.

Scheduling activities begin in the initial planning and cost-estimating stages of a software development project and continue through the early stages of review and negotiation. The data is continually refined and culminates in the initial program plan and schedule. The approval of this initial plan and schedule by cognizant managers, and subsequently the customer, is part of contract negotiations. The following sections discuss schedule interactions to be considered in schedule planning, define the structure of the milestone-type development schedule, describe other useful types of schedules, and provide general scheduling guidelines.

Schedule Interaction

The two principal tasks in the scheduling exercise are estimating the time required to complete various tasks and identifying the interrelationships that force or constrain schedule dates. These schedule constraints fall into two general categories: (1) interrelationships between tasks within the project and (2) constraints caused by external events outside project control. Identification of schedule interrelationships within the project is a product of the project task decomposition and scheduling activities.

External constraints should be carefully documented as a list of assumptions and shown on the formal schedule as critical events. The customer must be made aware of the impact of each external constraint on the development schedule.

Examples of external schedule constraints include:

1 Customer-supplied documentation.
2 Customer-supplied algorithms, techniques, or other defined inputs.
3 Customer formal reviews and approvals (i.e., customer must respond to design review material within a specified number of days after the formal review).
4 System engineering inputs (if outside the software development organization).
5 Subcontractor or vendor schedules.
6 Associate-contractor schedules.
7 Development computer installation schedule.
8 Computer time availability.
9 Hardware maintenance or downtime.
10 Special-purpose hardware development schedules (e.g., I/O boards).
11 Test data availability.
12 Formal test facility availability.

Schedule Structure

When developing a particular project schedule, two general categories of schedules should be produced: program schedules and detailed functional schedules. The detailed schedules must be documented in terms of the requirement or event, the organization or individual responsible, and the required date of compliance. The hierarchy of schedules developed should flow from a top-level correlation with the master program schedule requirements down to constraining schedules for the detailed work level. Four types of schedules which develop this top-down flow are defined below. The first two provide the program schedules and the last two constitute the detailed functional schedules.

Top-Level Schedule.   The top-level schedule is the schedule authority depicting the end-to-end plan for carrying out program objectives. It contains key program milestones (e.g., system level test dates), which are used to develop lower-level schedule plans. This schedule is developed at the project level and defines the end point requirements to the software development organization.

Interface Schedule.   Interface schedules expand the top-level schedule to provide all event information required for software development functional organizations, subcontractors and vendors, and interfacing organizations within the project. This information allows these groups to develop their schedules and provides the reference for interface status reporting. Interface schedules present all customer interface milestones and software development project external interface milestones.

Software Development Schedule.   The software development schedule presents the overall software development project milestones (PDR, CDR, etc.) consistent with the top-level and interface schedules.

Functional Schedules.   Functional schedules provide the lowest-level schedule control. These schedules extend the software development schedule (with cognizance of particular key items from the interface schedules) to organize specific measurable tasks into manageable activities. The functional schedules provide the framework for establishing and time-phasing detailed budgets, status reports, summaries, and cost and schedule performance. The functional schedules are prepared and maintained by the project organizations responsible for the lowest-level development tasks.

Other Useful Schedules

The schedules already described are commonly called milestone schedules. These schedules identify the major project milestones at each scheduling level. They identify the events that must occur to complete the project and their completion dates. They provide only binary data (often the milestone indicator is colored in when the event is completed) and do not provide level of completion information or task interactions needed to properly anticipate schedule problems. Bar charts and networks provide the latter information and are very useful supplements to the basic milestone charts.

Bar charts (also called Gantt charts) provide a graphic illustration of tasks to be performed. The status of each task (in terms of level of completion) is indicated either graphically or with numerical percentages. Status at any point in time can be shown by shading the bars. Though easy to read, the chart, like the milestone charts, fails to provide a picture of task interrelationships.

Networks overcome this shortcoming. One of the most successful procedurized network scheduling techniques is the Program Evaluation and Review Technique (PERT). PERT graphically illustrates the interdependence of project events. It identifies the project tasks, their sequence, and their interrelationships. It identifies which tasks must be completed before other tasks can begin.

Since PERT charts graphically present task interrelationships, they are useful in resource allocation planning. To accomplish this, resource estimates are made for each task in the PERT network. The project resources are then allocated on the basis of the task interrelationships shown in the PERT chart. This approach ensures that tasks upon which other tasks depend are scheduled earlier and have priority for project resources.

Scheduling Guidelines

Since the primary goal of scheduling is to specify how much time will be required to complete a task, a collection of tasks, or a complete project, particular care must be taken in developing the schedules. Considera-

tion must be given to the availability of people, computer time, interfacing equipment, data from organizations outside the project, design information for system elements to be modeled by software, and the time-phasing of tasks.

During the proposal period or internal company project definition period, preliminary schedules are prepared. This activity should develop a schedule for every major activity in the WBS structure. The task decomposition and scheduling activities help to identify problems with the WBS and to identify schedule incompatibilities. The schedule should incorporate tasks associated with the preparation of all deliverable items and design reviews. The proposal schedules should be sufficiently detailed to support the labor- and travel-estimating process.

At the start of the project more detailed schedules should be prepared for the first contract phase at the lowest WBS level. Similar detailed scheduling should be planned prior to the start of succeeding development phases.

Every project must have a written schedule, no matter how small the project. For small projects this may involve a one-page milestone schedule. For large projects it may consist of milestone schedules, at various levels, keyed to a master project milestone schedule with bar charts and networks to support the project planning and monitoring processes. The task of preparing the schedules requires decisions about the order in which activities will be performed and the time it will take to complete them. These decisions are fundamental to the project planning process and provide the basis for project control.

An important element in all project scheduling is maintaining task and nomenclature consistency between scheduling, task planning (WBS definition), budgeting, and organizing of project activities. Including a WBS identifier in each schedule or schedule line item and assigning specific WBS elements to organizational elements provides consistency between tasks, schedules, and budgets. This type of consistency in task decomposition, scheduling, and assignment of responsibility ensures not only that all events get scheduled, but that they can be readily monitored. It also facilitates change analysis and control.

Effective scheduling and schedule management are important responsibilities of the project manager. He is responsible for developing all project schedules. However, for large projects, review and approval of detailed schedules should be delegated to project control managers and subproject managers. The project manager should initiate the activity with the top-level master schedule and possibly the first one or two tiers below the master schedule. He should assign other project personnel to prepare lower-tier schedules and require consistency with the higher-level schedules. When lower-level scheduling constraints necessitate a change in the higher-level schedules, these revisions should be reviewed and approved by the project manager.

Since scheduling depends on and highlights the task and organizational interrelationships, success of the proposal (in terms of realistic costs) and of the project (in terms of on schedule completion at budgeted cost) is highly dependent on the validity and completeness of the scheduling activity. Do not treat it lightly during the proposal, project definition, or software development period.

3.3.3 Budget Planning

The budget is an important part of the Project Plan, but the fundamentals of budget planning fall under the project manager's contract management responsibilities.

The project budget description consists of a set of expenditure versus time plots (one plot for the overall project and one for each element). As work is completed or expenses incurred, the amounts are plotted on the same charts and the variations are noted. The project manager's job is to monitor these variations and understand and justify the reasons for deviations.

If the project had the same number of people working from start to finish and there were no other changes, the budget line would be linear. This rarely happens. Not only does the number of people vary throughout the project, but there usually are other changes. These are generally ODC (other direct charges), such as business trips, purchased equipment, and computer time. These charges seldom occur in a regular schedule. Nevertheless, the project manager should be able to estimate approximately when they will occur. ODC items present special problems, since they usually appear in the cost-reporting system long after they were incurred. This can tend to give the project manager a false sense of security, since the charts show him under budget. Proper budget planning and monitoring should prevent discovering overruns long after they occur.

The project manager's job is to manage to the final dollar. Uncontrollable variations—such as changes (seldom downward) to the company burden rates—that are applied to direct project costs (e.g., overhead rates) make precise budgeting impossible. Therefore, it is important, when possible, to maintain a management reserve and not allocate the total budget.

Typical budget plots for a software development project are shown in Figure 3.7. The predicted plots are included in the Project Plan and actuals are provided in the monthly project financial reports.

3.4 THE PROJECT ORGANIZATION

The basic resource for computer program system development is people. To successfully implement a system of computer programs, the project manager needs the right people with the right skills at the right time. The engineering manpower required for design, documentation, coding, and testing is only a part of the total staff requirement. In addition, needs for technical support personnel must be identified and such support commitments solicited within other company organizations. These functions deserve meticulous attention, as the lack of recognition of support functions required for the project may be a significant cause of schedule or cost problems.

The Project Plan should define the project organization, define specific responsibilities of each group within the organization, and identify key personnel. Key personnel are individuals the project manager places in charge of some aspect of the project. They are expected to exercise judgment and discretion in deciding how tasks are to be accomplished, who will be assigned a particular task, and when the task will be completed. The allocation of task responsibility should correspond to the project WBS. That is, the elements of responsibility delegated to key personnel should correlate to WBS elements so that the accounting system and schedule tracking functions in the project will provide direct measures of the success of the key personnel in managing their delegated tasks. In many projects the titles these people are given, such as Work Package Manager or Work Unit Manager, reflect the relationship of their responsibilities to the WBS work elements.

Putting the list of key personnel with their titles (responsibilities) in the Project Plan is not required in many companies, but it is a good form of insurance. Should the project manager be removed from the project for any reason (illness, accident, emergency, or sudden reassignment), the new project manager would quickly pick up the project reins if he can easily identify the key people and their responsibilities. This information, together with the rest of the Project Plan and the most recent status reports, should define the project status sufficiently for a rapid, successful takeover by a new project manager.

In planning and organizing the project, the project

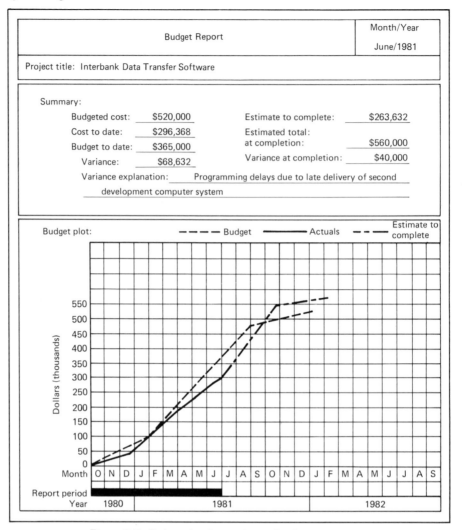

Figure 3.7   Budget plots for a software development project.

manager will be influenced by the corporate organizational structure and the provisions within that structure for supporting development efforts. The following sections briefly describe the impact of corporate structures on project organization, project organization alternatives, and project organizational responsibilities.

3.4.1   Corporate Structure Alternatives

The project organization is influenced by the organizational approach of the company. There are two basic approaches: the *functional organization* and the *project organization.* The functional approach groups people with particular specialties in departments or operations which provide the expertise of their specialty to projects. The specialists are essentially on loan to the project manager to do their part of the job. The special-

ist is responsible to his department or operations (functional) manager, not to the project manager.

This type of functional corporate organization, referred to as a *matrix organization,* is popular among the high-technology service and research and development companies. It allows the company to employ high-technology specialists who could not be hired to support a single project. When shared by a number of projects, these specialists can be used very effectively. The disadvantages of the matrix organization to the project manager are the following:

1   The project manager has little control over the working-level specialists because they are likely to be more concerned with their functional organization than with the project.

2   Typically, the project manager has little or no say

in the selection of personnel, only in the definition of the skills and level of experience required for his task.

3 There may be personnel substitutions before the tasks are finished.

4 There is little or no continuity of people on the job, compared to project-oriented organizations. Analysts, designers, and programmers are assigned to the project, do their job, and leave. It may be considerably more efficient to have less specialized people who can provide continuity between analysis, design, and implementation. This approach also avoids the higher project costs associated with bringing a larger number of people up to speed (learning curve costs).

The most common alternative to the matrix organization is the *project organization.* In this type of corporate structure, project personnel report only to the project managers. The advantages of this type of corporate organization are:

1 The project manager has complete control over people working on the job.

2 Continuity can be assured by having some analysts support both design and test-phase activities.

3 Staff problems can be resolved by the project manager by hiring, firing, and reassigning personnel within the project, without the necessity of negotiating with a functional manager who has little understanding of the current project requirements and who has other motivating goals.

4 Commitment to the project is fostered by the direct attachment of the individual to the project organization in a technical and administrative sense.

The major drawback of the project-oriented corporate organization, as opposed to the functional organization, is the additional placement responsibility assumed by the project manager. In the functional organization, when the assigned task is completed, the project manager returns the specialist to his or her functional organization, where someone else has the responsibility of locating a new assignment for the employee. Under the project scheme, the project manager is responsible for where the employee goes next. Also, during the project staffing period, large amounts of time for the project manager and key project personnel must be committed to hiring personnel from outside the company, as well as interviewing candidates being released from other projects. The interviewing and hiring is handled by functional management in the matrix organization, as is preliminary screening of current em-

ployees for available project positions. The major impact of these two corporate structure alternatives is on the project manager's level of staffing control.

3.4.2 Project Structure Alternatives

The structure of a project organization is mainly a function of four factors: *corporate structure, project size,* the *capabilities and management style of the project manager,* and the *capabilities of key personnel* in the project.

The extent to which various functions and tasks are separated into different groups under the project manager is determined by the size of the software development effort. A small project of three to six people may have no formal structure, with all personnel reporting directly to the project manager. Larger projects require increasingly greater task decomposition and more management levels. The most important criterion in defining management structure is the WBS; when management structure parallels the WBS, cost collection and status monitoring reflect the organizational responsibilities.

Though one of the major differences between small and large projects is the level of specialization of the groups within the organization, there is a higher-level organizational philosophy choice that is definitely influenced by project size. This is the choice between *functional project organization* and *job- or element-oriented project organization.*

The functional project organization, like the functional corporate organization, groups people with the same skills, as illustrated in Figure 3.8. The analysts are in one group, software systems engineers in another, programmers in another, product assurance personnel in yet another, and so on. The functional project organization has many of the advantages of the corresponding corporate organization. Specialists are used for each task, independent of which software or system element is involved.

Alternatively, the project can be structured along job- or system-element lines, which results in one group having responsibility for one element of the software, such as the display element, the data base management element, or the data reduction element. This group is then responsible for all analysis, design, code, and test tasks required to complete the development of that software element. The project is organized by breaking up the software into subsystems and assigning a manager and a group to the development of each subsystem. This approach is often referred to as the *"job-shop"* organization. It is quite successful for small, unrelated jobs, but is not recommended for larger sys-

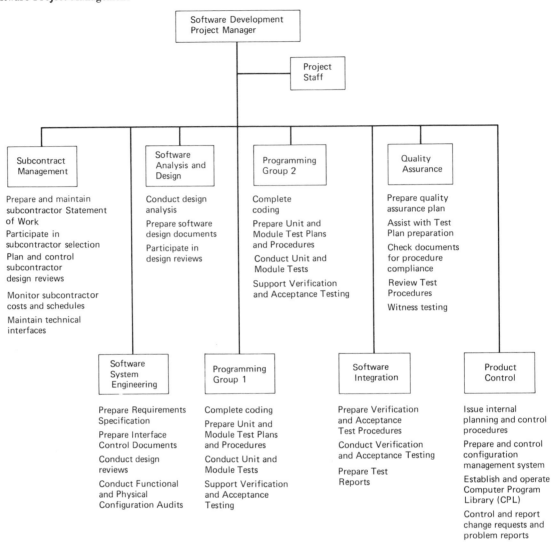

Figure 3.8 Functional project organization.

tem projects. Its major disadvantage is that all the subsystem managers are concerned about their subsystems, with no one having responsibility for system-level problems.

As is so often the case, most real-world projects, particularly larger projects, use a combination of these two basic project organization philosophies. Functional groups are often used for many of the system-level functions, such as software systems engineering, subcontract management, product assurance, and system-level testing, while the software development function is structured in a job-shop fashion, as illustrated in Figure 3.9. Within one of the job-shop elements, the tasks are usually structured functionally to take advantage of the available analysis, design, and test special-

ists. The specific responsibilities of each element identified in Figures 3.8 and 3.9 are described in Section 4.2.

The selected project organization must be described in the Project Plan. This description should recognize the possible need for organizational changes as the project moves from the requirements analysis through design and test to operations. Changes may occur for the following reasons:

1 As the project moves through the development phases summarized in Section 2.2, the emphasis shifts from analysis to design, to coding, and to testing. The organization should reflect these changes in project emphasis. For example, there is no need for a training or installation group early in

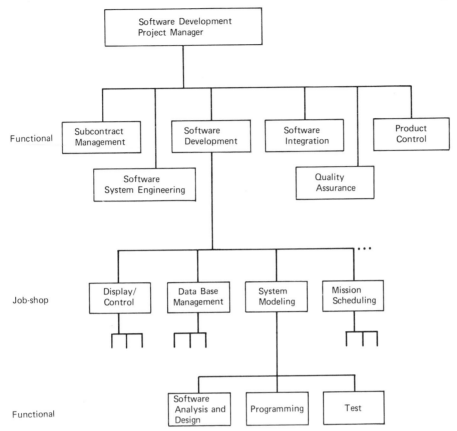

Figure 3.9 Large project organization.

the project, and there may be no need for requirements analysis or interface definition groups late in the project.

2 The organization should reflect the skills and strengths of the project staff, and adjustments should be made as needed to compensate for weaknesses, both individual and corporate.

3 For any number of reasons, the originally defined organization, as presented in the Project Plan, may prove ineffective. Often this results from conditions completely out of the project manager's control, such as organizational changes or weaknesses in the customer project organization. In these cases, the project should be reorganized, and the Project Plan should be updated to reflect the changes.

The most significant factor in organizing a successful project is not the particular structure, number of boxes on the chart, or selection of titles for each of the groups, but the extent to which the tasks have been clearly allocated in a workable manner and every member of the project staff understands his or

her goals, responsibilities, and relationship to other project staff.

3.4.3 Organizational Skill Requirements

A software development project has little hope of success if the project manager is unable to assemble a team with the proper skills and disciplines for each phase of the development effort. Figure 3.10 provides a summary of disciplines for a software development project. Examples are given for three different types of software in the aerospace field: on-board spacecraft microprocessor software, spacecraft test software, and ground support software to process data from the spacecraft and generate spacecraft commands.

Personnel in the five skill groups described in Figure 3.10 are phased during the project in accordance with the software development cycle to support the tasks described in Chapters 5–8. Figure 3.11 provides a generalized plot of the distribution of project personnel over the course of a typical software development project.

Function	General Skills	EXAMPLE: Flight Code	EXAMPLE: Spacecraft Test Software	EXAMPLE: Satellite Ground Support Software
1. Management – Project	– Software system development experience – Software system management experience – Software Product Standards and application – Customer interface – Ability to motivate and manage programmers – Understanding of peculiarities of software systems activities – Project budgeting, scheduling			
2. Software System Engineers	– Top-level system design – Ability to translate system level requirements into software – Ability to allocate functions between hardware and software – Interface with various types of hardware systems (both computing and non-computing) – Interface with specialists in key discipline areas – Experience in software system development – Ability to evaluate key features of candidate computer systems – Ability to produce clear, disciplined documentation – Software Product Standards and application	Problem: Control software for satellite on-board computer Special Expertise: – VWX/10 computer – Attitude control dynamics – Space Programming Language – Command and Control – Attitude System Hardware – Multi-level interrupt systems Problem Areas: – Memory Limited – Timing Critical – Error-Free Design Critical	Problem: Software for controlling and executing tests of spacecraft hardware Special Expertise: – Particular minicomputers (e.g., DG Eclipse) – Spacecraft subsystems – Sensor subsystems – System test language – Test procedures – Multi-tasking operating system – Multiple computer interfacing – Special hardware interfaces Problem Areas: – Large minicomputer memory management – Critical timing constraints – Solidifying requirements – Interfacing with spacecraft design and test schedule	Problem: Ground support computations required for launch and operation of synchronous satellite Special Expertise: – Large scale computer systems – Orbit Determination – Attitude Determination – Reaction Control Systems – AKM planning, station acquisition – Stationkeeping – Tracking and attitude data reduction – Large data base management – Computer-to-computer Interfaces Problem Areas: – Real-time control computer interface with commercial maxi-computer – Large integrated software system
3. Test Engineers, Product Assurance Staff	– Ability to relate system level test requirements to test sequences implementable through project Operating Instructions – Creative ability to minimize test expense by maximizing efficiency of individual tests – Ability to interface with programmers in their language to explain and help in isolating problems – Familiarity with applicable automated test tools – Ability to construct and implement structured, disciplined procedures – Overall understanding of system level requirements – Software Product Standards and application	Special Problem Areas: – Limited capabilities of VWX/10 for test visibility – Special purpose software simulation – Product must be error free – Continuous process testing	Special Problem Areas: – Features which can damage spacecraft hardware must be isolated for critical testing – Must be able to test without spacecraft for stimulus – Multiple computer interfaces – Multi-faceted testing: user control, generation of spacecraft inputs, analysis of spacecraft outputs	Special Problem Areas: – Large scale multi-overlay system – Exhaustive sets of input data conditions required to test all contingencies – Computer time expensive – Algorithm testing

4. Programmers	– Computer program design and development
	– Experience with computer and operating system for project
	– Familiarity with language(s) to be used
	– General understanding of system level problem area
	– Software Product Standards and application
	– Special experience required by project, for example:
	  – Real-time systems
	  – Data Base design and access methods
	  – Batch systems
	  – Interactive systems
	  – Reentrant programming
		– VWX/10 assembly language
		– Space Programming language
		– Cross assembly on off-line machines
		– Real-time interrupt driven program
		– Software development using host computer interfacing with VWX/10
		– Operating system integrated with application
			– Combination of real-time, batch background, and interactive software
			– Multi-computer and multiple hardware interfaces
			– Fortran and assembly language programs
			– Vender supplied general purpose operating system and utilities
				– Large scale Fortran models and algorithms
				– Data Base storage and retrieval system
				– Multi-overlay integrated system operating via automatic remote job entry
				– Real-time computer interface subsystem
				– Complex mathematical subsystems

5. Product Control Staff	– Software Product Standards and application – Applicable government standards – Ability to structure and maintain disciplined control system – Ability to interface with programmers to control product during development – Ability to understand and process change items	– Critical configuration control requirements for flight packages – Off-line machine for maintaining files – Customer Standards	– Multiple subcontractors – Customer Standards – Development machines for maintaining files	– File management through large remote computer complex system

Figure 3.10 Summary of disciplines and skills for a software development project.

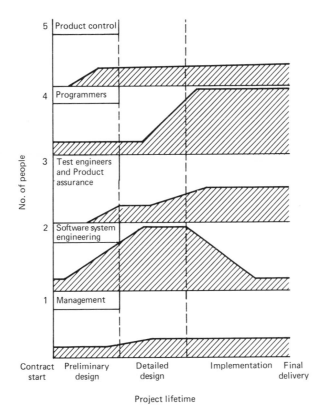

Figure 3.11 Distribution of project personnel over the course of a typical software development project.

chapter four

Managing the Project

Software project management has evolved rather slowly over the past two decades. The major reason for this is the persistent view that programming is an art, rather than a science. This view lingers among company and systems project technical and management personnel and has contributed to delays in the development of a well-defined, well-structured software management methodology. The problem persists despite the great advances in computer hardware technology, the introduction of software engineering, and the definition of new development approaches, such as design decomposition, structured design, structured programming, hierarchical input-output definition, and chief-programmer team management concepts.

These factors foster the perspective in corporate and project management that software management must continuously evolve and change to keep up with advances in software development technology. Yet, these conclusions are seldom applied to management of the rapidly advancing electronics field. Why can hardware development projects, in the midst of phenomenal technology advances, be managed in a disciplined, systematic manner based on past decades of project management experience while software projects apparently cannot?

Contributing to the general misunderstanding of software management is the much publicized view of the programmer as the unbridled creative genius, whose creative process will be stifled by any of the recommended project management controls, design standards, and programming standards. Forced to contend with this view is the software manager, often a recently promoted analyst or programmer who has worked on projects managed as a collection of creative artists doing their independent thing. Management's job in these projects was to try, somehow, to steer this collection of individualists in a common direction so that their products would accomplish the project goals, be able to interface with each other, be finished within the project cost and schedule constraints, and, perhaps most important, would come reasonably close to accomplishing what the customer had in mind for the software. The typical software manager of recent years has been well grounded in how a project should not be managed, but has had little exposure or training in the use of effective software management techniques.

It is the purpose of this chapter to provide the background and understanding required to manage a software development project successfully. The methodology presented is applicable to all software projects, commercial or government sponsored, large or small. For some projects, the Project Plan will be a three-page memorandum, the requirements will be documented in a similar fashion, and the design presented in a 30-page document. For others, the Project Plan will consist of three volumes to address in detail the required development, configuration management, and maintenance aspects of the project. For these projects, the requirements may necessitate a 100-page document, and the detailed design a six-volume, 3000-page set of documents. At either extreme, and everywhere in between, the functions performed, documents produced, and types of planning required are the same.

In this chapter we discuss the establishment of the project and describe the things that need to be done first (much like initializing the variables and tables before executing a block of code). We then describe the project management process and answer the following questions: What goes on during the project? How should the manager spend his or her time on any given day? How does the manager analyze the progress being made, if any? Lastly, we discuss what should be done during and at the end of the project to provide a legacy that will benefit future projects.

4.1 THE STARTING POINT

For each software development there are *two starting points;* one for the *company* and one for the *project.* The first is a necessary precedent of the second. The two major elements that establish the company starting point are (1) the *decision to proceed* with the project (in some cases this is a decision to compete, and the decision to proceed is actually made by the customer in his selection of the winning proposal) and (2) the *selection of the project manager.* The selected project manager usually has the responsibility for establishing the project starting conditions.

4.1.1   Company Starting Point

The decision to proceed with an internal project involves many factors, such as cost versus benefit trade-offs, considerations of various alternative approaches, definition of requirements for the selected approach, and establishing need dates and commitments from the supporting and using organizations. Most companies have established procedures for allocating company resources to investigate internal project possibilities to the point where go-ahead decisions and funding commitments are made. A funding commitment is required prior to the project decision. Resources must be allocated to prepare for the decision to proceed. The company should commit sufficient resources to progress far enough with the design to understand the scope and complexity of the project and price the effort. In doing so, the company must be prepared to treat the investment of resources as a necessary expense to support the decision making process, not as a justification to proceed because so much has "already been spent" on the project. As stated in the preface, the purpose of this book is to describe an approach to managing a software project, not to describe the procedures that lead to the project decision. Therefore, no more will be said about this first element.

Similarly, for a competitive proposal the decision to bid involves analysis of a large number of factors, such as company competitive position in the field, analysis of the company and competition weaknesses and strengths, analysis of the follow-on business potential, analysis of the project resource requirements compared to projected company resource capabilities, and analysis of the project risk factors. Further discussion of the bid decision process is also left to other publications.

The second element in establishing the company starting point, selecting the project manager, does warrant discussion to provide a complete analysis of project management. The selection of a good project staff is the most critical factor in the equation for successful software projects. The selection of the project manager could be thought of as an exponential element of this otherwise quadratic equation. A project may have some measure of success with a few unproductive analysts or programmers, but a project will not succeed with a poor project manager.

Selecting the project manager is a particularly difficult task, since each software project has a unique set of problems that tend to demand certain qualifications of the manager that may not be required for other projects. The qualifications required for any hardware or systems project manager also apply to the software project manager: leadership, technical understanding, management competence, alertness and decisiveness, versatility and flexibility, integrity, and foresight.

Leadership

Leadership is a requirement for any management position, but it is especially important for project managers, who must motivate a diverse collection of people temporarily working together as a team. A department manager in a functional organization may manage as many or more people, but in a much more stable environment with a more homogeneous character (e.g., a group of analysts in an accounting department). The project manager, on the other hand, must stimulate support for the project and project team within the transient project environment. He must accomplish this with a team having widely different backgrounds and skills, in an environment where change is more frequent and often very frustrating to the team member attempting to design an element of the software.

Technical Understanding

The project manager must be able to communicate with project technical personnel and administrative professionals, as well as with customers and company upper management. He must have sufficient grasp of the major technical issues, and the more subtle second-level technical issues, to see that the right technical decisions are made. As in many other types of projects, the technological issues predominate. For the manager to generate or evaluate cost estimates, schedules, and staffing requirements, he must have an understanding of the technical problems and know how to judge the critical technical issues, for which he should seek the advice of technical experts. He need not be highly creative, but must be able to *evaluate the creative products of others,* make the technical, cost, and schedule trade-offs, and communicate with the senior technical staff.

Management Competence

Independent of the technological level of a project, the manager must understand basic management skills and their significance to project success. Too often the highly technical project manager relegates keeping track of the numbers (the "bean counting") to a low priority, resulting in an elegant technical solution for a project that is cancelled due to cost or schedule overruns. In all projects, small or large, cost and schedule monitoring is as important as technical analysis. For small projects, the cost and schedule data is so straightforward and visible that little special effort is required by the project manager. For large, complex projects, much of the manager's time must be devoted to these nontechnical management activities. This is a major reason why many companies assign a chief engineer or deputy project manager to provide full-time direction to the technical efforts. In such cases, the project manager usually has less technical competence, but more administrative and management skill.

Alertness and Decisiveness

The project manager must observe, evaluate and decide. He must integrate data and concerns provided by various project personnel, including supervisory technical staff and administrative staff personnel, with data provided by formal and informal control systems. He must identify, assess, and evaluate the impact on the project of data, comments, and trends and decide what action, if any, is best. The project manager must recognize when decisions need to be made, gather the data needed to make the decision, and not postpone the decision unnecessarily. It is not the style or the *number* of decisions made at the project manager level that are important, but the *percentage* of good decisions made. Some managers will demand cognizance over detailed day-to-day technical decisions, while others will delegate much of this decision authority. Either method can be successful, depending on the manager's style and his technical abilities. Good judgment, both of people and with respect to technical and management decisions, is the key. Delegation may lead to failure if the manager is a poor judge of people and delegates much of the decision authority to staff members with poor judgement. On the other hand, retaining too much decision-making authority can stall a project as it waits for the project manager to make many of the detailed technical decisions.

Versatility and Flexibility

We have stated that planning is a key element of project success. Good planning and management require the ability to anticipate and adjust to unforeseen changes that come up in virtually every project. The project manager must be capable of putting unforeseen events into perspective, realistically analyzing their impact on every aspect of the project, and have the flexibility to change as required. This does not mean change the plan every time the actual costs deviate from the budget. It means a determination to meet the project objectives with the current plan, but with a willingness to adjust, when required, to assure that the plan against which status is measured is a realistic and accurate basis for management activities.

Integrity

To successfully recruit good people and to gain the confidence of the customer, the project manager must have a reputation of honesty and integrity. His job requires the trust of others to effectively complete the project. The fast-talking, shrewd operator may look good at first glance, but when project problems arise the character of the project manager will determine the project course. If he conceals project difficulties, their impact will be magnified when they reach the point when they can no longer be concealed. If his decisions reflect self-serving interests, instead of the best interests of the project and the company, this will soon be visible to the project staff. Morale problems will quickly set in, resulting in staff turnover.

Foresight

The ability to see ahead, anticipating potential problems and paths to solutions, is important for project success. Experience is a major contributor to management foresight.

4.1.2 Project Starting Point

Early in the project definition phase for internal projects, or during preproposal activities for competitive procurements, the selected project manager should take the lead in establishing the project starting point. This task includes identifying high-risk areas and establishing budgets, schedules, staffing plans, task allocations, support organization requirements, project interface techniques, subcontract requirements, and the project/customer interface approach. The results of these activities should be included in the management proposal and in the Project Plan.

The Project Plan, described in Chapter 3, defines the project starting point. When a project is initiated—whether an internal development effort, or a contract to develop software, or a system for a customer—the information defined in Chapter 3 should be available and documented in the Project Plan. As previously stated, *this plan provides a definition of what will be done, how, by whom, on what schedule, and which development and management tools and techniques will be used.*

The project manager controls the software development activities on the basis of plans prepared at the start of the project and updated as required. There are several management tools that assist the project manager in successfully completing the software development project: schedules, the WBS, documentation, reviews, configuration control, standards and conventions, organizational flexibility, and subcontracting.

The Project Plan includes sections for each of these areas, describing the intended use of each of these management tools to support the project manager tasks of *planning, progress analysis, problem resolution, and project coordination.* Each of the tools has been described in earlier sections, except for organizational flexibility and subcontracting, which are discussed in Sections 4.2 and 4.3.

4.2 ORGANIZATIONAL FLEXIBILITY

We have previously stated that the basic resource for software development is people, and have discussed the basic company organizational philosophy within which the project must operate. This chapter addresses the use of organizational flexibility within the project as a management tool to distribute responsibilities and project personnel resources more effectively.

In discussing cost estimating and defining the Project Plan, we stressed the importance of understanding the development phases, laying out a set of milestones, or measurable events against time, and estimating the project resources required to accomplish the tasks. These same activities constitute the first steps in the development of an effective project organization. For the software development project, regardless of the size and complexity of the software, the process includes transitions through the following stages:

1 *Software Definition.* Identifying software requirements and interfaces and defining a design approach to satisfy the requirements (Preliminary Design Phase).
2 *Software Design.* Performing the analysis, interface design, and detailed software design necessary to prepare for code of the software (Detailed Design Phase).
3 *Code and Test.* Often referred to as implementation and validation, including code, debug, lower-level programmer testing, and formal software verification and validation (Implementation and Operation Phase).
4 *Operational Support.* Performing software maintenance and operations support after the software has been accepted by the customer (Implementation and Operation Phase).

The software development phases just identified are summarized in Chapter 2 and described in detail in Chapters 5–8. For each of these phases, it may be necessary to have an organizational structure tailored to the performance of the work in that phase. The

following sections discuss the project organization during each of these phases. A clear distinction should be made between a Work Breakdown Structure (WBS) and the project organization charts. They serve two separate functions: task definition for cost accounting versus organization definition for performing the work. Obviously, to maximize the correlation between tasks, cost-accounting reports, and organizational responsibilities, the WBS and organization charts should parallel each other, with the WBS having more levels.

The software development organizational elements described in subsequent sections define the functions that must be performed to successfully complete a software development project. Organizational differences may be required because of the nature of the software or the size of the project, but the same set of functions must always be performed. The organizational plan for the project, however, must be documented in the Project Plan.

4.2.1 Preliminary Design Organization

A typical organization to accomplish the tasks associated with the Preliminary Design Phase is shown in Figure 4.1. The software project manager must emphasize requirements analysis, interface identification and definition, and planning functions designed to enhance the quality of the software product and the probability of success. For a large system project, much of the initial activity involves support of system-level requirements analysis tasks, followed by software analysis tasks. For a project established strictly as a software development activity, many of the system-level analysis activities precede establishment of the project.

The major activities of each of the organizational elements identified for the Preliminary Design Phase in Figure 4.1 are:

1 *Subcontract Management.* A subcontract management function should be set up as soon as its need is established through Make or Buy planning. The primary responsibility of the subcontract management function is to support subcontractor selection and provide control of and customer interface for the software and software-related hardware subcontractors.
2 *Software System Engineering.* The software system engineering function is responsible for requirements definition, system analysis, and the basic software design. This organization has responsibility for production of the Software Requirements Specification and the Functional Design Document. It is also responsible for planning and con-

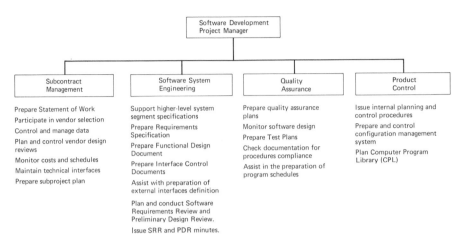

Figure 4.1   Preliminary Design Phase organizational functions.

ducting the Software Requirements Review and the Preliminary Design Review.

3   *Quality Assurance.*   The quality assurance function is the prime organization for assuring the development and delivery of a contractually acceptable product. It assists with program scheduling, monitoring design versus requirements, and developing the requirements-level test plans. All documentation should be audited by quality assurance, checking against the software documentation standards and contract requirements.

4   *Product Control.*   The product control function has primary responsibility for the mechanics of software configuration management. It also plans the Computer Program Library procedures for the project.

4.2.2   Detailed Design Organization

When the Preliminary Design Review is completed, the emphasis shifts from requirements and functional analysis to design analysis and verification planning. A typical organization to accomplish the tasks associated with this phase is illustrated in Figure 4.2. The transition from the type of organization shown in Figure 4.1 to that shown in Figure 4.2 will usually occur gradually, with the emphasis shifting from the software system engineering function to the newly formed software development function.

The major activities of each of the organizational elements identified for the Detailed Design Phase are:

1   *Subcontract Management.*   This function remains essentially the same, except for subcontractor selection, which should be completed during the Preliminary Design Phase.

2   *Software System Engineering.*   Changes resulting from the Preliminary Design Review should be incorporated into the documents that were produced during the Preliminary Design Phase. The software system engineering function continues monitoring the requirements and software design, and coordinates production of the Detailed Design Document in conjunction with the software development function. The software system engineering function also plans the Critical Design Review.

3   *Quality Assurance.*   During detailed design, the quality assurance function prepares plans for all formal software testing. This requires monitoring the software design activities performed by the software system engineering and software development functions. It also initiates preparation of the computer program verification and acceptance test procedures.

4   *Software Development.*   The software development function is established to prepare the detailed software design. Informal coding may be done and simulations developed to gain insight into elements of the design. The software development function prepares the test plans for all tests to be executed by the development programmer prior to formal verification testing. This function also participates in the Critical Design Review.

5 *Product Control.* The responsibilities of the product control function are essentially the same as during the Preliminary Design Phase; however, the amount of activity increases proportionally with the advance of the program stages.

4.2.3 Implementation Organization

After the Critical Design Review, the project emphasis shifts again. The software development function continues to grow, providing additional programming support to accomplish the code and checkout tasks. The test-related organizations are emphasized in preparation for and completion of the formal software testing. To accomplish the implementation tasks, a typical organization includes the functions illustrated in Figure 4.3.

The major activities of each of the organizational elements identified for the implementation period are described below:

1 *Subcontract Management.* The subcontract management function continues with relatively little difference from the Detailed Design Phase.

2 *Software System Engineering.* Prior to the beginning of this phase, all of the primary specifications and documents are completed. The software system engineering function incorporates the results of the Critical Design Review and revises the specifications and documents only as changes evolve in the software design. It prepares the final Operating Instructions Documents required to support the acceptance and delivery of the software end items and prepares for and accomplishes the Functional and Physical Configuration Audits with the customer.

3 *Quality Assurance.* The magnitude of this function increases greatly during this phase to maintain control of the various test activities. The quality assurance function is responsible for providing computer program verification and acceptance test procedures and testing activities. It is also responsible for witnessing and reporting on testing performed by the software development function and all testing done by the subcontractors.

4 *Software Development.* The large task of coding computer programs and the informal checkout of the code is the initial task performed by this function. The preparation of the development (unit and module level) test procedures and conducting the tests should be performed by the software development function prior to transferring the software and supporting materials to the Computer Program

Library. Subsequent higher-level testing is supported by the software development function as required.

5 *Product Control.* This activity continues with increased emphasis on version control and status reporting.

The quality assurance functions shown in Figure 4.3 perform independent quality monitoring and test functions in support of the software project. In the figure these functions are shown reporting to a program manager. These functions may be performed by an independent organization within the company, a separate company hired by the customer as an associate contractor to perform these functions, or by a group within the customer organization. The verification and acceptance test functions are often separated from the quality review functions and may be performed by separate organizations, called by such names as Formal Test, System Test, Verification Test, Independent Test, or Independent Verification and Validation.

The structure of the project organization after software acceptance is highly dependent on the level of studies and enhancement activity that the customer chooses to include as a part of the operations and maintenance activity. The project may consist of a small programming group to maintain the code, with support from a product control function (Computer Program Library operation, configuration control, and problem status reporting). If enhancement activity is included, small software systems engineering and software development functions may also be required.

4.2.4 Summary of Organizational Responsibilities

Figures 4.4 and 4.5 provide summaries of organizational responsibilities for documentation and test functions by development phase. These figures are based on the organizational structure defined in Figures 4.1, 4.2, and 4.3. Many variations on these organizational structures are possible, depending on the particulars of the project. Perhaps the most pronounced example is the definition of the test organizational structure. The organization defined here describes programmer control of unit-level testing and software development organization control of module integration testing, with monitoring and support from the quality assurance function, an independent group within the project. Testing against requirements, verification testing, and acceptance testing are performed by the quality assurance organization.

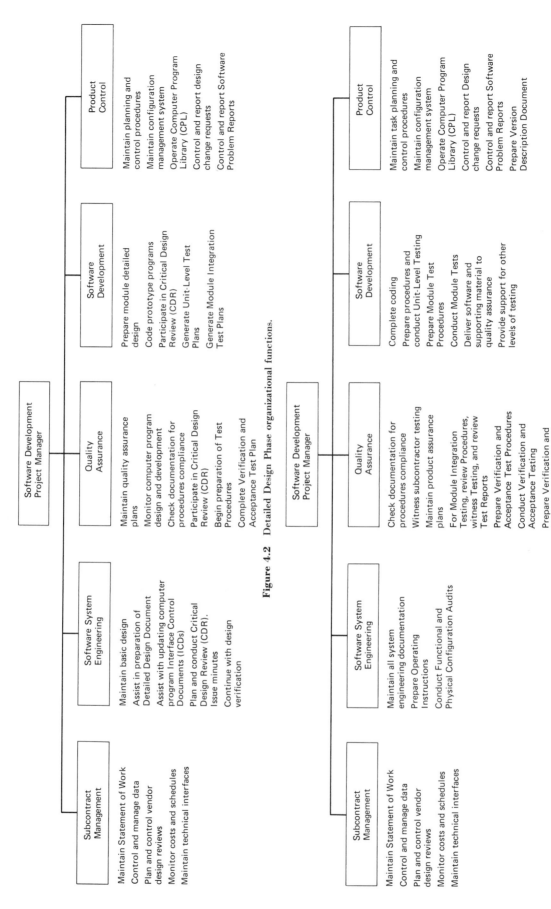

Figure 4.2 Detailed Design Phase organizational functions.

Figure 4.3 Implementation organizational functions.

50

Documentation	Development Phase	Organizational Function
Software Requirements Specification	Preliminary Design Phase	Software system engineering
Functional Design Document	Preliminary Design Phase	Software system engineering
Interface Control Documents	Preliminary Design Phase	Software system engineering
Test Documents	See Figure 4.5	
Detailed Design Document	Detailed Design Phase	Software development Software system engineering
Operating Instructions	Detailed Design Phase	Software system engineering
Version Description Document	Implementation and Operation Phase	Product control

Figure 4.4 Documentation responsibilities by organizational function.

Test Level	Test Plans		Test Procedures		Test Performance		Test Reports	
	Phase	Organizational Function	Phase	Organizational Function	Phase	Organizational Function	Phase	Organizational Function
Program Unit Testing	2	Software development	3	Software development	3	Programmer	3	Software development (programmer notes)
Module Integration Testing	2	Software development	3	Software development	3	Software development	3	Software development
Verification Testing	1 2	Quality assurance	3	Quality assurance	3	Quality assurance	3	Quality assurance
Acceptance Testing	1 2	Quality assurance	2	Quality assurance	3	Quality assurance and customer	3	Quality assurance
Reverification	3	Operations and maintenance group	3	Operations and maintenance group	3	Operations and maintenance group	3	Operations and maintenance group

1 — Preliminary design
2 — Detailed design
3 — Implementation and operation

Figure 4.5 Testing responsibilities by organizational function.

Many variations on this theme are possible. For example, the test duties assigned to the quality assurance function in Figure 4.3 and Figure 4.5 could be handled by a system test function, with monitoring by quality assurance. Alternatively, an independent test and verification group outside the software development project might be required by the contract or by the project manager. In small projects, even an independent quality assurance function may not be required, with these duties typically being assumed by the project manager, with additional support from the software development function.

The purpose of independent testing is to provide additional assurance of quality to the software product. Some errors are due to the subjectivity of the designer or programmer, and independent testing is a means of compensating for this subjectivity. Factors to be considered in determining the need for independent testing include: cost, amount of confidence that will be gained, criticality of the software to be tested, size of the software development effort, capability of the software developers, and the degree to which the implied test plan is straightforward (hence free of further subjective interpretation of test results).

The major advantages of an independent test group are: (1) more comprehensive and extensive testing, (2) the elimination of subjectivity and vested interest in the test procedures, (3) lack of fear of discovering poor implementation, and (4) experience in the discipline of software testing and its associated test and verification tools. The principal disadvantages of independent testing are greater overall cost, a longer required time, and possible inclusion of some unrealistic or irrelevant tests. In general, the advantages of independent testing far outweigh the disadvantages when the cost factor is eliminated. Independent testing will always help if the test team is truly independent in responsibility and separate from the software development function.

No matter how the testing and all the other functions in the preceding discussion are allocated organizationally, it is always important to clearly delineate each of the functions and assign the responsibilities. The selected organization must be clearly defined in the Project Plan.

4.3   SOFTWARE SUBCONTRACTING

There is virtually no difference between software project management and software subcontract management. The same rules of successful software development should be applied to the subcontractor, just as they are applied to all other elements of the project. The following key guidelines should be followed by the project manager who subcontracts some of the software development work:

1 The project manager should provide a *single point of contact* to manage the subcontractor: the subcontract manager.
2 The subcontract manager should be directed to impose the appropriate software development practices on the subcontractor (see Part 2), just as the project manager imposes them on his supervisors, group leaders, assistant project managers, or work package managers.
3 A subcontractor Project Plan, with the same contents as the Project Plan, should be required of the subcontractor. That plan should clearly define the following:

(a)   What is to be done (requirements and WBS).
(b)   By whom it will be done (organizational plan).

(c)   By what date (schedule).
(d)   How much it will cost (budget).

Note that the elaborateness of the plan required is at the discretion of the project manager and subcontract manager.

4.3.1   Subcontractor Considerations

The following important items should be considered when selecting a company as a software subcontractor:

1 Company strength and solidarity.
2 Company management skills and the degree of committed management support to your project.
3 Company reputation with other customers.
4 Experience and reputation of the particular individuals to be assigned to your job (this consideration usually outweighs many of the others).
5 Company experience and procedures with respect to formal software development.
6 Demonstrated ability to attract new people to satisfy company requirements.
7 Cost effectiveness.

4.3.2   Subcontractor Selection

There are basically two ways to use software development subcontractors: (1) as consultants and body-shop contractors (hourly; the subcontractor personnel become part of the in-house team and are typically managed by the project staff) and (2) by defining and contracting for a fixed portion of the job. The latter technique overcomes one of the two major disadvantages of subcontracting: lack of control over performance. The second disadvantage of subcontracting may be cost. Since the prime contractor generally applies administration fees and profit to the subcontractor cost, and since the prime contractor supplies personnel specifically to monitor and direct the subcontract, the net result can be higher cost to the customer. This higher cost may, however, be offset if (1) the prime contractor cannot perform the work (lack of staff or skills), (2) the subcontractor can perform the work more efficiently because of experience or some other marketplace advantage, or (3) the subcontractor has cheaper labor rates.

The selection of a subcontractor is an important task that can be, and often is, a lengthy process. Figure 4.6 illustrates the formal flow of activities involved in competitive subcontractor selection. Even though for small software subcontracts or noncompetitive subcontracts these formal steps may not be required, the chart

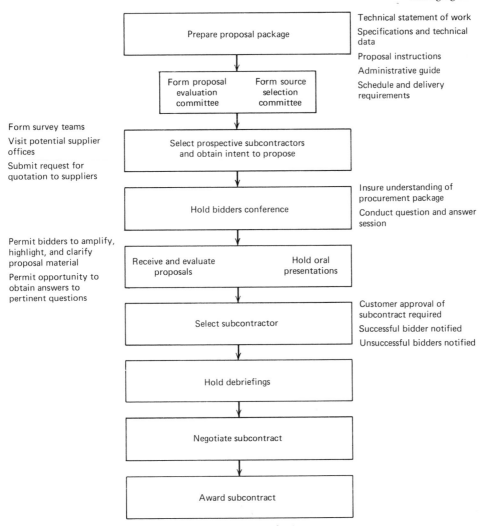

Technical statement of work

Specifications and technical data

Proposal instructions

Administrative guide

Schedule and delivery requirements

Form survey teams

Visit potential supplier offices

Submit request for quotation to suppliers

Insure understanding of procurement package

Conduct question and answer session

Permit bidders to amplify, highlight, and clarify proposal material

Permit opportunity to obtain answers to pertinent questions

Customer approval of subcontract required

Successful bidder notified

Unsuccessful bidders notified

Figure 4.6 Subcontractor selection process.

should be reviewed to remind the project manager of the steps generally required in subcontractor selection.

4.3.3 Subcontractor Management

Once the subcontractor is selected, the subcontract manager manages the subcontractor in much the same way that the assistant project manager or work package managers reporting to the project manager within the project manage each of their tasks. The subcontract manager should do the following:

1 Require a subcontractor Work Breakdown Structure.
2 Require an activity network that shows internal and external dependence of events. The subcontractor's dependence on external events becomes the responsibility of the subcontract manager.

3 Assure that the subcontractor properly controls the distribution of work within his own organization, using such techniques as a Project Work Authorization (PWA). The PWA is an intraorganization contract, and defines as precisely as the Project Plan what is to be done, by whom, by when, and for how much.
4 Impose the requirement for producing a master milestone schedule on the subcontract. This schedule is produced in conjunction with and usually as part of the subcontractor Project Plan.
5 Impose the requirement that the subcontractor provide budget status reports and review and understand all deviations. The format should be consistent with the project's contractual reporting commitments.
6 Conduct all subcontract reviews; these will usually

be the set of reviews identified in Chapter 2 (Figure 2.5) and described in detail in Part II.

7 Know who the subcontractor's key personnel are and understand the subcontractor's plan for replacements, if applicable.

Subcontracting software development tasks can be very productive if the subcontractor is carefully selected and is managed in the same rigorous manner as tasks within the project.

4.4 THE MANAGEMENT PROCESS

One of the prime attributes distinguishing software development from hardware development is the lack of physical reference points to help measure progress. This compounds the management problem and makes the management process much more complex. How then does one manage this kind project? Previous chapters provide part of the answer: careful planning, realistic pricing, effective organization, and constructive use of documents and reviews. This chapter addresses other very important elements of the software project management process: understanding the job of software project manager, managing the project manager, personnel management, technical management, cost management, and effective use of support services.

4.4.1 The Job

As project manager, you are responsible for project planning, staffing, progress analysis, problem resolution, and coordination. You *make the decisions* that determine the approach taken by the project team and ultimately determine the success of the project. You decide what needs to be done, when it should be done, and who or which project organization will perform the task. One of the most difficult concepts for the new project manager to understand is that he *does not decide how* the task should be accomplished.

For small projects, you perform more than one role. You may be chief engineer or technical lead, as well as project manager. In this case, you would indeed be involved in how a task is to be accomplished and the technical tradeoffs that lead to the selected solution. Too often, however, this approach is carried over to the larger project, where the project manager cannot effectively provide both technical and administrative leadership. The qualities of technical curiosity and performance, which led to promotion to project manager, must be suppressed. These must be replaced with qualities associated with management of, as opposed to performing, technical tasks. As a performer, the qualities

that brought attention and promotion might have been knowledge of a technical speciality, confidence in technical skill, enthusiasm and technical curiosity, and ability to work with minimum direction and solve assigned problems. These are the qualities that you would like to see in the people on the project. But as project manager, they are no longer qualities that will determine your success or failure. In fact, they may get in the way of your job.

When you become a project manager, your goals and your perspective must change:

1 You must focus your interests on results, not on how they are obtained. You have to let others decide how parts of the job will be done, even though your technical skills tell you how they "ought" to be done.
2 You must resist the temptation to do many jobs yourself (learn to delegate). You must watch others do jobs you "know" you could do better and faster.
3 You can no longer rely on others to tell you what should be done next. That is up to you.
4 You will have less chance to use your technical skills as you move to larger projects.
5 Your major concerns will be people problems—the management and motivation of people—not technical problems.

These outline some of the realities of the step to project management. How then does one make this transition? Mainly by being aware of the points just listed and utilizing the guidelines and checklists provided by your company project control policies, numerous journal articles on the subject, and books such as this one. Figure 4.7 provides an additional checklist of considerations for the job of software project manager. Every good manager should have a similar list, to which he can refer regularly, in his desk drawer—*a reminder of the responsibilities of the project manager.*

The essence of the list provided in Figure 4.7 is that the project manager must plan, review progress, resolve problems, and coordinate (lead) project activities.

4.4.2 Managing the Project Manager

As project manager for a software project or any other project, the first step toward success is *learning to manage yourself.* This involves learning how to manage your time, when to act, when to replan, and how to get your view of the project back into perspective.

Time Management
A major part of your job as project manager is to promote the effectiveness of others in the project. This

Prepare and maintain a written plan

Direct, but do not perform, the technical tasks

Listen to the project personnel

Be available to resolve problems

Clearly define assignments

Encourage creative thinking, approaches, and solutions

Control customer contract; buffer interference

Buffer organizational trivia

Set meaningful milestones

Check progress against the plan regularly

Insist on regular project reviews with your boss

Promote career development and training of staff

Interpret the contract

Constrain activities to those contractually required

Use meetings and reviews constructively

Establish project standards and require compliance

Utilize company resources such as contracts, product assurance, and industrial relations

Provide for contingencies

Manage your own time effectively

Figure 4.7 Software project manager responsibilities.

is accomplished by allocating much of your time to people, including being available for consultations on many subjects and keeping in daily touch with project personnel. On large projects it is easy for the project manager to become isolated from project activities as he interfaces with the customer, subcontractors, and other company organizations. As a result, he has no time to manage or direct the project. To avoid this isolation, the project manager must take steps to manage his own time.

Time management begins with an analysis of demands for your time, evaluation of the significance of each type of demand, and optimizing your use of available time. For the software project manager, this can be accomplished by defining three classes of activity and then allocating each of the time demands or activities to one of these classes. The three classes are:

1 *Primary Activities.*   Activities that have a significant effect on the project and can be neither delegated nor eliminated.

2 *Secondary Activities.*   Activities whose effect is proportional to the time required to accomplish them. These activities can and should be delegated for large projects. For small projects they should be delegated to the extent necessary to accomplish primary tasks.

3 *Busywork.*   Activities which have little effect on

the project. These activities should all be delegated or eliminated.

Good management of time requires the project manager to direct the major portion of his time to primary activities, delegate enough of the secondary activities to provide time to complete primary activities, and eliminate or delegate all busywork activities. Examples of the types of activities allocated to each class are provided in Figure 4.8.

Ironically, one of the problems of many project engineers, as well as project managers, is the strong tendency to spend a major share of the available time on busywork, even when they know there are serious problems to which their efforts should be directed through primary or secondary activities. There is a phrase that describes this phenomenon: "grazing on concrete." The phrase comes from an analagous phenomenon in the cattle industry. When cattle are brought to the loading pens and are about to be driven up the ramp into the railroad stock car, they often move to the far corner of the concrete pen and graze, even though there is no grass there. They know that the ramp is a real problem

Class	Activity Examples
Primary	Outline Project Plan
	Review and approve Project Plan details
	Allocate budgets
	Identify and recruit key personnel
	Review major problems and staff recommendations
	Interface and coordinate with customer
	Review customer requests against current requirements and the contract
	Direct top-level project activities
Secondary	Prepare Project Plan details
	Hold review meetings for each work element
	Attend detailed technical reviews
	Make or approve design decisions
Busywork	Attend all meetings to which invited
	Interview applicants who will not report to you
	Issue detailed instructions to each project team member
	Read all mail (independent of topic and size of distribution list)
	Review deliverable items for format and errors
	Set up meetings to provide communications between project team members
	Act as consultant to other projects

Figure 4.8 Activity classes.

for them, so they choose to ignore it by grazing nearby, on concrete.

We have all seen this occur in software projects. There is the project where great concern and much time and effort are spent debating display identifiers or printout headers, while serious questions of throughput or technical model fidelity are not addressed until too late. There are also projects where the project manager spends major portions of his time solving detailed technical problems of interest to him or reviewing decisions at the bit and byte level, while major software or project management problems go unidentified.

To avoid "grazing on concrete" or spending too much time on comfortable, easy, busywork activities, you, as project manager, can do several things in addition to classifying and assigning priorities to the activities competing for your time:

1   Start the habit of preparing a *"Things To Do Today"* list. Every evening before leaving the office make a list of the things to do the next day. Review the list, put all the primary tasks to the front, and use the list to guide your activities the next morning. You may not get very far down the list every day, but this technique ensures that you will be spending your time on the items of most significance to the project.
2   A good adjunct to the "Things To Do Today" habit is to complete the classification of the secondary and busywork items, as well as the primary items. Then delegate the secondary items and put the items in the busywork class in a hold basket or special file. When the file fills up, look those items over. You will probably find that most of them took care of themselves and did not really require your time.
3   Schedule uninterrupted blocks of time for planning and reflecting; these can be used to resolve an unexpected crisis. Do not let your whole day be booked. Be sure your secretary knows you want blocks of time allocated for planning your job, reviewing status materials, reviewing staff recommendations, and deciding on actions to solve current project problems.
4   Reserve a short block of time at the beginning of the day to rearrange your plan for the day, if necessary, and to delegate the secondary items on your list.
5   Set aside a block of time at the end of the day to review important mail, return phone calls, and set up your list of things to do for the following day.
6   Reserve some time to "walk the halls" each week to keep up with what is going on in the project, give

subordinates access to you, and provide an informal setting to raise questions or concerns. This time should be separate from that set aside to discuss in your office specific topics with subordinates at their request or yours.

Learning to manage your time well will provide more time for you to manage your project.

Action Versus Reaction

Good time management helps to reduce the tendency of project managers to be reaction or brush-fire managers. Having the time available to study problems and plan solutions reduces the stress that promotes hasty reactions. Often the quality of reacting quickly and decisively to all problems, sometimes with insufficient information, causes subordinates to conceal potential problems. This can happen if they are afraid the project manager will take quick, decisive action rather than listen to their plan for handling the potential problem. A good project manager must be able to determine when to act and when to support the actions of his subordinates. In the latter case, he should monitor the situation, reassessing his position if necessary, and bring other project resources to the problem only if required. Such thoughtful reaction encourages early identification of potential problems. Subordinates will then identify such situations, because they know that the project manager will not overreact by bringing in a task force, unless the problem really warrants such action. They will also be encouraged to surface such situations early, since they know that these pending problems will help to establish their priority for project resources and the project manager's time.

Having established himself as an action manager—one who wants to know about small problems to support their solution by subordinates, rather than react to the sudden discovery of a big problem—the project manager must refine his ability to judge the status of potential problems. Putting off all action under the guise of handling problems through subordinates is almost as bad as reacting to every problem as a crisis. A manager who refuses to make hard decisions can drift quickly from the calm waters into the rapids. When to react, take supportive action, or monitor the actions of subordinates depends on the seriousness of the problem and its impact on the rest of the development effort. Good time management will allow the project manager to divert time to understanding the problem and evaluating the alternatives, without disrupting the rest of the project. Where there is no time for reasoned evaluation, pressure from the problem area and other disrupted areas builds up like a series of sequential brush fires, successively more serious, until a crisis develops.

Replanning

It is mandatory that the project have a realistic plan against which to measure progress. It is also human nature not to want to look bad by having to report progress that falls short of the plan. The tendency of some managers is to declare the plan invalid and replan to make the actual situation match the plan. Most projects, however, have a few key dates and budget milestones, such as fiscal year funding and total budget, that do not change. Continual replanning merely tightens the time and budget available for later project phases. This approach can lead to a situation in which two thirds of the way through the project (according to the latest plan) the schedule or budget suddenly become critical, and the project ends up with delivery a year late and with a cost overrun.

Even if the customer is naive enough to allow such replanning, the project manager must seek the underlying cause of the schedule or budget problem. Replanning is usually in order when major project changes occur, such as changes in interfaces, late receipt of data from outside organizations, changes in fiscal year funding, or changes in the requirements. Note that most of these changes usually result in corresponding contract changes. However, when technical problems or staffing problems are the cause of the deviation from the plan, these are real and should continue to be reported and monitored. They should not be masked by rescheduling.

As project manager, you must carefully assess the motive and impact of all replanning. *Do not try to look good today at the expense of tomorrow.* Take your pressure today, so that when the most important milestone—delivery—is checked, the project will meet it.

Perspective Resets

Project managers tend to become very involved in the projects under their control, often to the point where they have difficulty seeing warning signs. In technical areas, the good project manager gets help from technical reviews by outside experts, even if they are not required by the customer. In project administration areas, this is not as easy or as automatic. Most large companies have now evolved software project standards that require technical reviews for all projects, but too often do not require similar and more frequent management reviews. The manager must often persuade his boss to hold regular reviews or attempt to change his perspective at regular intervals. We call this reassessment a perspective reset.

If your boss does not require regular project reviews with you or is often too busy to attend the reviews, it is up to you to manage yourself. In much the same way as you evaluate the demands on your time, you must step back from the detailed daily problems to assess the true project status. Look carefully at the top-level milestones, staffing plans, and budgets. Realistically assess the project against the plans. Ask yourself the kinds of probing questions you would expect from your boss or a company management review team.

This reset of your perspective serves to put things in their proper place. Your project goal is to complete the development as planned and as stated by a contract, either formally written with an outside customer or documented internally by agreements between organizations. The starting point of the perspective reset must be a review of the contract and an analysis of the project activities, plans, and problems against the contractual commitment. It is easy for software engineers to add extra features which they feel are needed, even though not provided for in the contract. Look for these items. Unless they are required by good design or there is a good reason to add them (and this can be done within the budget and schedule), discuss them with the customer. If the customer wants them, a change in the contract may be in order.

To accomplish a meaningful perspective reset that will improve your management of the project, ask yourself many questions about the project, your plans, the staff, and your understanding of the project tasks. Figure 4.9 provides an example of the kinds of questions that should be reviewed.

4.4.3 Personnel Management

In Section 4.1, we discussed the most essential element in starting a project—selection of the right project manager. Once this has been accomplished, the task of that individual is to recruit the project staff and to manage it until the project is successfully completed.

Recruiting

Definition of the project staffing requirements is usually done as part of the proposal preparation and cost-estimating process. If not, it is the most important item on the project manager's agenda at the start of the project. Depending on the organizational structure of the company, the project manager must then recruit within the company, and possibly also from outside the company, to meet the project staff needs. It is important for the project manager to identify high-risk areas that will require particularly talented people or unique experience. Emphasis can then be placed on acquiring

Is my management plan, as provided in the Project Plan, clear?

Is my project organization well structured and effective, or is it getting in the way of the work?

Am I, as project manager, providing the leadership and decision making required?

Am I supporting the actions of my subordinates, or reacting and overriding their authority?

Are the requirements and the operational environment definitions sufficient to direct the design effort?

Have the development risks been assessed, and are the risk areas being properly emphasized and managed?

Is the project staffed with personnel with the proper skills?

Is sufficient computing capacity being provided to support the development effort?

Are sufficient development support tools available to provide efficient use of project staff resources?

Have there been rapid and continuing changes in work assignments? Why?

Is there one crisis or "fire drill" after another on the project?

Has there been an increase in the turnover of project personnel?

Is there one individual without whom the project cannot meet its schedule? If so, what steps have been taken to remedy this?

Have there been a large number of major design changes?

Have the technical reviews been well planned and productive?

Have the right technical experts been in attendance at design reviews to make them productive design verification activities, not "dog and pony shows"?

Have the responsibilities and the authority of subordinates been clearly defined?

Have software quality assurance plans and procedures been developed, and is compliance with the procedures being enforced?

Have document standards been defined and enforced?

Have programming standards and conventions been defined and enforced?

Have measurable milestones been defined and progress realistically assessed?

Figure 4.9 Perspective reset questions.

key people for the project to cover these specific project areas.

The approach used to recruit the staff for the project can have a lasting effect on the attitude of the project staff. The first contact made by the project manager, the approach used, the information provided on the project, and the description of the candidate's project duties will determine if the project manager will be successful in transferring the candidate to the project or hiring the candidate from outside the company. These factors will also influence the attitude of the candidate once assigned to the project. Recruiting policies should be standardized and approved in advance by upper management. Commitments with respect to

job level (promotion), working conditions, compensation, and administrative arrangements related to travel, relocation, special working hours, and overtime should be obtained prior to beginning the recruiting effort to assure consistent commitments to all project staff.

The recruiting discussion or interview should include at least the following:

1 General information about the background of the project, its goals and the general type of work involved.

2 Information on the organization of the project, how it will interact with other company activities, the number of people to be involved, who will be assigned to the major technical and administrative positions.

3 A description of the project assignment being offered.

4 The reasons the candidate was selected for the assignment.

5 A description of the compensation changes and job classification changes, if any, included with the project assignment.

6 A discussion of administrative matters relating to relocation, working hours, and overtime, as appropriate.

7 Other pertinent information regarding the project, which may be different from other company projects with which the candidate may be familiar.

Much of the material identified for these recruiting discussions is common to most positions that are to be filled. It should be written down to avoid misunderstandings and to provide consistency when more than one supervisor or senior project staff member is involved in the project recruiting process.

After Recruiting—The Next Step

Having recruited the initial project staff, the project manager must begin one of the most important management activities—that of personnel management. The project manager must lead the staff toward the common goal of completing the specified development effort. An atmosphere conducive to open communication, pride, positive feedback, and a constructive attitude can be established through good leadership, fair treatment, and an honest effort on the part of project management to share the glory with the project staff who made it happen. People are motivated by the many intangibles that depend on the attitude of the project leadership toward the individuals on the project. The probability of project success is significantly enhanced when the people on the project feel that their contribution is important. It is the job of the project manager, once he has recruited a group of individuals for the project, to give them each a feeling of importance and build them into a project team. The first step in this process occurs during the recruiting activity. By telling the individuals why they have been selected for the project and clearly defining their job on the project, the feeling of importance and the team spirit begins. It can be nurtured during the project by a number of simple personnel management concepts:

1 *Remember commitments* made during project recruiting and reflect them in the project plans.
2 *Encourage communication* within the team—even conflict. Conflict left to fester will eventually surface in a destructive fashion. Brought out early in a problem-solving environment, conflicts can be resolved in a constructive, face-saving manner.
3 *Solicit ideas* from project team members.
4 *Provide opportunities* for project team members to demonstrate their expertise or knowledge before their peers, the customer, and upper management.
5 *Provide visible management acknowledgment* of individual accomplishments and completed milestones (i.e., do not show interest only in the trouble areas). Such positive feedback is a great moral booster and provides a strong incentive for continued high performance.
6 *Be consistent* in administering personnel policies.
7 *Give credit* to the performance of project personnel —do not take the credit yourself. Credit will come to the project manager when the project is completed on schedule and within cost.
8 *Provide time* in your schedule as project manager for the people problems.

These concepts, combined with an organized, well-planned effort, will contribute much to the success of the project. For larger projects, however, it is not sufficient for the project manager to use these personnel management concepts. Careful selection of subproject managers, work package managers, group leaders, or whatever levels of management are specified for the project is required to promote the team spirit and positive attitude throughout the project.

Reassignments

One approach too often taken by project managers, which frustrates project personnel, is that of frequent reassignment. The project manager is convinced that the organization must be restructured, or at the very least a number of reassignments be made, to meet each project crisis. Repeatedly reassigning staff from one task to another significantly reduces efficiency and individual motivation, tending to frustrate the reassigned individual. The feeling that the project is running out of control develops as the crisis reactions continue. Good planning, with provision for problem resolution, should considerably reduce the tendency to move people around to respond to each new problem.

The Next Step

When an individual's project assignment is completed, the project manager's personnel management functions may not be completed. Depending on the company policies, organizational structure, and the commitments made at the start of the project, the project manager may have some responsibility for aiding other company personnel in identifying an appropriate new assignment for people leaving the project. This responsibility, if ignored, will generate a reluctance on the part of employees to accept future project assignments under the offending project manager. Employees respect the project manager who follows through on all the personnel management commitments and responsibilities, as well as technical and administrative management responsibilities.

4.4.4 Technical Management

The level of direct technical management required of the project manager is a function of the size of the project and the type of project. For very small projects, the project manager provides technical as well as administrative management. For large projects, the project manager must, as described in Section 4.4.1, focus his activities on other nontechnical project issues. Usually a systems engineering subproject manager, a chief engineer, or a senior project analyst is delegated most of the authority and responsibility for the technical aspects of the project. However, major technical decisions which impact costs, schedules, interfaces, or other project elements cannot be delegated and should be resolved by the project manager. Technical, contractual, and administrative information needed to make the decisions and recommendations should be prepared by project specialists for consideration by the project manager.

The tools, concepts, and techniques for technical management were discussed in Chapters 2 and 3. The constructive use of documentation and design reviews is perhaps the most critical. It provides the environment wherein the project can benefit from the experience of technical specialists not directly supporting the development effort to validate the requirements, design, and test information.

Since some development concepts provide more technical visibility than others, the selected development approach does impact technical management. However, the major technical management concepts apply across the board. An environment must be provided for technical communication, documentation, review, and control. Standards for each must be established and enforced by the project manager. This book provides documentation and review guidelines that support successful technical management. Design, programming, configuration management, and test standards should also be established. The level of formality and complexity of the standards should be consistent with the size, complexity, and risk of the development effort.

Progress Assessment

Good planning facilitates technical progress assessment and reporting to aid the project manager in allocation of personnel to accomplish the required technical tasks. Important factors in technical planning are the designation of meaningful, measurable checkpoints, establishment of a progress-reporting mechanism appropriate to the project size, and establishment of a problem-reporting and tracking scheme tailored to the requirements of the project.

To make internal technical reporting work, the responsibilities of all staff members in the reporting process must be clearly defined and enforced. The weak link in the project reporting cycle is often the failure of team members or first-level supervisors to understand the significance of the progress-reporting system and how it is used in helping the project manager establish priorities and allocate project resources. This often results in the 90% completion syndrome, with team members reporting the task as 90% completed week after week. A better approach is to require estimated effort and time to complete the task. Being more quantitative and measurable, this provides the project manager with information by which he can more readily calibrate the estimating capabilities of each team member and more realistically interpret the meaning of status information. Then the project manager, working with the appropriate technical staff, can determine appropriate corrective action.

Meetings

The use of technical meetings can contribute to completion of the project or waste the time of many key people and hinder administrative activities, as well as technical progress. The project manager must control the tendency to try to accomplish technical work with meetings. Meetings, properly handled, can (1) educate those who need to know more about the current state of the design of a software element with which their product will interface, (2) serve to coordinate design or interface decisions (more rapidly and responsively than by project memorandum), (3) collect ideas rapidly on an impending decision, (4) provide essential information concerning changes, (5) surface hidden conflicts, and (6) reconcile conflicting views. The meetings then resolve issues, collect information, report status, or educate staff about the technical tasks, but do not accomplish specific technical work necessary to complete the project. With this in mind, the objective should be to hold only those meetings necessary to coordinate activities and maintain communications channels required to accomplish the development tasks.

When meetings are required to manage the technical activities, it is important that the project manager require the person calling the meeting to do the following:

1 Be sure the meeting has a *definite purpose* and that the participants understand the purpose.
2 Be sure the *participants know what is expected of them.*
3 Be sure the *right people are in attendance* to accomplish the stated purpose.
4 Be sure to *keep the meeting as small as possible* to provide for more effective communication. Only contributors, decision makers, and those tasked with carrying out the decisions should attend.
5 Be sure to *limit the length* of the meeting. If the issue is still unresolved, the possibility of scheduling a follow-up meeting with a smaller group should be explored.
6 Be sure to *bring the meeting to a definite conclusion.* Participants should leave understanding the decisions made, follow-up actions planned, and who has responsibility for subsequent actions. For an information meeting, the meeting should conclude with a summary of key points presented during the meeting.

Meetings are often the only effective way to get key people to focus on a technical issue so it can be resolved to keep from delaying one of the development tasks. This is productive if the meeting is well planned and not allowed to diverge into other areas. A meeting is not productive if:

1 The business of the meeting could have been more efficiently handled by individual telephone calls, a memorandum, or other less time-consuming means.
2 The meeting becomes a detailed technical discussion between a few participants.
3 The people necessary to accomplish the meeting objective are not in attendance.

4 The participants do not come prepared.

5 The cost of holding the meeting exceeds the value of the probable gains to be made at the meeting.

4.4.5 Cost Management

Cost management really begins during the cost-estimating process described in Chapter 3. Cost estimating, cost proposal preparation, final bid preparation, and negotiations lead up to the actual project cost-management activity. Realistic costing and negotiating can get a project started on the right foot. However, without cost reporting and cost consciousness on the part of the project manager, an otherwise successful project can become an albatross for the company and, perhaps, the career of the project manager.

The most important cost control consideration in setting up the project is to establish budgets for each technical task or work package. By basing the financial reporting on the same task breakdown as the technical management, the technical progress and financial reports can be readily correlated. By being able to readily compare the technical and financial information, the true state of the project can be easily determined without a massive conversion exercise.

Cost Reporting

Financial reports are usually generated by a company cost-accounting function for the project manager. The breakdown of costs and the level of the Work Breakdown Structure to which costs are tracked is somewhat at the discretion of the project manager. The important consideration becomes need and visibility. The project manager must decide at what level cost reporting is needed to provide the information necessary to control the project. Too much detail clutters things up and can mask what is really happening. However, data to a fairly detailed level are required to determine where the cost problems are in the project. A little extra time spent in setting up the project cost accounts at the beginning of the project can save a lot of extra effort and cost problems later.

The company cost accounting will normally provide budget data and actual expenditures to date by project cost account. The project manager should have these data plotted to provide a graphic representation, which is quicker to assimilate and indicates overrun/underrun trends more readily than reviewing the lists of numbers usually provided by the cost-accounting system. Carefully recording and tracking costs can also contribute valuable data as part of the project's legacy to the next proposal and project. A good record of actual expenses, used with the proposed budget, provides the basis for improved cost estimating.

Resource Allocation

The purpose of the project cost reports is to provide the intermediate cost information which, when compared to the budget, can be used to determine if management action is required. The budget represents a planned allocation of resources by task and by time period throughout the project. A cost problem in one area may require reallocating resources from another area or from a management reserve.

Management reserves are a mechanism used in many companies to provide the project manager with the ability to respond to cost overruns, for whatever reason, in one part of the project. By setting aside at the start of the project a certain percentage of the budget, the project manager has those resources available to support problem areas. The amount of management reserve is usually a function of the project risk (higher risk, larger reserve), contract type (fixed price, larger reserve than a cost-reimbursement type contract), company guidelines, and, occasionally, negotiated customer guidelines.

Commitment Recording

Particularly for smaller projects, the project manager can get a real surprise when the nonlabor costs finally get into the cost-accounting system. A project that appeared to be right on budget can suddenly turn into an overrun. The best way to avoid this situation is to track the nonlabor commitments as they are made with a Commitment Record. This record should have entries for each commitment, such as a hardware or computer equipment purchase, technical services from other company organizations, or travel expenses. As the commitments appear in the cost-accounting reports, they are cancelled from the Commitment Record. The record then contains only those commitments not already included in the financial reports from the cost-accounting system.

Project cost variances can be more precisely computed with the aid of the Commitment Record. The cost-accounting system reports plus the uncancelled commitments in the Commitment Record equals the actual costs to date. This approach should avoid surprise overruns due to the delays in getting nonlabor costs into the financial reports.

4.4.6 Support Services

The project manager may have specialized help available to support the project. Many companies maintain staffs of specialists in contracts, industrial relations, marketing, pricing, project planning and control, and configuration management to support all projects. The software project manager should seek out these sources of support and utilize them to the project's advantage.

Many companies also provide specialists in legal counsel, technical publications, patents, facilities planning, purchasing, security, and career development. When required by the project, these specialists should be enlisted by the project manager.

Another area that can be useful to a project is the corporate independent research and development (IR&D) activity. The project manager should be familiar with IR&D activities that may have produced results or tools useful to the project. He should also be alert to opportunities for exploring technologies or developing tools useful to the project through IR&D funded studies or development activities.

4.5 THE PROJECT LEGACY

Successful implementation of the planning and cost-estimating approach presented in Chapter 3 and project-management approach concepts discussed in this chapter requires development of an experience base from completed proposals and projects. It is not mandatory that the set of individuals preparing the cost estimates and Project Plan for the current project have personally experienced the completed projects. It is, however, required that personnel involved in the completed projects document the projects from a number of different perspectives in order for future projects to benefit. These perspectives should include an evaluation from the project manager's perspective, from the perspective of a senior technical or management staff expert close to the project, and from a cost/schedule planning perspective.

The product of this backwards look at each major proposal and project should include a description of the project, an evaluation of the Project Plan, an evaluation of the project as it was implemented, and recommendations for future projects. An outline of a project history document that covers these major topics is provided in Figure 4.10. For most software projects, this document will be no longer than a five to six page memorandum. However, for certain large software or system efforts, a considerably larger document may be required to evaluate the project in terms of various major software elements, with a performance evaluation and a set of recommendations in each area, as well as overall project evaluations and recommendations. It should be noted that certain of the topics included in this discussion apply to major proposals, as well as to the completed projects. That is, Sections 1, 5 and 6 of the outline in Figure 4.10 should also be completed for all major proposals, even the losing efforts, to help improve the quality of future proposal efforts.

PROJECT HISTORY DOCUMENT:
CONTENTS

Section 1   Introduction and Overview

1.1   Purpose
1.2   Project Description
1.3   Project Background
1.4   Document Sources

Section 2   Project Plan Evaluation

2.1   Actual Costs Versus Budget
2.2   Task Definition
2.3   Project Support Analysis
2.4   Labor Estimates
2.5   Schedule

Section 3   Management Techniques

3.1   Customer Coordination
3.2   Scheduling
3.3   Resource Allocation
3.4   Task Control
3.5   Progress Analysis

Section 4   Development Techniques

4.1   Requirements Analysis
4.2   Preliminary Design
4.3   Detailed Design
4.4   Code and Unit-Level Test
4.5   Test
4.6   Installation and Acceptance

Section 5   Lessons Learned

Section 6   Recommendations

Figure 4.10   Table of contents for a project history document.

Guidelines for each of the major sections identified in Figure 4.10 are presented in the following paragraphs.

Section 1   Introduction and Overview
The introduction and overview section of the project history document should provide the user of the document with sufficient background information to accurately assess the applicability of this project experience to specific future efforts. The description and background material should identify or describe at least the following:

1   Project title.
2   Period of Performance.
3   Customer.

4 Initial marketing efforts (if applicable).

5 Proposal environment, if applicable (competitive bid or sole source).

6 Contract type (fixed price, cost plus fixed, award or incentive fee, or other).

7 Fee structure and evaluation factors, as appropriate.

8 Customer monitor approach (monthly reviews, on-site representative, formal reviews, large or small customer technical support team, customer use of consultants, etc).

9 Major negotiations topics (specific areas where changes were made, the rationale, and associated cost/schedule impacts).

10 Special actions taken to acquire the contract in terms of corporate commitment of preproposal and proposal funds, personnel, research and development resources, teaming arrangements, and subcontractor selections.

11 Specific proposal evaluation factors in terms of strengths and weaknesses, with an indication of the factors most influential in the win or loss of the proposed contract.

In addition to the above, an important section to be included is one that identifies the document sources. This section should identify personnel associated with the proposal and/or project from whom additional information can be obtained. Personnel listed in this section should include:

1 The line manager directly involved in the decision to bid or proceed with the project.

2 For proposals, the proposal manager and senior proposal team members responsible for the technical and cost inputs.

3 The line manager to whom the project manager reported.

4 The project manager, senior technical, and senior financial project staff members.

5 If internal review teams or task-force support teams were used during the project, the chairman of such teams.

For completeness, if during the life of the project management changes were made, the period of involvement of each in terms of calendar time, technical tasks, and reviews accomplished should be included.

Section 2 Project Plan Evaluation

This section should provide an evaluation of the originally proposed tasks, labor and support estimates, schedules, and budget information by comparing them with the project actuals. The proposal data should be adjusted for any negotiated changes and then compared to the end-of-the-project actuals. Cost information from the proposal and the actuals data should be put into identical formats and then compared. A summary such as Figure 4.11 can be used for this purpose.

Subsections in this project evaluation section should provide sufficient information about the tasks, type of software development effort, equipment or support software problems, or unusual interface problems to allow future proposal cost analysts to interpret the summary financial data. In particular, the cost per instruction information must be evaluated carefully, together with project factors such as real time versus batch software, HOL versus assembly language, scientific versus data management, new design versus conversion effort, or support software versus a mature development system. This section must provide enough information to allow the user of this document to correctly compare the task and cost estimates and actuals for this project with other completed projects and use the data to improve proposal estimates.

Section 3 Management Techniques

This section should describe the management techniques used in the project, identify management problems encountered, describe corrective actions taken, and identify techniques that might have been beneficial in the project. The potential future use of this information should be considered when preparing this section. Specific management personnel should not be praised or criticized. In fact, the names of individual managers are unnecessary. The techniques used for customer coordination, scheduling, resource allocation (personnel, travel, equipment, and support services), task control, and progress analysis should be described and evaluated. In some cases, personalities will enter to the extent of recommending a person with particular strengths or avoiding a person with particular weaknesses for specific roles in the project. This type of information is valuable and should be included, but stated in a manner consistent with the previously stated intent and use of this document.

Section 4 Development Techniques

This section becomes increasingly more important during periods when a company is experimenting with new development approaches. The techniques used for the project should be described, their performance evaluated, and recommendations made. As with the section on management techniques, the future use of the project history information must control the level of detail to be included. This is not to be a sales pitch for the project manager's favorite new development technique. An attempt must be made to objectively evalu-

Project Phase	Manpower		ODC
	Hrs	$	$
Preliminary Design Software system engineering Quality assurance Product control			
Subtotal			

Detailed Design
 Software system
  engineering
Product assurance
Software
  development
Product control			

Subtotal			

Implementation
Quality control
Software system
  engineering
Product assurance
Software
  development
Product control			

Subtotal			
Totals			
Grand Total			

Project Function	Manpower		ODC
	Hrs	$	$
Project management Documentation System engineering Software design			
Software implementation			

Quality assurance test
  Unit level
  Module
  Verification
  Acceptance			

Quality control			
Product control			
Reviews and meetings			
Totals			
Grand Total			

—Should agree—

Total pages of documentation	Deliverable Nondeliverable	_____ _____
Total lines of code	Deliverable Nondeliverable	_____ _____
Documentation Cost per Page		_____
Total Cost per Machine Instruction		_____
Total Cost per Source Language Instruction		_____
Original contract price		_____
Overrun (+) Underrun (−)		_____
Follow-on/change of scope		_____

Figure 4.11 Cost statistics summary.

ate the techniques used in the project and, wherever possible, to suggest techniques that might have been effective in the project or that proved unsatisfactory.

The development techniques evaluation should address methods used to approach the major technical tasks in terms of personnel assignments, special training, technical review and audit techniques, and the use of design and development support tools.

Section 5   Lessons Learned
This section should summarize the important points from the first four sections in terms of lessons learned. It should identify techniques or approaches which proved to be unsatisfactory and those which proved to be effective. It should identify resource-estimating problems encountered on the project. If there was a cost overrun or underrun, or a schedule overrun, it should identify the major elements, tasks, or resource

requirements that were incorrectly estimated at the beginning of the project. If there were subcontractors, an evaluation of their performance, management techniques, and design techniques should also be addressed. Forms similar to Figure 4.11 could also be used for the subcontractor evaluation. Comparison of the subcontractor selection data with subcontractor performance would also be useful.

Section 6   Recommendations
This section should provide specific recommendations which will improve the estimates for and performance on future projects of a similar nature. This section and the previous one are the two most important sections of the project history document. The rest of the sections provide supporting details necessary to understand and apply the lessons learned and the recommendations to future projects.

part two

The Software Development Process

The software development process begins with the identification of the need for a computer software product and ends with the successful operation of the developed software in the user environment. Part 2 of this book describes a structured approach to the organization of the activities required throughout the complete design, development, and installation cycle.

The simplest analysis of the software development process might yield a three-phase approach. These three steps are common to the development and use of all computer programs, independent of the size, complexity, or application. In fact, these steps may be all that are required if the program is very small and used exclusively by the implementer. However, an implementation plan designed around these steps cannot succeed for larger software development efforts.

The major problem with this approach is the lack of intermediate measurable milestones to provide checkpoints for the development process. An attempt to introduce such checkpoints might produce the software development approach shown below. Introducing these steps into the process provides a major conceptual advantage over the three-step approach. Each step ends with a measurable milestone (i.e., complete problem definition, definition of how to solve the problem with a computer program, design of the computer program, the implemented code, and the corrected code). Furthermore, each step of the process may require iteration with adjacent steps, but, hopefully, not with steps

further back in the process. Therefore, fallback positions allowing effective use of earlier work in the development process are available.

The definition, refinement, and formalization of products and the monitoring techniques for these processes are the subject of the following chapters. Figure II.1 provides an overview of the software development process to be presented. The process is divided into three major phases: *Preliminary Design, Detailed Design,* and *Implementation and Operation.* These phases, their products, and their control and review are described in Chapters 5, 6, and 7, respectively. The testing process, which overlaps all three phases, is discussed separately in Chapter 8. Products and reviews that accompany the testing process occur in all three development phases. The timing of these test milestones is shown in each phase in Chapters 5–7 and may be easily correlated with the descriptive material in Chapter 8.

Chapter 9 describes a key element of the software development process, which is planned, implemented and utilized virtually over the entire life of the project: *software configuration management.*

Tasks performed within each phase of the software development process produce *documents* required to control and monitor the software design and produce coded programs, verified and delivered to the user. *Reviews* are used to formalize the development control process.

DEVELOPMENT DOCUMENTATION

During much of the software development process, the measurable product subject to review by project and

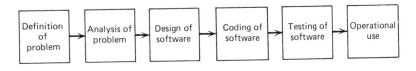

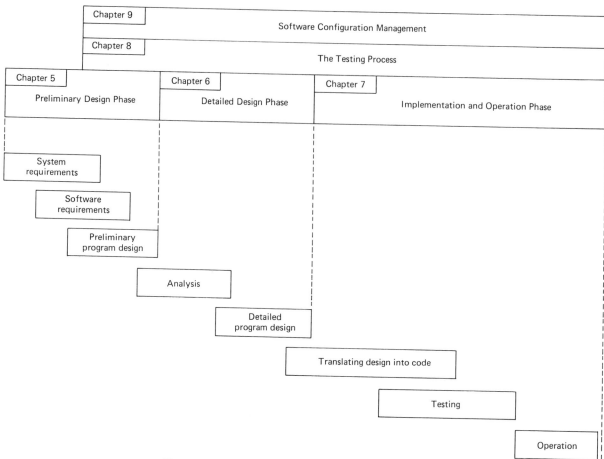

Figure II.1   Overview of the software development process.

customer representatives is documentation. These documents assist management in scheduling and monitoring the definition, design, and test preparation tasks. They provide continuity in the development process, even when personnel assignments are changed. They supplement the software engineering disciplines and provide the means by which the design can be audited prior to implementation.

For all software subsystems, the following information must be documented in accordance with the development phase descriptions provided in Chapters 5–8:

1   Definition of the requirements to be placed on the software subsystem.
2   Top-level design of the overall software subsystem.
3   Description of all interfaces to the software subsystem.
4   Plans and procedures for testing the subsystem and a report of the test results.
5   Detailed definition of the software design.

6   Instructions on the operation and usage of the software.
7   Description of the official configuration of the operational subsystem.

For small software projects, some of these documents may be short memoranda. However, the content described in the following chapters should be documented and reviewed. For large software subsystems, a series of separately bound documents may be required to accomplish the purpose of any one of the documents. A general overview of where each category of documentation is developed is provided in Figure II.2. Detailed descriptions of the documentation cycle are provided in Chapters 5–8.

The set of documents presented in this process has the following attributes:

1   Provides all the data required by the user, the software manager, and interfacing organizations at each stage in the software development process.

2 Is structured so that information originated or used by different organizations or available at different times in the development cycle is contained in separate documents.

3 Assists project and software managers in monitoring the development process by requiring well-defined outputs at key events in the software development cycle.

DEVELOPMENT REVIEWS

The software development process, as described in Chapters 5–8, requires periodic reviews. Their purpose is to evaluate the results of major tasks prior to initiating effort on subsequent tasks. The schedule and plan for the conduct of reviews should be included in the computer program Project Plan. Additional reviews may be conducted at the software manager's or project manager's initiative or at the customer's request.

The five major reviews required during the development process are summarized in Figure II.2. The figure shows the relative timing and the purpose of each review. After each review, review minutes should be promptly published and distributed to provide a formal record of the review. They should be brief, but carefully written, since they reflect important findings and actions to be taken. Each action item should state what is to be done, by whom, and by what date. The action items assigned are recommendations of the chairman of the review to the software project manager. They stand, unless modified by the project manager on the basis of cost, schedule, or other impact.

Each of the reviews may be conducted (1) at a single meeting, or a series of meetings, to satisfy a major program milestone requirement or (2) in increments, as the required information for the review becomes available. Regardless of the method used, accurate records should be maintained of the items reviewed and any required corrective action.

Each development review is conducted by a review chairman, who is responsible for selecting the review committee, ensuring that the review packages are adequate, conducting the review, recording action items, coordinating the post-review report and recommendations, and ensuring the satisfactory disposition of the action items. Care should be taken in the selection of

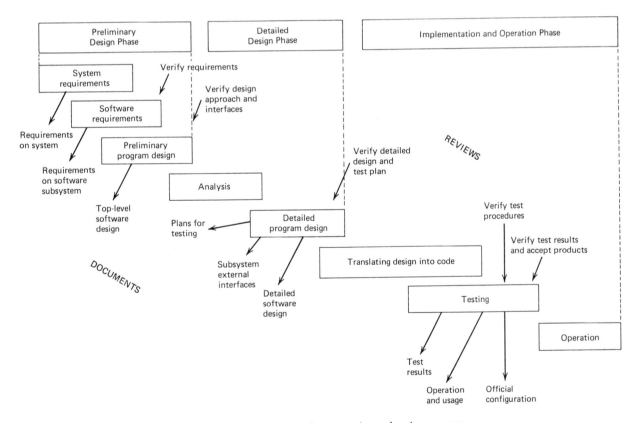

Figure II.2 Development documentation and review summary.

the review committee to ensure that members are experienced in the disciplines involved in the project under review and to exclude "noncontributors" from the review. During the review the chairman should maintain emphasis on *identification of problems* and should not allow extended discussions of potential solutions.

The chairman is responsible for ensuring that all reasonable questions are answered or recorded as action items, with both a schedule and responsible individual identified. Further, the chairman is responsible for ensuring that the list is limited to real, tangible, well-defined action items, not nebulous, all-encompassing investigations.

The post-review report developed by the review committee should include the attendee list, a statement of the committee's recommendations on the review (acceptable or unacceptable), the action items, any new information from the review which was not included in the documentation, and all committee observations, recommendations, and comments on the review material.

chapter five

Preliminary Design Phase

The first phase of the software development process is the *Preliminary Design Phase.* This phase has two major goals: (1) defining what job the software must perform and (2) generating a first cut at how the software should be structured to perform the job.

Defining the task that the software must perform is typically labeled *requirements definition.* Requirements definition has two basic objectives: (1) defining the user requirements that must be met by the software as a subsystem and (2) deriving implied requirements for the software which are necessary to meet the user requirements. For example: "The system shall provide a complete chronological summary of all operator activity over the most recent one hour time span on operator request" is a user requirement. A corresponding derived software requirement is: "The software must save all input keyboard commands on disk in a command file, generate and save the associated time of each command, purge commands older than one hour, and provide a time-ordered printout of the command file based on an operator input."

The second goal of the Preliminary Design Phase is to generate an initial computer program structure to perform the tasks. This is called the preliminary program design. This work is performed by software designers *prior* to the detailed analysis that will be required to fully design and implement the software system. Since the designers are working from the requirements alone, the preliminary design may be in error, but the top-level system considerations (memory availability, data storage, timing, data input and output rates, and interfaces to external components) will be solidified. This will permit the later detailed analysis and design to work within structured bounds and constraints, thereby leading to a realistic and implementable software subsystem. Total resources can therefore be evaluated at an early phase in the program, before a great deal of time and effort is spent trying to solve a problem with insufficient resources or unattainable operational requirements.

The preliminary design process, the associated documentation, and the formal program reviews are described in the succeeding sections.

5.1 THE PRELIMINARY DESIGN PROCESS

The Preliminary Design Phase of the software development process consists of three basic activities: (1) definition of *system requirements,* (2) definition of *software requirements,* and (3) *preliminary design* of the software subsystem. Figure 5.1 illustrates the relative timing of these three activities, the documentation produced, and the reviews required to verify the results of the Preliminary Design Phase.

The technical objectives of this phase are to completely specify the software requirements and *establish the basic design concept for the software in accordance with these requirements.*

5.1.1 System Requirements Definition

The system requirements definition activity consists of requirements analyses and trade studies to determine (1) the system functions to be performed, (2) how well the functions are to be performed, (3) how the system will be structured or segmented, and (4) the allocation of requirements to individual segments. The results of these tasks are documented in the *System and Segment Requirements Specifications.*

The customer or user is normally responsible for preparation of these specifications either directly or as products of advanced system studies. If the system is procured competitively, these specifications are normally issued with the Request for Proposal (RFP) against which prospective contractors bid. If the system is to be developed internally, the responsible user organization should produce the System and Segment Requirements Specifications before the software development group is asked to evaluate and cost the software implementation effort. Often, of course, assistance from software systems personnel is requested and desirable in this system definition work, even though the product is not specifically a software product, but is a higher-level specification from which software requirements will be allocated. Various hardware and software trade studies should be performed, operational sequences defined and examined, interface re-

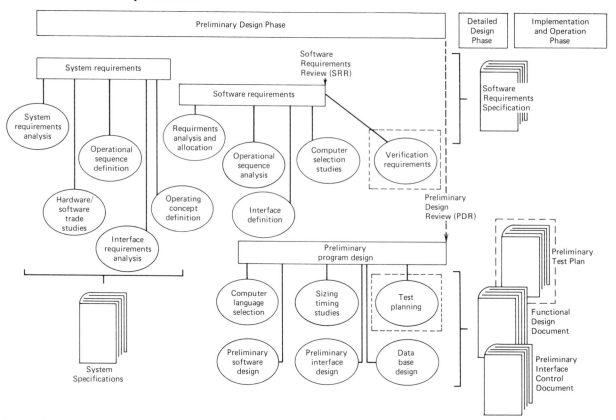

Figure 5.1 Preliminary Design Phase activities and products. Tasks or products that relate to testing (enclosed in dotted-line boxes) are described in Chapter 8.

quirements investigated, and system operating concepts defined. Iterative interaction between the user and the ultimate system designers at this stage will often result in a better product *if* some of the system level requirements are flexible. The key to this interaction, of course, is not to let potential design issues drive the system-level requirements, but rather to seek compromises that, first of all, meet the user's needs and, secondly, leave room for feasible solutions in the preliminary design process.

This system requirements analysis activity should analyze the end-to-end processing for each individual function to be performed throughout the entire system. A systematically executed functional analysis activity will fill the gaps in the specifications and expose any inconsistent requirements. The functional analysis should provide detailed diagrams and word descriptions for each major function to be performed. The analysis is not limited to software only. It involves the entire system and must define requirements for all subsystems. A properly conducted exercise will provide an end-to-end analysis of all functions and their relationships within the integrated hardware/software/operations environment.

For example, assume that a project consists of control of an airborne vehicle from a ground station. A function such as guidance of the vehicle would be traced from the guidance subsystem on board the vehicle through the entire system. The functional analysis would start with the guidance parameters to be measured and the instrumentation provided on the vehicle for measuring them. It would then trace the data generated through the on-board electronics, through the communications subsystem, over a transmission link to the ground, through a ground receiver, through the ground equipment into a computer. There the measurement data would be processed and outputs would be prepared for other computer programs and an operator. Commands would then be generated by further computer processing. The commands would be transmitted over a command link to the vehicle, received and processed by the on-board communications subsystem, and eventually by the guidance subsystem to provide appropriate corrections to control the vehicle.

Each of the affected engineering organizations in the example above describes the data or functions required to satisfy its particular responsibilities in relation to those of other organizations. The frequency of occurrence of the functions, concurrent operations, and any critical timing relationships between functions must be defined. Thus, additional requirements not apparent in the specifications for the affected subsystems, as well as software requirements, may be derived from the system functional analysis. These additional requirements are then recorded in the appropriate System and Segment Requirements Sepcifications.

5.1.2 Software Requirements Definition

When the higher-level specifications have been completed, the software requirements definition activity begins. This activity extracts software requirements from the specifications and derives additional detailed requirements. The derivation of software requirements is a complex activity requiring the active participation and cooperation of systems and software personnel, along with other affected design and staff support personnel. The primary sources of requirements are the higher-level specifications described in Section 5.1.1. In addition, operational sequence analyses, external interface and man-machine interface analyses, and computer hardware considerations provide inputs to the software requirements definition activity.

Requirements Analysis and Allocation
All major software functional requirements must be traceable to the next higher-level specification. These general system requirements are expanded in the software requirements definition activity to provide a clear definition of the functions and performance parameters for the software subsystem.

Operational Sequence Analysis
Operational sequence analysis takes the higher-level functional requirements described in Section 5.1.1 and extends them to a lower level of detail to describe the detailed functions of the system and the software. The emphasis is to derive detailed requirements as they relate to other system elements. In performing the operational sequence analysis, care should be taken to extract only requirements, and not a design. Possible design solutions can be evaluated against the operational scenarios later, during the design activity.

Interface Definition
Software interface identification and interface requirements analysis requires the support of interfacing organizations, systems engineering, and software personnel. Where human operators are a consideration in controlling the operation of hardware and software, man-machine interface analysis and human factors analysis and design tasks must be performed to derive

the associated software requirements. Control functions, sequences of operations, and displays required for performance of the operator's job must be defined.

These interface analysis tasks are usually the responsibility of systems engineering personnel and are often not performed until the design phase is well under way. Since the resulting software requirements may significantly impact the software design, the software organization must support and encourage early work in this area during the software requirements definition activity.

Computer Selection Studies
Computer hardware selection rightfully belongs in the preliminary program design activity, as discussed in Section 5.1.3. However, computer hardware is often selected prior to the software requirements definition activity for one reason or another (e.g., already available hardware, or overzealous salespersons). In this case, the available hardware capabilities and resources must be analyzed in deriving software requirements.

Verification Requirements
Those derived requirements against which the software subsystem will be accepted should be defined in the requirements definition activity.

The major product of the software requirements definition task is a Software Requirements Specification for each of the defined, deliverable computer programs (often called a Computer Program Configuration Item, or CPCI) making up the software sybsystem. The specification defines the functional requirements, quantitative performance requirements, interface requirements (often by referencing a separate Interface Control Specification), and verification requirements.

5.1.3 Preliminary Program Design

The final stage in the Preliminary Design Phase is the preliminary program design, which, as shown in Figure 5.1, overlaps in time with the end of the software requirements definition activity described in Section 5.1.2. In the early preliminary design activity, it is often difficult to isolate design issues from derived requirements issues. Care must be taken to ensure that design information is not included in the software requirements.

Preliminary program design is the process of defining the overall structural design at the software subsystem and computer program levels. This process includes the choice of computer systems, allocation of functions to program modules, definition of the computer program and module interfaces, development of the data base concept, and development of a verification plan. These activities are shown in Figure 5.1 and described below.

Computer System Selection

In many projects, either the computer, the programming language, or both are specified by the customer or by the software developer in the proposal. Computer and language selection often have a significant impact on overall software development costs and the ability to deliver software on schedule. The selection of the computer and the programming language to be used must be considered together, whether the selection is made as part of preproposal studies, proposal design activities, or as an early preliminary design task.

Some major considerations in selecting computer systems are:

1   Required computer storage.
2   Computational capability.
3   Input/output capability.
4   Growth capability.
5   Higher-order language support.
6   Off-the-shelf versus unique design.
7   Cost.
8   Availability and delivery schedules.
9   Operating system software features.
10 Development support software.
11 Vendor support.

Estimating the computer requirements in terms of storage, speed, input/output capability, and so on, is the first step in the selection process. The estimates must be based on the software requirements analysis and the basic preliminary design concept. It is important to note that first estimates tend to be optimistic. Probable growth requirements should be estimated and a spare capability reserved to assure that the expected growth will not cause the loading to exceed 65% of the available capability. Studies have shown that programming to optimize code beyond the 65% limit of hardware capacity greatly increases both the complexity and cost of software. This figure applies to computer loading at delivery. Since first estimates tend to be optimistic, the loading estimates should be closer to 40% of capacity at the end of the Preliminary Design Phase.

Similar selection criteria must be considered when choosing the programming language. Considerations for programming language selection between Machine Oriented Language (MOL), such as assembly or machine language, and Higher Order Language (HOL) include:

1   HOL is easier to learn and use.
2   HOL listings are easier to read and understand.
3   HOL programs are easier to debug and maintain.
4   HOL programs are easier to move to other computers.
5   Engineering problems are solved more quickly with HOL.
6   HOL object code is usually less efficient.
7   HOL may not be available for a given computer or the compiler may be highly inefficient for that computer.
8   HOL is not as well suited for some operating system functions, I/O handling, and bit manipulation.

If the decision is made to use HOL, there are a number of further considerations:

1   Suitability for the problem area and users.

   (a) Facilities for handling scientific equations.
   (b) Arithmetic capability, including floating point operations.
   (c) Degree of subscripting required for the application.
   (d) Sufficient variable and data naming capability.
   (e) Programmer expertise in language.
   (f) Special capabilities, such as character handling, report generation, and macros.
   (g) Sufficient diagnostic capability to aid in checkout.

2   Availability of the desired compiler and its computer configuration requirements.
3   Efficiency and use of the language. (A good language implemented by a bad compiler is of little use. Some compilers cannot be implemented efficiently on some computers.)
4   Reactions of previous users of language and compiler.
5   Ease of training and documentation.
6   Compatibility and growth (compatibility with other installations, ease of converting to a different computer, long-range growth potential).
7   Technical characteristics.

   (a) Method of describing data to be processed.
   (b) Use of operators.
   (c) Commands.
   (d) Compiler directives.
   (e) Delimiters.
   (f) Program structures.
   (g) Support of structured programming.

Preliminary Software Design

Functions specified in the Software Requirements Specification for a computer program are organized into functionally related groupings called modules, which are the first organizational level below the computer program. A module may or may not be an executable element within the computer program. Preliminary software design consists of breaking the computer program down into these functionally related modules, defining operational concepts (including modes, controls, and operational scenarios), and identifying interfaces between the modules. The primary thrust of this activity is to define what functions the computer program should perform and how it is to be structured to perform the functions. A first cut at the module-level design is necessary to accomplish this task. Ideally the computer program structure and operating concepts should require only minimal changes after the Preliminary Design Review (PDR), whereas module design could change significantly as a result of the detailed design analysis which follows PDR.

Establishing the operational concept involves defining how the computer program will be controlled to accomplish its function. The concept of control, sequencing of executable elements, interrupt handling, and input/output handling are developed at this point. Operational modes are defined and operational timelines generated which describe the expected sequence and timing of executable elements for normal and abnormal conditions.

Timing and Sizing Studies

When the operational structure has been established and the executable elements have been identified, the time required to execute each executable element and the amount of memory required during execution should be estimated. Modeling of critical elements may be required to improve the timing and sizing estimates. The sizing and timing estimates, combined with the operational timelines, provide the basis for the computer-loading studies performed in support of the computer selection task.

Preliminary Interface Design

Requirements for interfaces between the computer program and external sources, including other computer programs, are identified as part of the software requirements definition task. As part of the preliminary program design task, the types of data, data rates, special conditions, interface protocol, and specific data items are defined. If possible, even the specific data formats should be specified at this time. This interface design information then provides the basis for the top-level computer program input/output and processing design. Data developed under this task will be incorporated into the interface section of the Software Requirements Specification and into the preliminary Interface Control Documents.

Data Base Design

The first task in data base design is to define what comprises the data base. The data base may be defined as having a very narrow scope, consisting only of data that are formally controlled, or be defined very broadly to include computer program source files and load modules stored on disk and all communication data elements between each executable software element. If there is more than one computer program in the subsystem, the use of a common data base and special-purpose development tools to control the data definitions should be explored. The structure of the data base, access methods, updating methods, control, and protection features must be described in the Functional Design Document.

Test Planning

A preliminary plan for how the system will be tested is developed for presentation at the PDR. This test plan will be finalized during the Detailed Design Phase. This plan is described in detail in Chapter 8.

5.2 PRELIMINARY DESIGN PHASE DOCUMENTATION

As shown in Figure 5.1, the products of the Preliminary Design Phase of the software development process are the four documents described below. As previously discussed, various *system-level specifications* are also produced early in the Preliminary Design Phase. These documents are considered *inputs* to, not products of, the software development process. The detailed contents of each of the following documents are found in Appendix B.

5.2.1 Software Requirements Specification

The purpose of the *Software Requirements Specification* is to document the functional, performance, interface, design, and verification requirements for each computer program to be developed. The requirements must be specified to the level of detail necessary to establish the *limits of design*. These requirements are allocated from higher-level system and interface specifications or are derived from the analysis of system-level requirements.

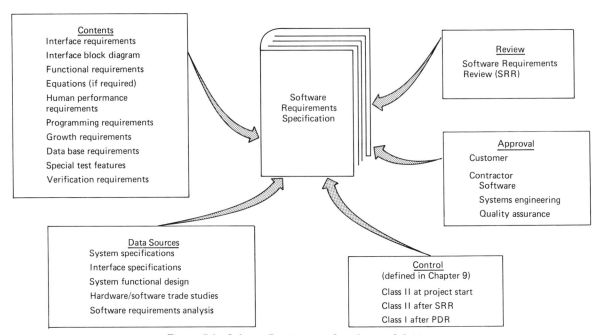

PURPOSE: Establish functional, performance, interface,
design, and verification requirements
Provide basis for design and development of
the software

Contents
Interface requirements
Interface block diagram
Functional requirements
Equations (if required)
Human performance
requirements
Programming requirements
Growth requirements
Data base requirements
Special test features
Verification requirements

Software
Requirements
Specification

Review
Software Requirements
Review (SRR)

Approval
Customer

Contractor
Software

Systems engineering

Quality assurance

Data Sources
System specifications
Interface specifications
System functional design
Hardware/software trade studies
Software requirements analysis

Control
(defined in Chapter 9)

Class II at project start

Class II after SRR

Class I after PDR

Figure 5.2 Software Requirements Specification definition.

SOFTWARE REQUIREMENTS SPECIFICATION: CONTENTS

Section 1   Introduction

1.1   Identification
1.2   Scope
1.3   Functional Summary
1.4   Assumptions and Constraints

Section 2   Applicable Documents

2.1   Customer Documents
2.2   Other Documents

Section 3   Requirements

3.1   Interface Requirements
3.2   Functional Requirements
3.3   Special Requirements
3.4   Data Base Requirements
3.5   Identification and Marking Requirements

3.6   Requirements Traceability

Section 4   Quality Assurance Provisions

4.1   General Requirements
4.1.1   Definitions
4.1.2   Software Version Integrity
4.1.3   Software Test Procedures
4.1.4   Test Software Validation
4.2   Verification Requirements

Section 5   Preparation for Delivery

Section 6   Notes

Appendix A   Acronyms and Abbreviations

Appendix B   Definitions and Nomenclature

Figure 5.3 Sample table of contents for the Software Requirements Specification.

Figure 5.2 summarizes the contents, approval, and control events associated with the Software Requirements Specification. A sample table of contents is provided in Figure 5.3.

5.2.2 Functional Design Document

The purpose of the *Functional Design Document* is to establish the functional design of the software at the computer program level. It is the basis for subsequent detailed design of the computer program. It must therefore provide sufficient design information to accomplish the goals of the Preliminary Design Review, as defined in Section 5.3.2. To do this, the Functional Design Document must:

1   Provide a description of the overall software subsystem design concept, showing how the computer program fits into the design.
2   Provide definitions, flow diagrams, and descriptions of the modules making up the computer program hierarchy.
3   Provide top-level data flow diagrams and narrative to describe the data paths and major events in the operational system. The flows should define all interface data paths between the computer program, hardware, operators, and other computer programs.
4   Assign each unique requirement in the Software Requirements Specification to specific modules and routines, or groups of logically related routines within a module, and explicitly identify the mapping from requirements to software design.
5   Identify and name all the levels of software organization (e.g., subsystem, computer program, module, program unit) required for the software to be developed.
6   For each level of software organization through the module level:

    (a)   Identify by name and function the components at that level.
    (b)   Specify the control interfaces affecting components at that level.
    (c)   Specify the data interfaces affecting components at that level.
    (d)   Identify the data-processing flow at that level from point of input to point of output.
    (e)   Describe the required development/modification approach for each of the components to be adapted from existing software.

7   Specify the data-processing resource budgets (e.g., timing, storage, accuracy).

8   Identify all required major algorithms and their location within the computer program design.
9   Identify and name the levels of data base hierarchy (e.g., data base, file, record, array), down to the individual parameter level. For each level of data base hierarchy, the Functional Design Document identifies the name, contents (description and units), and size of the data base components.
10   Demonstrate that the aggregate data-processing resource budgets (e.g., timing, storage, and accuracy) are within the total available resources.
11   Include a user-oriented description of the design of the interfaces between the human users and the computer program, computer hardware, and system equipment.
12   Include a definition of all design standards and conventions adopted for use in the design presented in this document and those to be observed during the Detailed Design Phase. These design standards may include flow chart or program design language standards, naming conventions, interface conventions, message format conventions, and so on.
13   Include a definition of all standards and conventions to be observed during coding, such as languages, prohibited coding practices, required coding practices, and recommended coding practices.

The contents, approval, and control events associated with the Functional Design Document are summarized in Figure 5.4. A sample table of contents is provided in Figure 5.5.

5.2.3 Preliminary Interface Control Document(s)

The *Interface Control Document* (ICD) establishes responsibility between organizations or contractors for the functional and performance requirements of specific interfaces external to the software subsystem. The ICD specifies these interface requirements and establishes the design of the software components supporting the interfaces. The requirements portion of the document should be available for review and approval at the Software Requirements Review. It may be developed and bound separately as an Interface Control Specification (ICS) if desired. The design portion of the ICD is developed in parallel with the software design. Therefore, the ICD is delivered in preliminary form at the end of the Preliminary Design Phase and in final form at the end of the Detailed Design Phase.

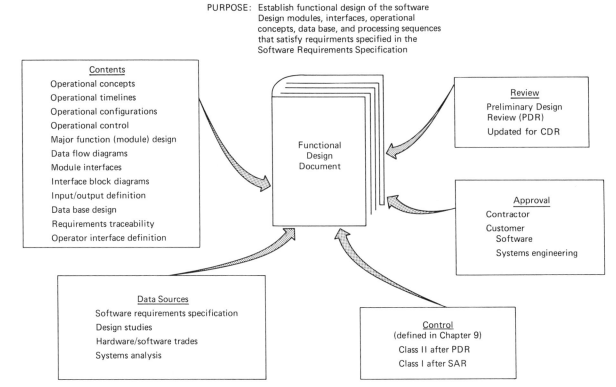

PURPOSE: Establish functional design of the software
Design modules, interfaces, operational
concepts, data base, and processing sequences
that satisfy requirments specified in the
Software Requirements Specification

Contents
Operational concepts
Operational timelines
Operational configurations
Operational control
Major function (module) design
Data flow diagrams
Module interfaces
Interface block diagrams
Input/output definition
Data base design
Requirements traceability
Operator interface definition

Functional
Design
Document

Review
Preliminary Design
Review (PDR)
Updated for CDR

Approval
Contractor
Customer
  Software
  Systems engineering

Data Sources
Software requirements specification
Design studies
Hardware/software trades
Systems analysis

Control
(defined in Chapter 9)
Class II after PDR
Class I after SAR

Figure 5.4 Functional Design Document definition.

FUNCTIONAL DESIGN DOCUMENT: CONTENTS

Section 1   Introduction

1.1   Purpose
1.2   Scope
1.3   Design Overview

Section 2   Related Documents

2.1   Applicable References
2.2   Development Documents

Section 3   Design Description

3.1   Computer Program Description
3.2   Computer Program External Interfaces
3.3   Computer Program Internal Interfaces
3.4   Computer Program Operational Concept
3.4.1   Operational Configurations
3.4.2   Operational Modes
3.4.3   Operational Control
3.4.4   Operational Timelines

3.5   Data Flow
3.6   Computer Program Data Base Design

Section 4   Module Descriptions

4.*M*   [Module Name *"M"*] Module
4.*M*.1   Purpose
4.*M*.2   Functional Description
4.*M*.3   Inputs and Outputs
4.*M*.4   Limitations
4.*M*.5   Messages
4.*M*.6   Method and Processing Sequence
4.*M*.7   Sizing and Timing Estimates

Section 5   Development Conventions

5.1   Design Conventions
5.2   Coding Conventions

Appendix A   Acronyms and Abbreviations

Appendix B   Definitions and Nomenclature

Figure 5.5   Sample table of contents for the Functional Design Document.

76

A single software ICD or an ICD for each major software interface may be written. This decision should be made in the project planning phase and the result documented in the computer program Project Plan. The size of the project, the complexity of the interfaces, the number of interfacing organizations, the status of the interfacing element (existing versus under development), and customer requirements must be considered in establishing the project approach to ICDs. For small projects, the ICD may be a memorandum coordinated between the organizations developing the interfacing elements. In any case, the important point is that the ICDs be produced in this phase to establish interface agreements.

The contents, approval, and control events for the ICDs are provided in Figure 5.6. A sample table of contents is included in Figure 5.7.

5.2.4 Test Documentation

The preliminary Test Plan produced during the Preliminary Design Phase defines the methods to be used in testing the software subsystem. This document is described in detail in Chapter 8.

5.3 PRELIMINARY DESIGN PHASE REVIEWS

As shown in Figure 5.1, two major reviews are held during the Preliminary Design Phase: (1) the *Software Requirements Review* (SRR), held at the end of the requirements definition portion of the Preliminary Design Phase, and (2) the *Preliminary Design Review* (PDR), held at the conclusion of the Preliminary Design Phase. The responsibilities, contents, format, and expected results of these reviews are discussed in the following sections.

5.3.1 Software Requirements Review

The first formal review between the software developer and the customer is the *Software Requirements Review* (SRR), which is conducted after completion of the requirements analysis and allocation of requirements to computer programs in the software subsystem. Its purpose is to obtain mutual agreement between the user or customer and the software developer that the requirements specified for the software subsystem or computer program are complete and accurate and that they represent the development commitment for the software item.

The review is based on the Software Requirements Specification, described in Section 5.2.1, which must be completed prior to the review. Review of the completed specification is the basis for agreements that can be enforced, controlled, and communicated. The *approved specification* is the basis for computer software design and test.

Preparation for the SRR includes analyzing and evaluating the Software Requirements Specification for its technical and contractual acceptability and developing a response to each problem identified in this analysis or in customer review comments received prior to the Software Requirements Review. The review preparation activities include the following:

1 Analysis of top-level requirements for completeness, consistency, testability, and technical feasibility.

2 Analysis of each requirement with respect to the following:

   (a) *Clarity.* All requirements allocated to the computer program(s) should be clearly stated in the specification.

   (b) *Presentation.* The requirements should be stated in a language understandable to the user community in general, rather than in computing or software jargon.

   (c) *Traceability.* Each requirement should be traceable to a higher-level specification.

   (d) *Compatibility.* Each requirement must be compatible with system-level objectives.

   (e) *Technical Feasibility.* Each requirement must be within the capabilities of present technology or technology projected to the development time period.

   (f) *Completeness.* As the requirements are stated, anything that is yet to be determined must be identified explicitly, not merely implied.

   (g) *Verification.* Each stated requirement should be verifiable by test, analysis, or demonstration.

   (h) *Verification Method.* The software specification should identify the general method to be used in verifying each requirement.

   (i) *Validity.* Only true requirements should be stated; the specification should be free of design information.

3 Analysis of the requirements to determine compatibility with contract schedule, funding, and other project resources.

The SRR review committee reviews the presentation of the results of the requirements analysis to determine

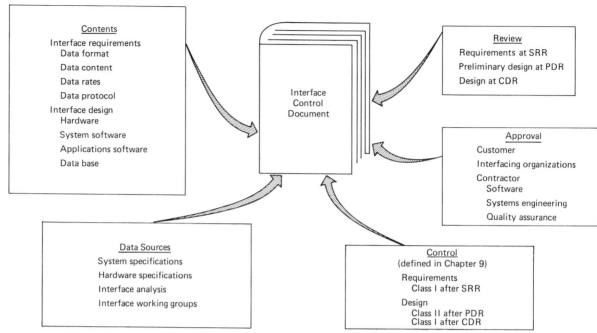

PURPOSE: Establish concurrence of customer and development organizations on interface requirements and design

Contents

Interface requirements
Data format
Data content
Data rates
Data protocol
Interface design
Hardware
System software
Applications software
Data base

Review

Requirements at SRR
Preliminary design at PDR
Design at CDR

Interface Control Document

Approval

Customer
Interfacing organizations
Contractor
Software
Systems engineering
Quality assurance

Data Sources

System specifications
Hardware specifications
Interface analysis
Interface working groups

Control
(defined in Chapter 9)

Requirements
Class I after SRR
Design
Class II after PDR
Class I after CDR

Figure 5.6 Interface Control Document definition.

INTERFACE CONTROL DOCUMENT: CONTENTS

Section 1   Introduction

1.1   Purpose
1.2   Scope
1.3   Summary

Section 2   Applicable Documents

Section 3   Interface Requirements and Design

3.1   Interface Block Diagram
3.2   Interface Requirements
3.2.1   [Interface "1"]
3.2.2   [Interface "2"]

. . .

3.2.*M*   [Interface "*M*"]
3.3   Data Base Requirements
3.4   Special Requirements
3.5   Requirements Traceability
3.6   Requirements Allocation
3.7   Interface Data Definition

3.8   Interface Design
3.8.1   [Interface "1"]
3.8.2   [Interface "2"]

. . .

3.8.*M*   [Interface "*M*"]
3.9   Data Base Design

Section 4   Quality Assurance Provisions

4.1   General Requirements
4.1.1   Definitions
4.1.2   Software Version Integrity
4.1.3   Software Test Procedures
4.1.4   Test Software Validation
4.2   Verification Requirements
4.3   Acceptance Test Requirements

Appendix A   Acronyms and Abbreviations

Appendix B   Definitions and Nomenclature

Figure 5.7 Sample table of contents for the Interface Control Document.

that each requirement has been analyzed and defined in sufficient detail to begin software design.

5.3.2   Preliminary Design Review

The preliminary program design activity and the Preliminary Design Phase culminate in a *Preliminary Design Review* (PDR). The materials reviewed at PDR include the Functional Design Documents, Interface Control Documents, and results of trade studies performed to support the preliminary program design activity. (In addition, Test Plan material is reviewed at PDR time, as described in Chapter 8.) When these materials, which document the overall design, have been reviewed, detailed software design can proceed.

The purpose of the Preliminary Design Review is to evaluate the basic design approach prior to proceeding with the detailed design effort. This review is conducted to determine whether the design approach satisfies the requirements of the Software Requirements Specification and whether the interfaces are compatible with other interfacing systems. The review is held when design has progressed to the point where functions have been allocated to computer program modules, and operational flows, showing the data flow between functions, have been completed.

The following materials must be available to the reviewers prior to the PDR meeting:

1   Any proposed changes to the Software Requirements Specification.
2   Functional Design Document(s).
3   Interface Control Document(s).
4   Preliminary performance estimates.
5   Preliminary software Test Plan (see Chapter 8).

The documentation review prior to PDR and the discussions at PDR should accomplish the following:

1   *Review of Design Approach.*   This review should confirm that the computer program design approach presented in the Functional Design Document incorporates and satisfies all requirements stated in the Software Requirements Specification. Particular consideration should be given to the allocation of specification requirements to software elements (modules) and to the definition of storage allocations, operational concepts, and the data base design.
2   *Review of Interfaces.*   This review should uncover and resolve incompatibilities and inconsistencies among external interface specifications for both functional and physical interfaces.

3   *Review of Verification Requirements.*   This review should comprise an evaluation of the preliminary software Test Plan (as defined in Chapter 8) to ensure that it complies with the quality assurance provisions of the Software Requirements Specification. It should also provide assurance that all test support requirements have been included in the test planning, particularly those which require a long lead time for development or procurement.
4   *Review of Supporting Data.*   This review should determine whether the design approach, as documented in the Functional Design Document, has sufficient supporting data and whether the development schedule is realistic. The following should be included in the supporting data: the development schedule; results of design trade studies, including simulations and analyses; operational sequence diagrams; system functional flows; and results of timing and sizing analyses.

The PDR meeting generally consists of a presentation addressing, as a minimum, the following issues:

1   An overview of the design, identifying software structure, supporting design rationale, software operation in the system environment, and user interface.
2   An overview of the implementation and test plans.
3   Critical technical and contractual issues, followed by a resolution of these issues and an agreement with the customer to proceed with the Detailed Design Phase.

5.4   PRELIMINARY DESIGN PHASE CHECKLIST

The following checklist provides a topical summary of the information that should be available at the end of the Preliminary Design Phase to support the detailed design activities in the next phase:

1   Performance and external interface requirements at a sufficient level of detail to form the basis for the software design.
2   Functional allocation of requirements to design.

   (a)   A description of the overall data-processing requirements.
   (b)   Allocation of performance requirements (from the Software Requirements Specification) to individual software elements.

(c) The sequence of operations within software elements at a level sufficient to show fulfillment of performance requirements.

3 Software environment.

(a) A description of the hardware configuration.
(b) A description of the operating system and any other system support utilities.
(c) A description of any existing software to be utilized in the development.
(d) Details of critical dependencies on any of the above software (e.g., operating system timing).
(e) A description of any software to be developed that will not be a part of the operational system (e.g., test tools or development support tools).

4 Program structure.

(a) A description of the overall hierarchical structure of the software elements.
(b) Reasons for adopting the specific structure.
(c) Methodology to be used in implementing the structure (e.g., top-down).
(d) Functional allocations to the module level, with supporting rationale.
(e) A description of executive control and program sequence of operation.

5 Resource allocations.

(a) Allocation of available memory to individual software elements.
(b) Allocation of storage to the data base and transient data.
(c) Description of how timing, sequencing, and hardware constraints have been considered and satisfied in determining storage allocation.
(d) Timing analysis for critical software sequences, input data rates, and interrupt handling.
(e) Analysis of concurrent processing requirements, tasking, and overlay structures.

6 Data structure.

(a) Format of all data interfaces.
(b) Definition of operator displays, actions, and responses.
(c) Definition of file structure, including name, size, location, and timing implications.

7 Operational concept.

(a) Start-up procedures.
(b) Backup/recovery procedures.
(c) Error handling, fault detection, and recovery techniques.

8 Security considerations.

(a) Identification of security requirements that may influence or constrain the program design.
(b) Description of the design techniques for implementing and maintaining security requirements.

9 Identification of risk areas.

(a) Identification of elements critical in terms of impact on operations.
(b) Identification of elements with high technical or cost/schedule risk in their development.

chapter six

Detailed Design Phase

The second phase of the software development process is the *Detailed Design Phase.* The major goal of this phase is to *develop and document* a detailed program design for the complete software subsystem to form the baseline for software implementation. The key point here, and perhaps the key point of the entire book, is that *program design comes first.* The program design should be accompanied by *complete documentation.*

The level of design documentation required at this stage of the software development process is sufficient for program documentation of the final product. That is, if the world were perfect, the implemented software delivered at the conclusion of the project would exactly match the description in the Detailed Design Phase documentation and, furthermore, this documentation would be at a sufficient level of detail to support operations and maintenance after program delivery. This implies that the program designers are actually working at the program flow/individual subroutine logic level and documenting this work through flowcharts, program design language, or some other logic documentation method, rather than through actual code.

The most important part of managing this phase is to enforce the detailed documentation requirements without exception and without discrimination. *The documentation is the design.* If the documentation is incomplete or poor, then the design is incomplete or poor. If it does not exist, then the design does not exist, even though many people may have many ideas and may spend many (mostly lost) hours talking about it.

This chapter describes the detailed design process, the associated documentation, and the formal reviews.

6.1 THE DETAILED DESIGN PROCESS

The Detailed Design Phase of the software development process consists of three basic activities: *analysis, detailed program design,* and *pre-CDR coding.* The relative timing of these activities is illustrated in Figure 6.1. For scientific, highly analytical computer programs, the overlap of the analysis task with the detailed program design may be considerably more than illustrated in the figure. For logic-oriented programs with no critical resource problems, the analysis phase may be nonexistent. Detailed design of the program control structure, input/output routines and some processing routines can proceed while the analysis is being completed.

The technical objectives for the Detailed Design Phase are to complete and review the design of the computer program(s), and the computer program interfaces. Additional objectives are to complete and review the design and begin coding support software, utility routines, and any modeling software required to support the detailed design activity.

6.1.1 Analysis

The analysis activity includes equation or algorithm derivation, data base content analysis, data storage and access analysis, throughput analysis, and software design analysis. The equation or algorithm derivation task of the analysis activity consists of those scientific, mathematical, or numerical analysis tasks required to specify precise equations or algorithms to be implemented in the detailed program design task. This is one of the few tasks in the software development process that has traditionally been approached in the past by using the concepts presented in this book. That is, (1) the problem is defined, (2) the work is done to define a solution (derive techniques or equations), (3) the solution is documented and reviewed by experts in the field, (4) the solution is tested analyticaly or with a simulation, and (5) the solution is finally released for implementation in the software.

Generally, the special technique or algorithm derivation task is well managed and reviewed. Often, specialist groups are dedicated to the analysis, and when they have completed their sometimes difficult and complex work, the resultant code may be as small as a few instructions. If an error is made in the analysis, it is often corrected with a change in a single instruction, or small set of instructions, with minimal disruption to the

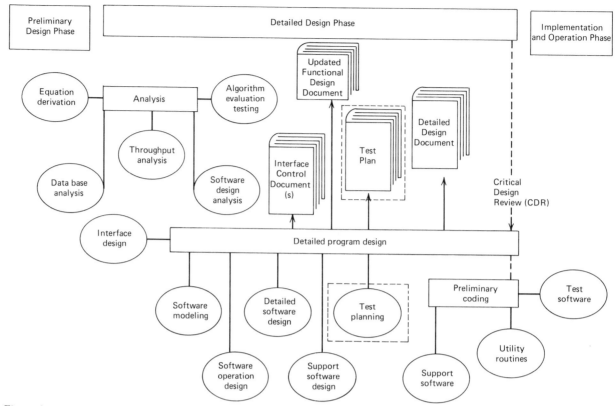

Figure 6.1 Detailed Design Phase activities and products. Tasks or products that relate to testing (enclosed in dotted-line boxes) are described in Chapter 8.

computer program development process. However, if the basic premise on which the analysis is based is incorrect, the entire software design concept may have to be changed. For this reason, the Preliminary Design Review (PDR) includes a complete review of the analytic basis for the design concept prior to performing the detailed analysis and detailed program design. For critical data processing techniques or algorithms, prototype code may be developed for algorithm evaluation testing to verify algorithm design prior to completion of the detailed design as a step in the design verification process.

The other analysis tasks are more directly related to the software implementation and are necessary to verify that the design concept reviewed at PDR can be implemented as proposed. Data base analysis involves studies of timing, access constraints, format problems, error handling, and recovery design features to support the implementation of the PDR concepts in the detailed design process.

The analysis activity also includes a detailed system throughput analysis, based on the PDR design, and any additional software design analysis tasks that may be required to support the detailed program design activity.

6.1.2 Detailed Program Design

Detailed program design is the process of developing a complete design and operational description of each computer program, down to the subroutine level, based on the design concepts presented in the Functional Design Document and reviewed at PDR. The design and operation description, presented in the form of a Detailed Design Document, is reviewed at the Critical Design Review (CDR). The selection of the computer and the programming language, the development of the basic software structure and operating concept, and the design of the software interfaces are all completed before PDR. The remaining design effort focuses on the design of the executable elements of the program modules and the details of their operational use.

The detailed design process may use modeling techniques to analyze critical design solutions, interface data flow diagrams to ensure compatibility among the executable computer program elements, Interface Control Documents for controlling external interface design, computer resource management techniques for controlling the computer resources of storage and computational capacity, and design integration techniques to assure continuity of design. After these system design techniques, which are discussed in the following paragraphs, have been employed and the results evaluated, the design of each of the executable elements within the module progresses to a point which ensures that the module design reflects all of the required functions assigned to it. The design is described through detailed logic flow diagrams, a program design language, or other logic documentation techniques.

Interface Design

The Preliminary Interface Control Documents (ICDs) reviewed at PDR contain detailed design descriptions of the external software interfaces. These documents may include algorithms and equations, as well as specific data message content, rates and formats. The algorithms and equations in the ICD are requirements for the software and must be implemented in the detailed design of the appropriate module.

During the detailed design of the software, there is usually some iteration of the specifics of the interface design. For this reason, the ICD's are republished in this phase in final form. Clearly, during the design process proposed changes to the preliminary interface design should be coordinated with those responsible for the design of the system elements on each side of the modified interface.

Software Modeling

Many software systems have requirements, such as precise timing, that are difficult to implement and for which it is difficult to verify that the design is adequate. In the event that the design solution cannot be fully evaluated by analytical means, it may be necessary to prove the adequacy and feasibility of the proposed design by modeling. This modeling and analysis of the results is part of the detailed design process.

Modeling consists of experimental coding of the functions to be evaluated and dummy representations of the interfacing elements not required to verify the design solution in question. Where computer loading is one of the items in question, the dummy elements are coded to be representative of the expected memory and processor loading of the final products. Parametric controls are included so that the impact of variations in the loading estimates can be evaluated. The results of the modeling are used to verify proposed design solutions and provide improved sizing and timing estimates.

Software Operation Design

The use and operation of the software must be finalized during this phase. This information, including all operator/user interfaces, is then incorporated into the design of the appropriate software elements. This design activity addresses support of both initiation and operation of the computer program.

Initiation involves activating the software, controlling its execution, and operating backup configurations. Operation design involves the detailed definition of all interactions with human users of the software, including display formats, command inputs, operational restrictions, and error conditions. These operation considerations are incorporated into the software design. Detailed procedures for operation and use of the software are documented in the preliminary Operating Instructions Document, which is delivered during the next phase.

Detailed Software Design

On the basis of the results of the analysis activities, the requirements derived from the ICDs, and the results of the software modeling activity, the detailed design of each software module is developed. This level of design includes logic flow documentation for all levels of software, including all subroutines. The logic flows define all branch points, processing iteration, entry points, recovery logic, and external storage access and usage. For all subroutines, calling sequence arguments, assumptions, interaction with other subroutines, data and control interfaces, restrictions, and limitations are described. This design information is documented in the Detailed Design Document. Useful tools in the preparation of the detailed design are data flow diagrams and computer resource management.

Data Flow Diagrams. Data flow diagrams are useful tools in the development of the detailed design, particularly when several software designers are involved in the detailed design process. Data flow diagrams should be developed for each level in the software hierarchy to enable any interface data element (input/output) to be traced to the creating or using subroutine. These interface data elements vary with the application, but generally they are data routes, data blocks, queues, buffers, tables, data sets, data files, and so on, that are used to collect, transfer and store data.

Of necessity, data flow diagrams are normally prepared on large sheets of paper, so that all the data flow paths and subroutines can be shown. The diagrams should be posted on the wall in the project area and should be used by and be familiar to each software designer. These data flow diagrams are used as figures in the Interface Control Documents and the design documents developed during this phase. Figure 6.2 shows a sample data flow diagram.

Computer Resource Management. The detailed design process requires keeping track of the estimated memory and external storage, data channel and computational capability, and the latest estimated requirement for each of these resources. Sizing and timing estimates for programs and sizing and access rates for data must be established and kept up to date. These must be consistently compared against the available memory, on-line storage, execution speed, and data channel capabilities. If the limits are approached, corrective action must be taken. Reserve requirements must be considered in determining if corrective action is necessary. This action may include restructuring the executable elements, the data base, or the operating concept, or increasing the available resources. Computer resource management is an important part of the

detailed design process. Impact on these resources should be a major factor in considering various detailed design alternatives.

Support Software Design

An important element of software development planning is defining the required software development facilities. This includes not only special computer hardware facilities, such as tape drives, extra disks or printers, or extra terminals not included in the operational computer configuration, but also development support software. This may include assemblers, compilers, precompilers, data base generation software, environment simulators, interpretive computer simulators, test data generation programs, test data reduction programs, and debug aids, such as dump and trace capabilities. During this phase, the detailed design of these support elements must be completed and, in most cases, reviewed and approved for coding prior to CDR. This is necessary in order to have the support software verified in time to support code and test of the product software.

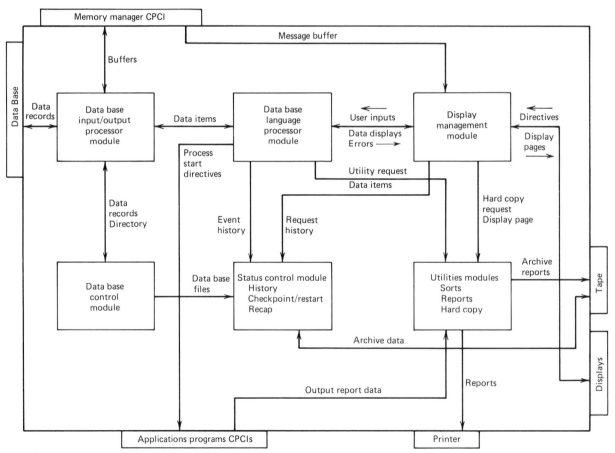

Figure 6.2 Sample data flow diagram (high level).

Test Planning

The final plan for how the software will be tested is developed for presentation at CDR. This plan is described in detail in Chapter 8.

6.1.3 Pre-CDR Coding

In order to meet development schedules, it is normally necessary to begin coding selected software elements prior to CDR. The elements for which this is done should be carefully selected and should not be exempted from the CDR type of design scrutiny. It may be desirable to document these elements in a separate Detailed Design Document for review at an early mini-CDR held to review the design of these elements, namely the development support and test software. Additional routines, such as utilities, may also be considered for early coding.

The pre-CDR coding should be subjected to the same programming language considerations and project programming standards as the rest of the code. It is extremely important that comments be written with the code to permit easy traceability from the listings back to the logic flows.

6.2 DETAILED DESIGN PHASE DOCUMENTATION

As shown in Figure 6.1, the products of the detailed design of the software development process are three documents, described below. The detailed contents of each of the following documents may be found in Appendix B.

6.2.1 Interface Control Documents (Final)

The *Interface Control Documents* produced during the Preliminary Design Phase and described in Chapter 5 are completed during this phase and delivered in final form.

6.2.2 Updated Functional Design Document

The *Functional Design Document* developed in the Preliminary Design Phase must be updated to reflect any changes in the top-level design that occurred during the development of the detailed design.

6.2.3 Detailed Design Document

The software top-level design presented in the updated Functional Design Document is expanded to a coding-level design in the *Detailed Design Document* for re-view at the Critical Design Review. The content, review, approval, and control requirements for this document or set of documents are presented in Figure 6.3.

The Detailed Design Document establishes a detailed ("build to") design from which the code will be generated. The Detailed Design Document must:

1 Update and expand the design baseline established at PDR, including the details of program operation and control and the use of common data. The detailed design must be described through the subroutine level of software organization and lowest logical level of data base organization (i.e., field or bit level, as appropriate). Refer to the updated Functional Design Document for overview design information.

2 Adhere to the basic control structure provided in the programming standards defined in the Project Plan.

3 Emphasize the details of timing, storage, and accuracy.

4 Allocate functions to each software element at each level of the software hierarchy (module, program unit, subroutine), with a description of how the subroutines and program units operate to accomplish the functions allocated to each module.

5 Provide detailed design descriptions of each program unit in each module, including the following:

(a) *Functional Description.* What the program unit does.

(b) *Usage.* Calling sequence and/or operating procedures, meaning of messages or printouts, error returns or stops and appropriate actions, and special input or output features or operating requirements.

(c) *Subroutine Usage.* Identification of all subroutines called by the program unit.

(d) *Inputs.* Detailed description of all external data, data base, and operator or hardware interface inputs, including control words, detailed formats, options, timing, and so on, either explicitly or by reference to other documents.

(e) *Outputs.* Detailed description of all outputs, including options, formats, limits, timing, and so on.

(f) *Processing Method.* Description of all mathematical and logical processes used. Presentation should be in the sequence that the actual programming will take and should utilize the design concept information of the

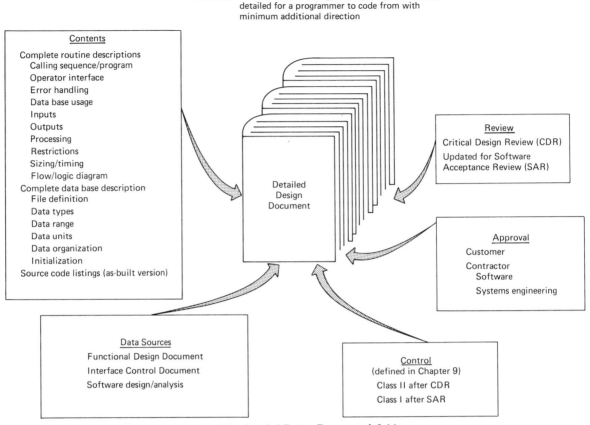

Figure 6.3 Detailed Design Document definition.

Functional Design Document, by reference, for the methods employed. Logic flow presentations (flow charts, process flows, or design languages) are used to describe the processing flow in sufficient detail for an experienced programmer to code the program unit. The logic flow includes or references any equations used and identifies all constants, options, and decisions. It defines all branch points, processing iterations, entry points, recovery logic, and external storage access and usage. Accuracy tolerances inherent in numerical processing or mathematical models and those that arise from the implementation technique must be specified.

(g) *Limitations.* Program unit restrictions, such as limits to volume or transfer rates for input or output data, minimum hardware components required, accuracy and logic limitations, error checks not made (if any), and any conditions that must be satisfied prior to execution of the program.

(h) *Sizing and Timing Estimates.* Program unit

resource requirements, both code and data, to be used as a basis for updated software subsystem and computer program estimates.

(i) *Subroutine Description.* Definition of the same type of information as specified above for the program units for each subroutine designed as an element of the program unit.

6 Provide detailed design descriptions for utility subroutines used by a number of program units. These descriptions should provide the same information as specified in item 5 for program units and their subroutines.

Listings of all computer programs described in the document are added as an appendix when the document is updated to reflect the final configuration in the next phase. This process is described in Chapter 7.

A sample table of contents for a Detailed Design Document is shown in Figure 6.4. The Functional Design Document, defined in Chapter 5, provides the overall computer program structure, module-level descriptions, and module interface definition. The De-

DETAILED DESIGN DOCUMENT: CONTENTS

Section 1   Introduction

1.1   Purpose
1.2   Scope
1.3   Design Overview

Section 2   Related Documents

2.1   Applicable References
2.2   Development Documents

Section 3   [Module Name] Design

3.1   Purpose of Module [Module Name]
3.2   Functional Description
3.3   Program Units
3.3.1   [Program Unit Name "1"]
3.3.1.1   Identification
3.3.1.2   Functional Description
3.3.1.3   Usage
3.3.1.4   Subroutines Required
3.3.1.5   Inputs
3.3.1.6   Outputs
3.3.1.7   Processing Method
3.3.1.8   Limitations
3.3.1.9   Sizing and Timing Estimates
3.3.1.10   Subroutine Descriptions
3.3.2   [Program Unit Name "2"]

. . .

3.3.*P*   [Program Unit Name *"P"*]

. . .

3.4   Utility Subroutines

Section 4   [Module Name] Design

4.1   Purpose of Module [Module Name]

. . .

Section *N*   [Module Name] Design

N.1   Purpose of Module [Module Name]

. . .

Section *N* + 1   Data Base

Section *N* + 2   System Resource Allocation

Section *N* + 3   Functional Flow

Section *N* + 4   Formats

Section *N* + 5   Utilities

Section *N* + 6   Notes

Appendix A   Acronyms and Abbreviations

Appendix B   Definitions and Nomenclature

Appendix C   Computer Program Listings

Figure 6.4 Sample table of contents for the Detailed Design Document.

tailed Design Document describes the design for the program unit and subroutine levels within each module. For large computer programs, it may be desirable to use separate documents to describe each module. It is also sometimes desirable to separate the data base information into a Data Base Design Document. Another useful approach is to separate all the logic flow representations into another volume, keyed to the text by section number. This technique allows the reader to have the two volumes side by side, making it easier to relate the prose to the logic. Also, readers not desiring to get into the logic details have a less cumbersome and easier to follow volume to work with.

6.2.4   Test Documentation

The final version of the Test Plan is produced during the Detailed Design Phase. This document, which was

begun during the Preliminary Design Phase, is described in detail in Chapter 8.

6.3   DETAILED DESIGN PHASE REVIEWS

During the Detailed Design Phase, the design of the software evolves, culminating in a final detailed design. To support this process, two types of reviews are held in this phase: *Internal Design Reviews and the Critical Design Review.* These reviews are discussed in the following sections.

6.3.1   Internal Design Reviews

As the overall computer program design matures and individuals focus more intensively on design of their own modules, it becomes increasingly difficult to keep a systems perspective. In addition, the flow of information about useful techniques and module interfaces becomes less effective on an *ad hoc* basis.

In order to address the above problems, the project should hold a series of *Internal Design Reviews* (IDRs). An IDR is an informal presentation that focuses on a specific area of design, whether a module, an interface, or an overall computer program capability. An IDR should provide a concise conceptual view of the area under discussion and a presentation of any special techniques or special features involved.

An IDR should never involve more than an hour or two of preparation or lead to more than half an hour of actual review. All project members should be invited, but attendance is usually optional, except for those directly concerned with the review material. The review is not a test or a demonstration, but a presentation of a piece of the software: its purposes, general structure, and current state as seen by the person responsible for its creation. It should never become a design-by-committee session, although problems that must be addressed outside the review may surface.

Briefly, the goals of the IDR are (1) to acquaint all staff members with overall software structures, (2) to show techniques found to be effective within the project (especially use of the hardware equipment), and (3) to explain special problems and considerations, pooling the knowledge of all project members.

6.3.2 Critical Design Review

As shown in Figure 6.1, the Detailed Design Phase of the software development process culminates with the *Critical Design Review* (CDR). The CDR is a formal technical review of the design. It is conducted when the detailed design for the software is completed and the Detailed Design Documents are ready for release. The Critical Design Review verifies design adequacy.

To accomplish the design verification, the following materials must be available to the reviewers prior to the scheduled CDR meeting:

1 The updated Functional Design Document.
2 The Detailed Design Document.
3 The current Software Requirements Specification.
4 Interface Control Documents.
5 Negotiated changes to the Software Requirements Specification and associated Interface Control Documents.
6 The final version of the software Test Plan.

7 Design evaluation or trade study results.
8 Updated performance estimates.

The documentation review prior to CDR and the discussions at CDR should accomplish the following:

1 *Review of Detailed Design.* This review should establish that the detailed design reflected in the Detailed Design Document satisfies the requirements of the Software Requirements Specification.
2 *Review of System Compatibility.* Reviewers should compare all detailed block diagrams, schematics, and logic diagrams with Interface Control Documents (and System Interface Description Documents, if available) to determine system compatibility.
3 *Review of Design Changes.* This review should consider all changes to System Requirements Specifications and Interface Control Documents made after the Preliminary Design Review to verify that the design adequately reflects the changes. The review should consider the functional design, as documented in the Functional Design Document and approved at PDR, to ensure that changes in the top-level design are acceptable.
4 *Review of Verification Plan.* This review should comprise an evaluation of the software Test Plan for completeness and technical adequacy (see Chapter 8).

The Critical Design Review generally consists of a presentation of at least the following topics:

1 An overview of the detailed design, identifying software structure, component interface and interaction, supporting design rationale, software operation in the system environment, and detailed user interface descriptions.
2 An overview of the implementation and test plans.
3 Resolution of critical technical and contractual issues, leading to an agreement with the customer to proceed with the coding phase and to an agreed-to test program.

For a large complex software project, the CDR is sometimes conducted on a progressive basis, with individual computer programs or modules reviewed and authorization granted to proceed with implementation and test at a series of separate reviews. Care must be taken that the design of the separable modules is not dependent on the design of modules to be reviewed at a later date.

6.4 DETAILED DESIGN PHASE CHECKLIST

The following checklist provides a topical summary of the information that should be available and approved at the end of the Detailed Design Phase to support the subsequent implementation and test activities.

1 Performance requirements and external interface design at a sufficient level of detail to form the basis for implementation.
2 Detailed allocation of requirements to the designed software modules (update of PDR material, if required).
3 Software environment.

    (a) Design of all software interfaces with the hardware configuration.
    (b) Design of all software interfaces with and usage of the operating system and any other system support utilities.
    (c) Design of all software interfaces with and identification of any existing software to be utilized in the development.
    (c) Analysis of critical dependencies on the hardware and any software.
    (d) Design of any software that will not be a part of the operational configuration (e.g., test or development tools).

4 Software design details.

    (a) A written description and detailed specification of the function and performance of each module.
    (b) A block diagram showing the structure of each software module down to the algorithm level.
    (c) Module flow diagrams or an equivalent logic flow description at a sufficient level of detail to begin coding.
    (d) A block diagram showing data transfer between program modules and between hardware and software.
    (e) A detailed definition (description) of control interfaces between each pair of modules.
    (f) A detailed definition of all inputs and outputs for each module, including data formats and valid ranges of data.

5 Resource allocations (expansion of PDR material; see item No. 5 in Section 5.4).
6 Data structure.

    (a) A definition of the structure of the data base and all other data files and data interfaces.
    (b) Details of the structure and design of each data file, including its name, origin, content, length, resident device, access method, and so on.
    (c) A definition of each item or group of items in the data base, data files, or other data interfaces, including the item or group name, prose definition, format, units, and usage.

7 Operations Procedures.

    (a) Detailed design of procedures and data interfaces for operation of the computer hardware, use of the operating system, and initialization and control of the computer program.
    (b) Detailed design of backup and recovery configurations and procedures.
    (c) Detailed design of the procedures and data interfaces for use in the computer program.

chapter seven

The Implementation and Operation Phase

The Implementation and Operation Phase of the software development process includes (1) the translation of the documented, reviewed detailed design into executable code, (2) the validation of this transformation through various levels of testing, and (3) the formal verification that the result satisfies the documented requirements in the Software Requirements Specification. The key events in this phase are the completion of the implementation and testing of the software and the formal acceptance of the software by the customer. The testing and acceptance process supporting these activities is described in detail in Chapter 8. Following the successful conclusion of these efforts, which culminate with the installation of the software in the operational configuration, the software is ready to perform the functions for which it was implemented.

Normally the postdelivery software operation and maintenance activities are contractually and organizationally distinct from development and are separate with respect to specific personnel involved. However, a brief summary of the types of activities required is provided in this chapter, since awareness of the operations and maintenance requirements may influence design decisions and the emphasis placed on various development-phase tasks. For example, a simulation tool used to support design and test of a large system, which will be operated by its developers, may require a different level of detail in documentation and testing than a commercial software system, which will be operated by clerical personnel with a high employee turnover rate.

In addition to test documentation and the delivered code, several documents produced during this final phase of software development are used to support software operation and maintenance. These include updates of the design documentation to reflect the "as-built" software, a description of the operation and usage of the software, and documentation clearly identifying each version of the computer programs.

7.1 THE IMPLEMENTATION AND OPERATION PROCESS

The Implementation and Operation Phase of the software development process consists of three basic activities: *translating design into code, testing,* and *operation.* The relative timing of these activities is illustrated in Figure 7.1. The basic objectives of this phase are to *implement the design in code, test the resulting software, and formally deliver, use, and maintain the software in the operational environment.*

There is a great deal of overlap in the functions and iteration through various steps in the activities performed during the Implementation and Operation Process. For example:

1 Coding and testing activities (and sometimes even design) are continually iterated as errors are uncovered in testing.
2 Particular consideration and understanding of the operational environment and expertise of the operators and users of the system is required during the complete software development cycle. This will ensure the least complicated and costly design and implementation that is appropriate to the environment in which the computer program is to be operated.
3 System operations and software maintenance disciplines are exercised heavily during coding and testing. The operation of the software is refined continually during the later phases of verification testing. The procedures for maintaining the software in the operational environment are established and utilized after configuration control is instigated during development.
4 The test definition process must consider software maintenance activities to ensure that a subset of tests will be appropriate for retesting in the operational environment. This will eliminate the need for

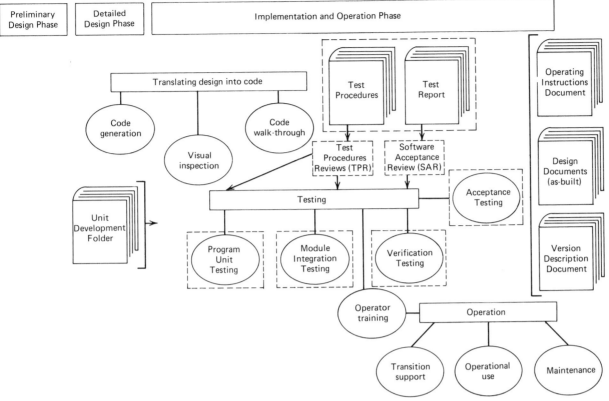

Figure 7.1 Implementation and Operation Phase activities and products. Tasks or products that relate to testing (enclosed in dotted-line boxes) are described in Chapter 8.

later rework of test generation. For example, if simulators are required for the predelivery testing, the tests should be easily adapted to the use of real data in the operational system.

5 Superimposed on the entire Implementation and Operation Process is the configuration management activity described in Chapter 9.

7.1.1 Translating Design Into Code

The first step in the implementation process consists of tasks involving code generation, visual inspection, and code checking. These activities are directed at preparing the code for testing.

Code Generation

The coding process is the conversion of the logic flows from the Detailed Design Document to the assembler or Higher Order Language (HOL) statements for input to the assembler or HOL compiler. Coding either is performed according to the project programming standards included in the Project Plan, or according to a separate standards document produced at the start of

the project. It is extremely important that sufficient comments are written during coding to permit easy traceability from the program listing to the logic flows. Coding includes correction of all compilation or assembly errors.

Visual Inspection

The compiler or assembler provides only diagnostics for errors in syntax or use of the programming language. It cannot verify that the code is a correct translation of the logic flow. An important step in the software development process—which is often skipped—is to compare the assembled (compiled) code with the logic flows. This simple visual inspection can save hours of computer programmer time in the verification process by locating many simple logic translation errors.

Code Walk-Through

An important concept to be implemented in the coding process is the code walk-through (sometimes called peer code reviews). In this process, programmers examine each other's code in a structured manner before testing begins. In addition to aiding in the discovery of errors in coding, interfaces, and requirements implementation, the process also reduces management dependence on the support of individual programmers.

7.1.2 Testing

The testing process is intended to ensure that the coded program satisfies the performance and design requirements specified in the Software Requirements Specification. The testing process is defined in detail in Chapter 8. This phase of the testing process culminates in the formal verification and customer acceptance of the software.

7.1.3 Operation

System operation consists of utilizing the software in the operational environment to produce the results or control the processes that were originally defined in the system specifications. The operations phase typically begins with three major activities.

Transition Support

After acceptance of the software or, in some cases, prior to acceptance, a period of parallel operation and tuning may occur. If the software is replacing an old hardware, software, or manual system, there may be a period of parallel operation where the outputs of the new system are compared with the old. The new system can then be used operationally, with the possibility of reverting to the old system at any time, or it can be implemented incrementally, gradually phasing out the old system.

During the transition or system activation period, data base parameters may be tuned to provide optimal operations support. This adjustment or refinement of parameters can often be done only after the system has been observed in operation for some time. It is important that all software changes during this period be formally controlled. The system is operational, and hastily implemented changes could prove disastrous.

For formal software development procurements, the transition support may be specified as part of the development contract, or it may be a separate "labor hours" support contract. In the former case, care must be taken to specify explicitly what is to be covered by the transition support portion of the contract. It is very easy for the customer to regard missing capabilities or special features as errors to be fixed

during this phase of the contract, whereas they are really upgrades that should be covered as a contract change.

Operator Training

Training of personnel to use the new software may also be covered under the development contract or follow-on operation and maintenance (O & M) contracts. In either case, the extent and type of training, the amount of special materials (visual aids, workshop materials) to be prepared, the number of people to be trained, the number of hours (classroom, laboratory, and on-the-machine) to be provided, and the background of the trainees should all be specified in advance.

If properly structured, the Functional Design, Detailed Design, and Operating Instructions Documents should provide the major elements required for the training courses.

Operational Use

When the software is finally put into operational use, it is usually exercised by personnel who were not part of the development effort (e.g., computer operators and persons familiar with the functional discipline that the software supports). For this reason, misunderstandings of the requirements and usage of the system often occur in the early operational phase. Whenever possible, software development personnel should provide on-site assistance during this time to answer questions, cope with unusual conditions, and clarify system usage to the operational personnel. This close support will prevent unwarranted problem reports and complaints and ensure a smoother transition into the operational environment.

Maintenance

The final key activity during the operation phase is software maintenance. A major component of software maintenance is the configuration management process. This process is discussed in Chapter 9.

Software maintenance involves *fixing errors* that show up during operational use of the software. This work is best done under a separate contract. The most common is a "labor hours" contract, under which a level of effort is provided to fix whatever the customer requires, and the customer pays for the expenses incurred. This type of contract avoids warranty questions and arguments as to whether the fixing is a correction or an upgrade. Upgrades typically require a contract change if the effort is being performed under the development contract.

A hardware warranty means that the hardware will be fixed if it fails to meet specifications at some point during operation. The same is true of software product. That is, the software is guaranteed to meet the requirements as defined in the software acceptance test criteria. These tests are sufficient, since the customer has agreed that meeting the acceptance tests is equivalent to meeting the requirements. Therefore, in a carefully structured and managed software development process, any errors found after acceptance are not under warranty, since they did not occur in the acceptance tests, and, if the software is the same, will not occur in a rerun of the acceptance tests. In reality, however, errors that should have been discovered earlier do occur, since it is usually too costly to perform totally exhaustive acceptance tests. Therefore, early agreement with the customer on a funded software maintenance contract, together with a rigorous approach to the test process as defined in Chapter 8, is the most inexpensive and efficient approach to software reliability and maintenance.

Software changes after delivery will often be made by persons different from those who developed the software. Therefore, the documentation is extremely important. It is the basis upon which the maintenance personnel acquire the necessary design and operations understanding to make changes without introducing new errors. Clear, explicit processing descriptions in the Detailed Design Documents will reduce the number and severity of the operational problems caused by incorrect maintenance changes. Tight configuration control of the code and documentation updates, reflecting all changes, is necessary to support continuing software maintenance activities. These control procedures are defined in detail in Chapter 9.

In addition to fixing errors encountered during software usage, the software maintenance activity may include *software enhancements.* Minor upgrades to the delivered software system may be accomplished under the auspices of the software maintenance contract. Chapter 9 provides guidelines for controlling the resulting configuration changes. Larger changes, however, should be treated separately. They should be priced, scheduled, documented, and controlled in the same manner as the original development. The product may be a new release of some elements of the software system or a complete redelivery of the entire software system, not unlike the original system delivery.

As with software maintenance, a key element in reducing enhancement risks is the quality of the design documentation.

7.2 IMPLEMENTATION AND OPERATION PHASE DOCUMENTATION

As shown in Figure 7.1, the baseline documents for the Implementation and Operation Phase are the Operating Instructions Document, the Unit Development Folder, the final Functional and Detailed Design Documents, and the Version Description Document. These documents may be updated as changes occur during operation and maintenance of the software. The detailed contents of each document may be found in Appendix B.

7.2.1 Operating Instructions Document

The purpose of the *Operating Instructions Document* is to describe the operating procedures to load, start, operate, restart, and stop the computer program. Complete operating instructions include machine requirements, inputs, outputs, control card image or keyboard input formats, options, limitations, halt and recovery procedures, on-line listings, and special parameters.

There are two categories of operating procedures for software. The first category, *computer program operations,* shows the steps required to bring the computer program from its quiescent state in program storage to a dynamic state capable of performing the intended functions. The second category, *major function operations,* describes how the capabilities of the software are exercised. The first category is often documented in an "Operator's Guide", while the second category is included in a "User's Manual".

For each major function, a brief technical discussion of the program operation in that mode is given. This is accomplished either by referring to detailed documents, such as the Software Requirements Specification or the computer program design documents, or by including some or all of the detail normally contained in these documents. The general content, review, approval, and control requirements for this document are presented in Figure 7.2. A sample table of contents is provided in Figure 7.3.

Throughout the preparation of the Operating Instructions Document, the skills and expertise of all probable users must be taken into consideration. Accordingly, there is a need for clear, unambiguous descriptions in the most easily understood wording. Illustrations, graphs, charts, and tables should be used liberally to facilitate comprehension and to provide rapid reference material. The Operating Instructions Document is the one manual that *must be accurate*

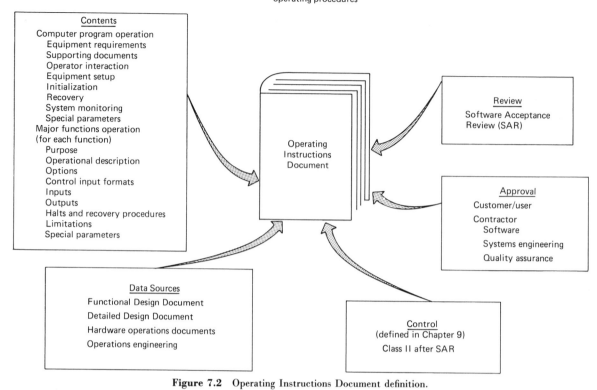

PURPOSE: Describe the computer program
operating procedures

Contents
Computer program operation
    Equipment requirements
    Supporting documents
    Operator interaction
    Equipment setup
    Initialization
    Recovery
    System monitoring
    Special parameters
Major functions operation
(for each function)
    Purpose
    Operational description
    Options
    Control input formats
    Inputs
    Outputs
    Halts and recovery procedures
    Limitations
    Special parameters

Operating
Instructions
Document

Review
Software Acceptance
Review (SAR)

Approval
Customer/user
Contractor
    Software
    Systems engineering
    Quality assurance

Data Sources
Functional Design Document
Detailed Design Document
Hardware operations documents
Operations engineering

Control
(defined in Chapter 9)
Class II after SAR

Figure 7.2 Operating Instructions Document definition.

OPERATING INSTRUCTIONS DOCUMENT: CONTENTS

Section 1   Introduction

1.1   Purpose
1.2   Scope
1.3   Operational Overview

Section 2   Related Documents

2.1   Applicable References
2.2   Development Documents

Section 3   Computer Program Operations

3.1   System Components
3.1.1   Hardware Description
3.1.2   Software Operation
3.2   System Configurations
3.3   Equipment Setup
3.4   Computer Operator Interaction
3.4.1   The Operating System
3.4.2   External Interfaces
3.4.3   Software
3.4.4   Operator Messages
3.5   Operating Procedures
3.5.1   Initialization
3.5.2   Monitoring
3.5.3   Shutdown
3.5.4   Standby Operations
3.5.5   Backup
3.5.6   Recovery

3.5.7   Special Procedures
3.6   Parameters
3.7   Analysis of Error Conditions

Section 4   Major Function Operations

4.1   [Major Function Name "1"] Major
           Function
4.1.1   Purpose
4.1.2   Operational Description
4.1.3   Program Options
4.1.4   Operations Request Formats
4.1.5   Inputs
4.1.6   Outputs
4.1.7   Error/Recovery Procedures
4.1.8   Limitations
4.1.9   Special Parameters
4.2   [Major Function Name "2"] Major
           Function

. . .

4.X   [Major Function Name "X"] Major
           Function

. . .

Appendix A   Acronyms and Abbreviations

Appendix B   Definitions and Nomenclature

Figure 7.3 Sample table of contents for the Operating Instructions Document.

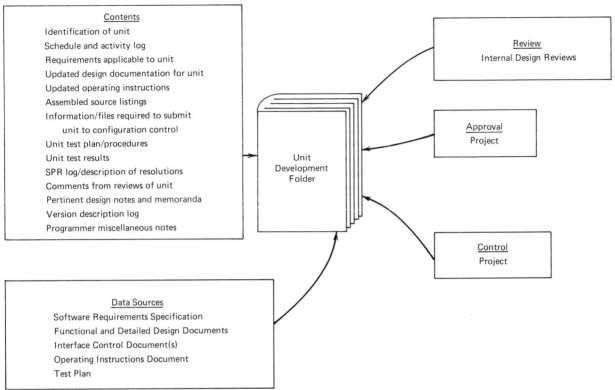

PURPOSE: Record software development activities
associated with a program unit
Provide basis for final as-built documentation

Contents

Identification of unit
Schedule and activity log
Requirements applicable to unit
Updated design documentation for unit
Updated operating instructions
Assembled source listings
Information/files required to submit
    unit to configuration control
Unit test plan/procedures
Unit test results
SPR log/description of resolutions
Comments from reviews of unit
Pertinent design notes and memoranda
Version description log
Programmer miscellaneous notes

Unit
Development
Folder

Review
Internal Design Reviews

Approval
Project

Control
Project

Data Sources

Software Requirements Specification
Functional and Detailed Design Documents
Interface Control Document(s)
Operating Instructions Document
Test Plan

Figure 7.4 Unit Development Folder definition.

UNIT DEVELOPMENT FOLDER: CONTENTS

Section 1 Unit Status

Section 2 Requirements Specification

Section 3 Detailed Design

Section 4 Operating Instructions

Section 5 Code

Section 6 Unit Test Plan and Procedures

Section 7 Test Results

Section 8 Software Problem Report Changes

Section 9 Audits and Reviews

Section 10 Notes

Figure 7.5 Sample table of contents for the Unit Development Folder.

over the life of the software, and it is subject to continual change. Therefore, the document should be organized and bound in a way that will make it convenient and inexpensive to maintain.

7.2.2 Unit Development Folder

The *Unit Development Folder* (UDF), often called the Programmer's Notebook, is a record of specific software development activities associated with a program unit. It is established in skeletal form at the start of the program and becomes an important management tool for monitoring progress during software development and testing activities. The Unit Development Folder also serves as the vehicle by which the software design may be incrementally reviewed by the customer throughout the software development process.

The programmer responsible for a program unit maintains the related UDF in a notebook. The most convenient format is a loose-leaf binder with tabbed sections. The UDF is the central place for maintaining all the necessary information about a particular unit and will be heavily relied on when generating the "as-built" system documentation included in the final design documents. The UDF will also be used to accomplish the following:

1 Ensure consistent documentation of the program unit testing process.
2 Track any modifications to the original design of the program unit.
3 Document design and coding decisions that might affect the final system capabilities or performance.
4 Reduce time required for program unit familiarization during system maintenance.
5 Provide a vehicle for monitoring project progress on a program-unit basis.

Figure 7.4 summarizes the contents of the Unit Development Folder. A sample table of contents is provided in Figure 7.5.

7.2.3 Design Documents (As-Built)

The final versions of the *Functional and Detailed Design Documents* have exactly the same content as the preliminary versions defined earlier. The earlier versions are not considered preliminary because information is missing, but only because of the recognition that changes will occur in the design during the implementation process. Producing the final documents is a straightforward job if the Unit Development Folders have been properly maintained. The final Detailed Design Document should also contain the final program listings. The listings are added as an appendix to the document (they may be separately bound).

7.2.4 Version Description Document

The purpose of the *Version Description Document* is to record and describe the content and capability of each delivered version of the software system. It identifies the items delivered and records additional pertinent data relating to status and usage of the computer program or the changes to a previously delivered program. It identifies the applicable design and test documents, lists the versions of each separately compilable element of the software, identifies the adaptation data associated with the version, and gives instructions for generating new object code from the source program and data.

The content, review, approval, and control requirements for the Version Description Document are sum-

marized in Figure 7.6. A sample table of contents is provided in Figure 7.7.

7.2.5 Test Documentation

As described in Chapter 8, the remaining test documentation is developed during this phase. This includes the preliminary and final *Test Procedures Documents* and the *Test Report.*

7.3 IMPLEMENTATION AND OPERATION PHASE REVIEWS

Three types of reviews are held to support the activities of the Implementation and Operation Phase: (1) *Internal Design Reviews* and code walk-throughs to review software design and completed code, (2) *Unit Development Folder audits* to verify completeness of the UDF and compliance to established standards, and (3) *Test Reviews* to review the testing process and to verify correct software operation. The quality assurance organization should be represented at all reviews to assure that the quality assurance program is being implemented. The content, format, and expected results of these reviews are discussed in the following subsections.

7.3.1 Internal Design Reviews

The *Internal Design Reviews* (IDRs), introduced during the Detailed Design Phase, should be continued throughout the implementation process. The purpose, content, and format of the IDRs during the Detailed Design Phase are described in Section 6.3.1. The reviews have the same purpose and should follow the same format during the implementation process, but should focus on more detailed design issues and implementation information, including completed code. Code walk-throughs should be conducted after a program unit is coded, but before spending any extensive effort in Program Unit Testing (see Section 8.1.3).

7.3.2 Unit Development Folder Audits

The *Unit Development Folder* (UDF) for a program unit should be reviewed by the quality assurance organization and the programmer responsible for the program unit prior to submittal of the program unit to configuration control. The UDF should be reviewed to verify completeness and adherence to established stan-

PURPOSE: Describe the content and capability of each
delivered version of a computer program

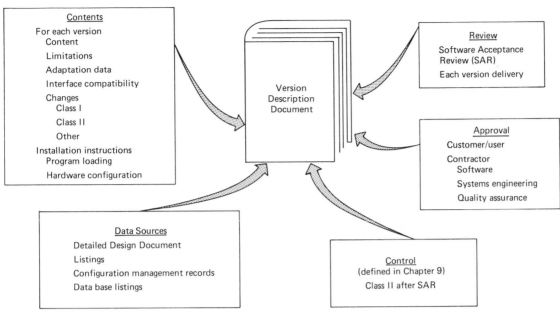

Figure 7.6 Version Description Document definition.

VERSION DESCRIPTION DOCUMENT: CONTENTS

Section 1 Introduction

1.1   Identification
1.2   Scope
1.3   Summary of Differences

Section 2 Related Documents

2.1   Applicable References
2.2   Development Documents

Section 3 Version Descriptions

3.1   Version 1
3.1.1   Change Summary
3.1.2   Limitations
3.1.3   Adaptation Information
3.1.4   Interface Compatibility
3.1.5   Changes
3.1.5.1   Class I Changes
3.1.5.2   Class II Changes
3.1.5.3   Other Changes
3.1.6   Installation Instructions
3.2   Version 2

. . .

3.*V*   Version *"V"*

Figure 7.7 Sample table of contents for the Version Description
Document.

dards. Special attention should be paid to the Unit
Testing Plan/Procedures/Results to assure adequate
testing at this level (see Section 8.1.3). The updated
documentation may be critical to the correct implementation of other program units. Therefore, the
UDF must be submitted to configuration control and
made available to everyone on the project at the same
time that the program unit is submitted to configuration control.

7.3.3   Test Reviews

Most of the test reviews are held during this phase.
These reviews include the *Test Procedures Review* and
the *Software Acceptance Review* (see Chapter 8).

**7.4   IMPLEMENTATION AND OPERATION PHASE
CHECKLIST**

The following checklists provide a topical summary of
the information that should be available and approved
at the Implementation and Operation Phase reviews.

Internal Design Reviews that review module design
should provide the information listed in the checklist in
Section 6.4. Those reviews at which actual code is reviewed should also verify the following:

1 That each program unit is prefaced by a header containing at least the following information:

(a) Name.
(b) Programmer.
(c) Purpose and description of the processing performed by the program unit.
(d) Description of the data to be processed.
(e) Call structure and parameters passed.
(f) External interfaces.
(g) Revision history.

2 That there are sufficient comments within the body of code to describe the processing being performed, including decision comments in every area of code that involves a change in process direction.

3 That acceptable control structures are used, have clearly defined boundaries, and are not obscured by comments.

4 That program units have a single entry and a single exit.

5 That uniform notation and terminology are used to provide consistency and ease of traceability of requirements to software elements.

6 That the integrity of shared data is maintained.

7 That the code is an accurate translation of the requirements and design documented in the UDF.

If an Internal Design Review including a code walkthrough has already been held for a program unit, the Unit Development Folder audit consists of a review of the items checked at the IDR and a final pass through the UDF to verify completeness. Otherwise, a code review, utilizing the checklist above, must be performed during the UDF audit. The following items should be checked to verify the completeness of the UDF:

1 That all sections are present and clearly identified.

2 That the UDF contains all related documentation from the Software Requirements Specification (can be by reference), Functional and Detailed Design Documents, Interface Control Document (can be by reference), and the Operating Instructions Document.

3 That all documentation has been red-lined as required to reflect the design of the tested code.

4 That the unit test documentation satisfies the checklists given in Section 8.4.

5 That all Software Problem Reports related to this program unit are closed.

Checklists for the Test Procedure Reviews are given in Section 8.4, along with the testing checklist that is the major part of the Software Acceptance Review. Checklists for other items reviewed at the SAR, such as documentation, are found in the chapters related to those documents.

chapter eight

The Testing Process

The testing process is performed throughout a software development project. The activities include test planning and implementation of the test program. The purpose of the test planning activity is to establish a means to formally demonstrate that the computer software to be delivered satisfies the contractural requirements and performs according to the approved Software Requirements Specification. This activity is separate from design, but conducted concurrently with the preliminary design activity and highly dependent on the design. An essential element of test planning is early definition of the tests that must be successfully executed for acceptance of the software product—the end product acceptance tests. These tests and other acceptance requirements should be defined and agreed to with the customer early (prior to PDR if possible, certainly prior to CDR).

The plans and procedures for the testing process are written early in the development cycle and carried out during implementation. The testing process has three major goals:(1) verifying that the software product performs as specified in the design documentation, (2) verifying that the software product satisfies all the requirements specified in the Software Requirements Specification, and (3) providing project management with project progress status throughout software implementation. The testing process consists of two test phases and four testing levels:

1 Development testing.

    (a) Program Unit Testing.
    (b) Module Integration Testing.

2 Validation testing.

    (a) Verification Testing.
    (b) Acceptance Testing.

Development testing of a computer program is defined as an iterative process of determining whether the product of each step of a Computer Program Configuration Item (CPCI) development process fulfills all of the requirements levied by the previous step. It de- monstrates that the software performs as specified in the design documentation and is performed throughout the implementation process. Development testing activities are primarily controlled by the software development organization.

Validation is defined as the evaluation, integration, and test activities carried out at the software subsystem level to ensure that the developed software satisfies the performance requirements and design criteria specified in the Software Requirements Specification. Validation of the software is controlled primarily by the quality assurance (QA) organization. Note that a separate test support organization, under control of the project, may be utilized for Validation testing, as discussed in Chapter 4. In this chapter, however, we assume the function is performed by the quality assurance organization.

Test results are used as progress milestones during software implementation. Milestones are easily defined by the successful completion of a defined test and are fully documented in test result reports.

The testing process, the associated documentation, and the formal program reviews are described in the succeeding sections.

8.1 THE TESTING PROCESS

The testing process is performed across the phases of a software development project and consists of three basic activities: (1) the generation of detailed test plans and procedures, (2) the performance of testing activities, including resolution and retest of deficient software, and (3) the documentation of test results for progress tracking. Figure 8.1 illustrates the relative timing of these three activities within the project phases, the documentation produced, and the reviews required to verify the results of the testing process.

The Test Plan describes the complete software test program and is based on the Software Requirements Specification. It is delivered in preliminary form and reviewed at PDR. During the Detailed Design Phase, comments from the PDR on the preliminary Test Plan are incorporated into the Test Plan, and additional

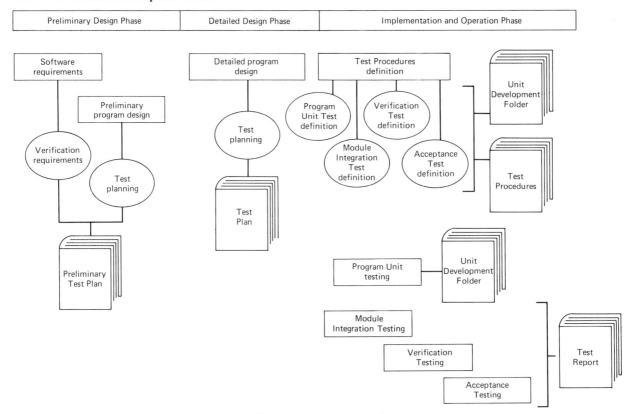

Figure 8.1   Testing process activities and products.

details concerning test configurations, test software, and specific test cases are developed and incorporated into the document. The Test Plan is delivered in final form at CDR. After CDR the Test Plan is under formal configuration change control. On the basis of the Test Plan and the Detailed Design Document, the preliminary Test Procedures are written and reviewed at the Test Procedure Review (TPR). The Test Procedures are updated on the basis of the TPR and are delivered in final form prior to formal testing. During the testing process, the Test Procedures are under configuration control, but can be modified if found to be incorrect. The Test Reports are generated during the testing process and are reviewed at the Software Acceptance Review (SAR).

Multiple organizations are involved in the testing process, both in the group producing the software product and the users. In the following discussion, the user organization responsible for accepting the final software product will be referred to as the "user." This organization usually consists of both quality assurance personnel and actual end users of the system.

The most influential organization in the testing process is the quality assurance organization for the group producing the software. In a small project, this organi-

zation may consist of a single person on the development team, such as the project manager, while in a larger project the organization may consist of a group of people not responsible for the development of the product and possibly from a totally different organization within the company.

A number of verification methods are employed by the testing organization. The choice of which verification method to use will depend on the requirement being verified and the testing level being performed. The testing organization, the verification methods, and the test levels are described in the following sections.

8.1.1   Quality Assurance

In order to maximize the effectiveness of the quality assurance (QA) program, the QA personnel should be independent of the organizations responsible for product development. This can be accomplished by establishing the QA organization directly under the control of corporate management, rather than under software project management. The following sections describe a quality assurance program and an alternative to formal QA.

Quality Assurance Responsibility and Authority

The QA organization is involved in all phases of program development, from proposal preparation through final acceptance and delivery. Its specific responsibility and authority are summarized in Figure 8.2. The organizational independence of QA assures that the checks and balances necessary for a successful QA program are inherent in the management structure. Since the ultimate responsibility for the delivered products usually rests with the development organization, the independent QA provides a separate reporting channel for monitoring development progress. The QA organization has the authority to accept or reject all deliverable products, as well as to conduct in-process audits and reviews. In the event of conflict between QA and the developing organization, resolution should be accomplished at the corporate management level.

Software Quality Assurance

Quality can only be built into software by its designers and programmers, but independent reviews can contribute to software quality by discovering and reporting problems, or potential problems, and by following up on the resolution of such problems. By using modern programming techniques and including the QA personnel in frequent technical reviews, errors can be uncovered early and corrected before their effect cascades through the system.

As discussed in Chapter 9, software configuration management is maintained through a Computer Program Library (CPL). Software quality assurance personnel use the CPL reporting procedures to document software problems and track changes to correct the errors.

The software QA group is responsible for:

1 Maintaining strict control over specifications, design documentation, software code, and test configurations to assure that performance and design requirements are being incorporated and that traceability of requirements to higher-level specifications is being documented.
2 Reviewing software design prior to coding.
3 Participating in technical reviews and audits of design and development activities.
4 Conducting reviews to ensure adherence to software standards and procedures.
5 Reporting software problems and discrepancies and monitoring corrective actions.
6 Reviewing and approving qualification test plans and procedures.
7 Monitoring test conduct to ensure that procedures are followed and all success criteria are satisfied.

Software QA reviews test procedures to ensure that they are consistent with the software test plan and current documentation, that they test all requirements, and that they contain adequate success and acceptance criteria. Software qualification testing leading to program acceptance is monitored by software QA to ensure that:

1 Test procedures are approved prior to the start of testing.
2 Test hardware and software are acceptable and controlled.
3 All tests are conducted in compliance with the test procedure.
4 All software and test deficiencies discovered during testing are recorded.
5 All software corrections are retested.
6 All test data are recorded and reflect the actual findings of the test.
7 All test documentation is maintained to allow repeatability of the tests.
8 Test status reports are accurately maintained.
9 Test reports reflect the requirements of the test.

Responsibility	Authority
Participate in requirements and design reviews; review documentation for compliance with standards and incorporation of adequate quality assurance provisions	Recommend improvements to design specifications, drawings, documents, Test Plans, and Test Procedures
Survey in-plant product development and test, identifying nonconforming items	Stop production of products that do not meet contract or design specifications
Track failure reports and verify that corrective actions result in problem resolution	Approve corrective actions
Ensure that the software subsystem complies with contract and design specifications	Release the software subsystem for delivery when all contract and design specifications have been met
Verify that configuration control and accountability are maintained for the software subsystem	

Figure 8.2 Quality Assurance responsibility and authority.

10 All design documentation is updated to reflect changes made during testing.

11 All testing is complete, problems are resolved, and software is acceptable for the next phase of testing or for delivery.

In the conduct of each test, measurements, observations, and outputs for the test procedure are recorded and verified by QA. Test reports are reviewed and certified by QA to ensure correlation between test objectives and results.

Software QA reviews the following software documentation for consistency, completeness, compliance with standards, and incorporation of change information:

1 Project Plan.
2 Software Requirements Specification.
3 Interface Specification.
4 Functional Design Document.
5 Test Plan.
6 Test Procedures.
7 Test Reports.
8 Detailed Design Document.
9 Operating Instructions Document.
10 Version Description Document.

All deliverable computer programs are certified by software QA. This certification is made before turnover to the user. Software CPCIs are formally certified when the following conditions are satisfied:

1 All relevant documents and drawings are complete, current, and under change control.
2 QA file copies are controlled according to established procedures.
3 All qualification testing is completed; test documentation is updated and rereleased as required.
4 All Software Problem Reports have been closed.

Alternative to Formal QA

Smaller projects, with a total software staff of less than approximately 20 people, can be successfully managed without formal quality assurance, as described above. A substantial cost saving is possible by modifying the formal QA procedure described above as follows:

1 The project manager, rather than an independent QA organization, authorizes delivery of documents and software.
2 There is no independent review or monitoring of the technical work and progress.
3 No QA audit trail is produced.

4 Review of materials is accomplished through peer reviews and project management reviews.

8.1.2 Verification Methods

Verification must be performed for all software subsystem requirements by the use of one or more of the methods presented below:

1 *Inspection.* This method is used to verify that the software meets those requirements that cannot be demonstrated through operational testing. It includes examination of software hierarchy and functional flow diagrams, program listings, Program Design Language (PDL), and associated narrative descriptions. These requirements include hardware and software configuration and adherance to programming and design standards.

2 *Comparison.* This method compares the execution of the new software element with a known standard program, followed by an analysis of results.

3 *Analysis.* This method includes an analysis of program outputs to evaluate algorithm performance at various stages of processing. It is used to validate complex equations and logic whose results are not directly related to inputs. Analysis consists of independent computation of expected results and comparing these results to the actual program results.

4 *Prior Qualification.* This method is based on a demonstration that the CPCI elements have passed qualification in other user systems.

5 *Demonstration.* This method includes observation of performance of the system within a controlled environment. It provides for the verification in real-time of discrete functions, such as lights turned on or off, alarms sounded, color displays varied, and so on.

6 *Usage.* This method involves the repeated execution of the software in conjunction with one or more of the methods described above.

7 *Test.* This method is accomplished by conducting a series of tests with known inputs that should generate known outputs. The test results should be capable of examination after the tests are completed.

8.1.3 Test Levels

The testing process consists of four distinct levels, which, together, satisfy the testing requirements for the delivered software system. These levels are (1) Program Unit Testing, (2) Module Integration Testing, (3) Verification Testing, and (4) Acceptance Testing.

Program Unit Testing is performed by the programmer and is intended to verify that a single program unit performs according to its intended design. Module Integration Testing is performed by the development organization and is intended to verify that individual program units interface with each other correctly and that, as a group, they perform the functions defined in the design documentation. Verification Testing is performed by the quality assurance organization and is intended to verify that the "as-built" system satisfies the requirements specified in the requirements documentation. These three levels are performed at the development site, which often differs from the operational site.

Acceptance Testing is performed in the user's operational environment, as a joint effort between the quality assurance organization and the user, and is intended to provide the user with the final assurance that his system performs as specified in its intended environment. Figure 8.3 describes the four software test levels discussed in the following paragraphs.

Program Unit Testing

The purpose of Program Unit Testing is to verify that the "as-built" program unit performs as specified in the Detailed Design Documentation. A unit is defined as a single computer program that can be described in terms of inputs, processes, and outputs. For example, in Fortran a unit would correspond to a main program or a subroutine. Formal test plans, procedures, and results for Program Unit Testing are not generated unless the unit test verifies that the software meets a requirement not verified later in the test program. Informal test plans, procedures, and results are generated by the programmer when designing and coding the program unit and are documented in the corresponding Unit Development Folder. The primary input to the test plan and procedures is the Detailed Design Document.

Program Unit Testing is performed separately from the testing of other units and consists of two phases. The first phase involves compiling the unit and correcting the errors indicated by the compiler. This includes using other compiler aids, such as a cross-reference listing, to verify that no variable definition errors have been made. The second phase is intended to find any logic errors within the unit. Its purpose is to verify that each program branch, each equation, and the logic flow is properly executed. Testing is continued until all known errors have been eliminated and the coded program unit logic matches the design.

Test Level	Test Basis	Performed and Controlled By	Purpose
Program Unit Testing	Design	Programmer (informal)	Verify program unit logic Verify computational adequacy Verify data-handling capability Verify interfaces and design extremes Execute and verify every branch
Module Integration Testing	Design requirements Interfaces	Software development organization (formal)	Integrate program units into modules Verify modules through anticipated range of operating conditions Demonstrate that modules meet acceptance criteria Integrate modules into software system Verify software system through anticipated range of operating conditions Turn over test of software to independent test group
Verification Testing	Requirements Interfaces	Quality assurance organization (formal)	Formally verify software performance and interface requirements
Acceptance Testing	Requirements	Quality assurance organization and user (formal)	Test software end-to-end scenario Demonstrate that software satisfies the set of predetermined acceptance criteria

Figure 8.3 Software test levels.

Design deficiencies that affect released documentation must be handled in accordance with the defined quality assurance standards. In general, design deficiencies that do not affect functions other than those within the software system are corrected in the code, and the change is "red-lined" in a copy of the appropriate Detailed Design Document section, which is maintained in the Unit Development Folder. When the design deficiency affects interfaces with other organizations or requires a specification change, the formal change process is started immediately.

Although the testing is informal (i.e., conducted without formal written procedures), it is a planned activity. Planning is necessary for efficient use of the computer and the programmer's time. Planning should include defining what the programmer intends to accomplish for a given test, what inputs are required, what outputs are expected, and how the test will be conducted. The programmer should prepare a list of tests to be conducted for each unit and maintain this list in the Unit Development Folder. Estimated completion dates for the tests should also be noted. When the tests are successfully executed, the completion date should be noted. The Unit Development Folder thus provides an internal, up-to-date status of the informal testing process. Much of the testing at this level is very detailed and will not be repeated again in higher-level tests; therefore, the record of informal testing in the Unit Development Folder and the corresponding test results should be preserved for reference purposes.

The Program Unit Tests are completed (1) when the programmer has completed his planned test program and is satisfied that the code matches the design, (2) when all known errors have been eliminated, and (3) when the code has been reviewed by a review team in a code walk-through. The review team can consist of one or many reviewers, with some of them preferably from the development team. Aside from finding bugs in the code, the review has the added advantage of providing other programmers with enough knowledge to take over the further testing of the module if the programmer who wrote the program is for some reason unavailable. A checklist to confirm that Program Unit Testing is complete includes the following:

1 Each equation has been tested using all applicable parameters with nominal values, values at the specified limits, and values outside the limits where appropriate. These equations should include loop control equations.
2 Every program branch has been executed.
3 All known coding and design errors have been corrected.

4 All successful tests have been recorded in the Unit Development Folder.
5 Test results from successful tests have been saved.
6 All paperwork for design changes has been initiated.

Once Program Unit Testing is completed, the programmer fills out a Computer Program Library Transmittal Form (CTF) and submits the CTF and the code to the computer program librarian (see Chapter 9). The unit is then combined with related units and Module Integration Testing begins.

Module Integration Testing

Module Integration Testing consists of building the entire software subsystem by iteratively adding program units, then, as the program units are integrated, testing to ensure that the implemented software subsystem matches the one described in the design documentation. (Module Integration Testing is also referred to as Module Testing, Integration Testing or Preliminary Qualification Testing.) If software is implemented using a top-down approach, Module Integration Testing consists of integrating the top-level program units first and using the tested modules as a framework for testing each successive program unit.

Module Integration Testing uses a building-block approach to integrating and constructing the computer program and, if applicable, software subsystem. The top-level modules of the software subsystem hierarchy are integrated first. Integration progresses in stages according to a schedule based on the functions to be performed by the modules, their interdependencies, their availability, and input interface data. Stubs are substituted for low-level routines to isolate the functions under test. The stubs are replaced in stages by actual modules until the software subsystem is complete. A major advantage of the top-down integration and testing approach is that the major subsystem interfaces are defined at a high level in the hierarchy, and are therefore verified early in the project. Once the interfaces are verified, the implementation and testing of the different subsystems can be done independently.

The purpose of Module Integration Testing is to verify that:

1 The individual program units interface with each other correctly to form the modules described in the Detailed Design Document.
2 The modules have been properly coded, so that all equations function properly and all logic paths operate as designed.
3 The modules interface with each other to form the

software subsystem described in the Detailed Design Document.

4 There is an orderly progression toward the final software capabilities that will be verified during Verification Testing.

Formal test procedures are prepared jointly by software development and software quality assurance groups and are documented, reviewed, and approved. Software quality assurance groups should perform a review of the procedures prior to their use by the software development organization. Software QA should ensure that all tests are conducted in compliance with documented procedures. Any deviations should be documented.

Module Integration Tests are conducted using the static and dynamic input data necessary to execute the intermodule and executive interfaces and to exercise operational functions. It is desirable to have access to the actual or target processor during Module Integration Testing. At this point, the operating system should be fully capable of supporting these tests. Where Module Integration Testing is conducted using a target processor simulation, the target processor should be phased into testing as soon as it becomes available. Sufficient retesting should be accomplished to ensure full compatibility.

A full complement of math and utility routines, including test and debugging aids, should be available for Module Integration Testing. The test hardware should include all needed peripherals: user terminals, line printers, disk and tape controllers and drives, operator consoles, and so on. This complete test environment may not be required during the initial stages of testing, but will be required as testing progresses.

Test input data should come from actual hardware/software interfaces, if available. Otherwise, the input data should be representative of the actual interfaces. Test drivers and other test programs required for Verification and Acceptance Testing should be used during Module Integration Testing. These are validated for use during formal Verification Testing as a result of successful operation during Module Integration Testing.

Module Integration Testing consists of two elements: Integration Testing and Functional Verification Testing. Integration Testing verifies the correctness of program interfaces by testing that each program can call and be called by the programs it interfaces with, and pass parameters properly. The primary purposes of Module Integration Testing are (1) to establish compatibility between interacting computer programs and

modules, and (2) to establish the compatibility of the programs with their external interfaces.

Functional Verification Testing consists of examining the collection of program units already implemented and testing to see that they function as an integrated module and perform the functions assigned to them in the Detailed Design Document. Functional Verification Testing is usually performed after all the program units comprising a module, as defined in the design documentation, have passed Integration Testing.

Satisfactory completion of Module Integration Testing establishes that the implemented software properly performs the functions specified in the design documentation and is ready to be verified against the requirements specified in the Software Requirements Specification.

Verification Testing

Verification Testing consists of tests, demonstrations, and analyses performed to confirm that the software satisfies all the requirements set forth in and derived from the Software Requirements Specification. The Detailed Design Specification, used during earlier testing, plays only a minor role in Verification Testing. Instead, the early documents stating the mission or product objectives and software or system requirements are the main source from which test cases are derived. A correlation between the Software Requirements Specification and the Verification Test Plan is provided in the Test Plan. Formal test plans and procedures are written for Verification Testing. Analysis is performed for those requirements that are too costly to verify by testing or demonstration.

Verification Tests are conducted in the same test environment as Module Integration Tests, using full complements of support software, peripheral hardware, and operator devices, plus the target processor, with full operating system capabilities and realistic or actual hardware interface data.

Before the start of Verification Testing, the computer program listing should be released, the computer program code should be under formal configuration control in the Computer Program Library, the test software should be validated and be under configuration control in the Computer Program Library, and the test procedures should be approved. All Verification Testing is conducted under the surveillance of the project quality assurance group. Because of the extensive testing that precedes these tests, it is expected that relatively few errors will be uncovered during Verification Testing.

Redundancy of tests and superfluous testing should

be deliberately avoided. At the conclusion of these tests, all requirements that can be verified at this level will have been verified and the test results analyzed and released. The tests verify external interfaces, demonstrate that the computer program satisfies the specified functional and performance requirements, and demonstrate computer program performance under simulated operational conditions similar to those expected in actual operations.

The three test levels described above are implemented in serial with respect to a particular program unit, but are performed simultaneously throughout the testing phase of the project. A program unit enters the Module Integration Testing phase as soon as it has passed Program Unit Testing. At any time during software implementation, a Verification Test may be run to demonstrate that overall software subsystem requirements are being met.

Acceptance Testing

Many of the Verification Tests are repeated during Acceptance Testing to verify that the software performs in the operational environment as it did in the test environment. In many instances, Acceptance Testing is the only testing in which the software operates with the actual external interfaces, rather than with test software and hardware. At PDR agreement should be reached with the user that the execution of these test cases in a manner described in the Test Plan—using an approved data base and producing test results that satisfy the defined acceptance criteria—will result in acceptance of the software system.

At the conclusion of Acceptance Testing and after the Test Report has been written, the Software Acceptance Review (SAR) is held. At this review the software products, code, documents, and test results are reviewed. If all items are satisfactory and in accordance with the acceptance plan included in the Test Plan, the software is accepted. The SAR requirements are described in Section 8.3.3.

Final documentation should be planned for delivery after successful execution of all Acceptance Tests so that corrections necessitated by errors detected late in the formal test program can be included. The alternative is to deliver the documents earlier and have the expense and inconvenience of issuing errata sheets or change pages. The latter approach is not recommended. Therefore, at acceptance time, the final "as-built" Detailed Design Document should be prepared and the Operating Instructions Document should be finalized. With each delivery of the software, a Version Description Document is also required.

8.1.4   Test Control

Program Unit Testing is performed and controlled by the programmer who implemented the unit. Prior to coding the unit, the programmer should study the Detailed Design Document description of the program unit and prepare informal test plans and procedures. These are incorporated into the Unit Development Folder. If any problems are found during Program Unit Testing, the programmer fixes the unit and documents the changes. The programmer continues to test the program according to the test plans and procedures until all known problems are solved. The results of the tests are documented in the Unit Development Folder. Once the unit passes Program Unit Testing, it is submitted to the Computer Program Library. The unit is then integrated into the system, and Module Integration Testing is performed by the development group, assisted by the QA organization. If any problems are found, they are documented on a Software Problem Report (SPR) form (see Chapter 9) and the unit is returned to the programmer for modifications and subsequent program unit retesting.

If Module Integration Testing for a program uncovers a problem in already tested programs, these programs have to be removed from the test bed (the collection of tested software modules) and returned to the programmer for modification and testing. Depending on the seriousness of the problem, all or part of Module Integration Testing has to be rerun that involves the faulty program. The decision of what tests need to be rerun is made by the software development organization. Once a program completes Module Integration Testing, it becomes part of the test-bed system and is used as part of the framework to test other programs.

When the entire software subsystem has passed Module Integration Testing, Verification Testing is performed. The user should be involved as much as possible in Verification Testing in order to become familiar with the software operations. The quality assurance organization performs Verification Testing. If any problems are uncovered, they are documented in a Software Problem Report (see Chapter 9), and the faulty program(s) are isolated and returned to the programmers. The programs must be fixed and retested according to the procedures specified above. The failed Verification Test is then rerun until the problem is solved.

It is the responsibility of the quality assurance personnel to decide which completed Verification Tests need to be rerun to ensure that no side-effects were caused by software changes made to solve the identified problems. The software should be designed to require minimal interdependence between modules, so that changes in one module would not affect other modules. This would allow testing to continue in unrelated areas of the software while problems are fixed.

Acceptance Testing is conducted by the quality assurance organization and the user in the operational environment. If any problems are found, the user has the right to request that the entire Acceptance Test procedure be restarted (unless other procedures were specified in the Test Plan).

The testing process is controlled by the following test documentation: (1) informal Program Unit Test Plan and Procedures in the Unit Development Folder and (2) formal Test Plan and Procedures for Module Integration Testing, Verification Testing, and Acceptance Testing. It is the responsibility of the quality assurance organization to ensure that all testing is done in accordance with these documents and that all results are documented. The configuration control placed on these documents is described in Chapter 9.

8.2 TEST PROCESS DOCUMENTATION

The purpose of the test planning activity is to establish a means to formally demonstrate that the computer software to be delivered satisfies the contractual requirements and performs according to the approved Software Requirements Specifications.

The product of the test planning activity is the test documentation. The required formal test documentation consists of a Test Plan, Test Procedures Document(s), and Test Reports. Figure 8.4 provides a summary of the parameters associated with the formal test documentation.

The purpose of the Test Plan is to establish detailed requirements, criteria, general methods, responsibilities, and overall planning to confirm that the "as-built" system fulfills the requirements specified in the Software Requirements Specification. It defines the test activities to be performed by the software developer to achieve software acceptance by the user. The purpose of the Test Procedures is to define in detail the actual procedures to be employed to perform the tests outlined in the Test Plan. The Test Reports document the results of the testing process and are used to formally convince the user that the system operates as specified.

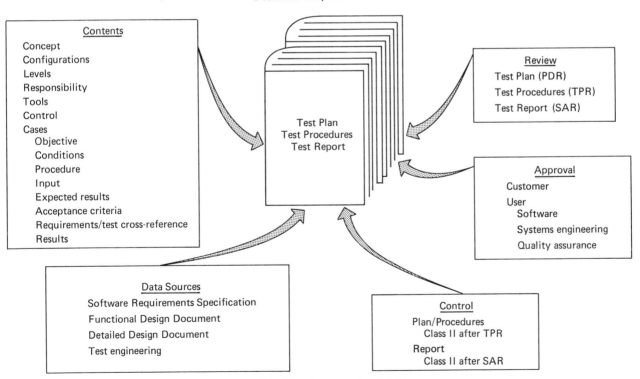

Figure 8.4 Test documentation definition.

The detailed contents of each of these documents may be found in Appendix B.

8.2.1   Test Plan

The *Test Plan* describes the complete software test program. It defines what development testing will be performed by the programmer, what Module Integration, Verification, and Acceptance Tests will be executed, and the conditions under which each of the elements of the test program will be accomplished.

The Test Plan defines the test configurations, test schedules, and the test levels, identifies required test equipment and test software, defines the roles of various organizations in the test process, defines the configuration control to be implemented at each level of testing, and identifies the test cases to be executed at each test level. Detailed descriptions of the test cases are provided in the Test Procedures. Specifically, the Test Plan describes:

1   The organizational responsibilities for the various tasks in the test program.
2   The methods to be employed to review test plans and procedures, monitor and control test execution, report and correct test discrepancies, report test results, and determine readiness for acceptance.
3   The top-level concepts and goals for development and Acceptance testing and the strategy for fulfilling these goals, including a description of the test levels and the development philosophy.
4   The data generators, test drivers, environmental simulators and test analysis programs required for each level of testing. (Note: All test software must be verified and under configuration control prior to its use for formal verification.)
5   The concept and methods of stressing the software (e.g., with noisy and otherwise imperfect input data, or with peak data loads) during each level of testing.
6   The test schedules, which provide a detailed description of the sequence of all test activities. Test schedules must be established to ensure that the required testing will be completed within the allotted time period. The test schedules must be compatible with:

(a)   Availability of the computer facility.
(b)   Availability of the software to be tested.
(c)   Availability of supporting test software.
(d)   Availability of interfacing software and hardware.

(e)   Availability of special test equipment.
(f)   Overall project test schedules.

7   The test environment, including hardware configuration, test software configuration, and required verified new software elements. The test environment must be established as part of the test planning process before test cases can be defined. Block diagrams, showing the progression of testing configurations, should be prepared for each level of testing.
8   The individual tests to be performed to demonstrate compliance with the requirements. The description of each test case includes the requirements to be verified, the test configuration to be used, and the test software required. The test procedure will be prepared later for each test case identified.
9   A subset of the test cases defined in the Test Plan. These tests should be identified as the Acceptance Test cases to provide the means for software acceptance. These cases should be agreed upon with the customer as the Acceptance Test Plan.

A sample table of contents for a Test Plan is provided in Figure 8.5.

8.2.2   Test Procedures

Test Procedures Documents are developed to describe the Module Integration, Verification, and Acceptance Test Procedures. These procedures may be combined into one document for small computer programs, one document for the procedures at each test level, or, for large systems, additional separate volumes.

For each test case identified in the Test Plan, the Test Procedures define the test configuration, test conduct, and test results. The test configuration specifies the specific test materials, input data, test routines, and hardware configuration. Test conduct describes the step-by-step sequence to be followed in performing the test, how and when test data are to be input, and expected results. Expected results include acceptable tolerances and a supporting discussion of how these results show that the test objective has been satisfied. Where applicable, additional information on program options and estimated run times should be identified. A sample table of contents for the Test Procedures Document is shown in Figure 8.6.

Whereas the Test Plan gives an overview of the test program, the Test Procedures Document gives the detailed step-by-step procedures required to test the software. Since the Test Plan is delivered in final form at

TEST PLAN DOCUMENT: CONTENTS

Figure 8.5   Sample table of contents for the Test Plan Document.

CDR, it cannot include a detailed description of all the required user interfaces. The Test Procedures contain references to the Test Plan, where appropriate, to avoid duplication of information. They have many of the same sections as the Test Plan, but contain more detail about the actual design of the tests.

For ease of tracking and documenting the testing process, each test level can be broken down into test phases. In Module Integration Testing, these test phases represent major functional milestones in the development process. In Verification and Acceptance Testing, these phases represent major milestones in the testing process. The phases can be defined by completed modules or by functional milestones within one subsystem when a new testable capability is added to the subsystem. The test phases should be small enough for the testing to be accomplished in two to four hours.

8.2.3   Test Reports

The *Test Report* documents the results for each of the test cases defined in the Test Plan and described in detail in the Test Procedures. The test results for each test case are described with a synopsis of the problems encountered, SPRs written against the test, disposition of the SPRs, and disposition of the test outputs of the final successful test execution. Also included are any recommended changes to the previous documentation, including change pages and waiver requests. A sample table of contents for the Test Report Document is provided in Figure 8.7.

8.3   TEST REVIEWS

Three types of reviews are held to support testing: (1) *Preliminary and Critical Design Reviews* to review the design and the Test Plan, (2) *Test Procedures Review (TPR),* held before formal testing (may be held incrementally), and (3) *Software Acceptance Review (SAR),*

TEST PROCEDURES DOCUMENT: CONTENTS

Section 1   Introduction

1.1   Purpose
1.2   Scope
1.3   Summary

Section 2   Related Documents

2.1   Applicable References
2.2   Development Documents

Section 3   Test Objectives

Section 4   Manning and Responsibilities

Section 5   Equipment and Computer Program Requirements

Section 6   Test Operating Procedures

6.1   Initiating the System Operation
6.2   Maintaining the System Operation
6.3   Termination and Restarting the System Operation

Section 7   Detailed Test Procedures: Module Integration Testing

7.1   Test 1
7.1.1   Module Description
7.1.2   Test Description
7.1.3   Test Inputs
7.1.4   Test Conduct
7.1.5   Expected Results

. . .

7.*n*   Test *n*
7.*n*.1   Module Description
7.*n*.2   Test Description
7.*n*.3   Test Inputs
7.*n*.4   Test Conduct
7.*n*.5   Expected Results

Section 8   Detailed Test Procedures: Verification Testing

8.1   Test 1
8.1.1   Test Description
8.1.2   Test Inputs
8.1.3   Test Conduct
8.1.4   Expected Results

. . .

8.*n*   Test *n*
8.*n*.1   Test Description
8.*n*.2   Test Inputs
8.*n*.3   Test Conduct
8.*n*.4   Expected Results

Section 9   Detailed Test Procedures: Acceptance Testing

9.1   Test 1
9.1.1   Test Description
9.1.2   Test Inputs
9.1.3   Test Conduct
9.1.4   Expected Results

. . .

9.*n*   Test *n*
9.*n*.1   Test Description
9.*n*.2   Test Inputs
9.*n*.3   Test Conduct
9.*n*.4   Expected Results

Section 10   Data Reduction and Analysis

10.1   Recording and Reduction Requirement
10.2   Data Reduction and Analysis Procedures

Appendix A   Acronyms and Abbreviations

Appendix B   Definitions and Nomenclature

Figure 8.6 Sample table of contents for the Test Procedures Document.

TEST REPORT DOCUMENT: CONTENTS

Figure 8.7   Sample table of contents for the Test Report Document.

held after Acceptance Testing is successfully completed and all required documentation has been prepared or updated to the "as-built" configuration. The quality assurance organization attends all reviews to ensure that the quality assurance program is being implemented. The content, format, and expected results of these reviews are discussed in the following subsections.

8.3.1   Preliminary and Critical Design Reviews

The Test Plan is reviewed in preliminary form at the *Preliminary Design Review* (PDR) and in final form at the *Critical Design Review* (CDR). The purpose of the Test Plan review is to ensure that all significant design features will be tested and that all specification requirements will be verified. The test program philosophy presented in the preliminary Test Plan is reviewed in detail at the PDR. The details of the actual tests are in the final Test Plan reviewed at CDR.

8.3.2   Test Procedures Review

Software Test Procedures are reviewed at *Test Procedures Reviews* to ensure that adequate testing will be performed on each component. These reviews provide formal approval for the procedures to be used in testing and ensure that they carry out the intent of the Test Plan.

Two series of Test Procedures Reviews are conducted: Development Test Procedures Reviews and Validation Test Procedures Reviews. These should be conducted separately. Development Test Procedures Reviews are conducted before Module Integration Testing and review the procedures to be followed during Module Integration Testing. Validation Test Procedure Reviews are conducted before Verification Testing to review procedures to be followed during Verification and Acceptance Testing. Development tests are conducted to ensure that the individual modules with their interfaces perform as designed. Validation tests are conducted to ensure that the completed computer program satisfies its stated performance requirements. Thus, development tests evaluate the computer program against its design documentation (Functional Design and Detailed Design Documents), while validation tests evaluate the computer program against the requirements in the Software Requirements Specification. The items to be examined in evaluating these test procedures are listed below:

1   *Test Procedures/Plan Compatibility.*   The procedures should be consistent with the Test Plan and cover all required test areas.

2 *Test Inputs.*   The test inputs should be delineated; the inputs defined for test conduct should be capable of testing the design at its limits.

3 *Test Completeness.*   The documented tests should satisfy all test objectives. All significant aspects of the software design should be exercised during testing and should be documented.

4 *Procedure Clarity.*   The operator instructions should be stated clearly, concisely, and unambiguously.

5 *Software Configurations.*   The configurations of the software to be tested should be accurately and thoroughly described.

6 *Success Criteria.*   Success criteria should be defined for each step in each test procedure; they should be consistent with the objectives of the test.

7 *Test Hardware Configuration.*   The test hardware configuration should be adequate for the conduct of the test and defined in sufficient detail to evaluate its adequacy.

8 *Test Software Configuration.*   The required test software configuration should be adequately defined. Coverage should include the test setup, data inputs, peripherals, displays, data sampling criteria, data rates, and so on.

8.3.3   Software Acceptance Review

The *Software Acceptance Review* is a formal meeting held to audit the software product prior to user acceptance. Completion of this audit signifies that the software is ready for operation and that the development phases are complete. The review normally consists of two audits: a Functional Configuration Audit (FCA) and a Physical Configuration Audit (PCA). These audits may be conducted incrementally as the necessary information becomes available. If they are conducted incrementally, most review items will be a matter of record at the time of the formal meeting. The SAR will then consist largely of examining the records to ensure that all audit items have been completed.

Functional Configuration Audit
The objective of the FCA is to verify that the software performance complies with the software specification performance requirements. This is accomplished by reviewing the test data accumulated during software testing. Each software configuration to be delivered may be subject to an FCA. The audit should determine the following:

1 *Completeness of Verification.*   The FCA should include an audit of the test plans, procedures, and

results to confirm that the test data and results comply with the test plans and procedures. If deficiencies are noted, repeat tests or additional testing should be recommended. Where there is partial completion of verification requirements, the status should be established and the plans for completion should be presented.

2 *Validity of Simulations.*   The FCA should confirm that software and hardware interface simulations used in the conduct of tests have been validated.

3 *Validity of Analyses.*   Where analyses have been used as a substitute for testing, the analysis methods and their results should be validated.

4 *Validity of Configuration.*   Functional and Detailed Design Documents and the Version Description Document should be reviewed to ensure that the configuration of the software audited is the same as that verified.

5 *Design Change Status.*   All changes, as documented by Software Problem Reports, should be reviewed to ensure that they have been incorporated and verified.

Physical Configuration Audit
The PCA is conducted prior to item delivery. It consists of an examination of the detailed design documentation against the "as-built" software configuration. It is conducted to ensure the adequacy, completeness, and accuracy of the technical design documentation. The review also includes an audit of the current change status, change records, and version description records to ensure that the "as-built" configuration is compatible with the released documents.

The PCA team should review the items described below. The necessary documents and records should be provided by the software development organization.

1 *Design Documentation.*   An audit of the design documentation should be performed to ensure that they exactly represent the to-be-delivered configuration. The design documentation consists of the Functional Design, Interface Control, and Detailed Design Documents. Examination of the documentation should ensure the following: correlation of module flows to top-level flows, proper entries to flows, and correlation of interface data to ICDs. The examination should also ensure adequate definition of data base characteristics, storage allocation provisions, timing and sequencing characteristics, and necessary cross-checking of flows to computer program listings.

2 *Test Documentation.*   Test documentation to be reviewed consists of the Test Plan, the Test Proce-

dures, and Test Report. Changes to Test Procedures made during testing should be reviewed to determine the validity of the tests performed using the amended procedures. Test data should be examined to make sure that all required test data are present and certified by the quality assurance organization. The Test Plan is reviewed to ensure that all approved changes to the Test Plan have been reflected in the Test Procedures.

3 *Version Description Document.* The Version Description Document should be audited to ensure the completeness of the descriptions of the delivered version. A complete list of documents, version numbers, and subroutine identifiers required to build the computer program version should be included.

4 *Operating Instructions Document.* The Operating Instructions Document should be certified for operational use.

5 *Supporting Documentation.* All deliverable supporting documentation should be reviewed.

6 *Change Status.* A list of all design changes incorporated into the computer program since the start of testing should be reviewed to ensure their completeness.

7 *Configuration Items.* The configuration item package should be reviewed to certify that all tapes, cards, documents, lists, and so on are present and labeled with the required markings and identification.

8.4 TESTING PROCESS CHECKLIST

The following checklist provides a topical summary of the information that should be available in the test documentation. This information ensures that the final software meets the requirements stated in the Software Requirements Specification and the design described in the Detailed Design Document.

1 Testing philosophy and methodology employed and alternate test methods considered to achieve acceptance of the software.

2 Personnel required to support the test program, including the number of people and their qualifications in terms of training, organizational affiliation, and experience.

3 Computer facilities required, including a block diagram of the test bed on which the software will be tested.

4 Test software required to support the test program.

5 Test schedules, including location, test configuration, and test flow diagram.

6 Correlation of all software and design requirements to individual tests.

7 Performance, interface, and test requirements upon which the test plan is based.

8 Test plan for checkout of each software module written, as well as a test plan to verify that the system meets the system requirements.

9 Description of all tests to be performed including inputs, test conduct, and expected results. The expected results should include the measurement tolerances and acceptance criteria.

10 Test results obtained in each test.

The testing documentation is reviewed in part at PDR, CDR, TPR, and SAR. When reviewing this documentation, the review team should ensure that:

1 The test plan encompasses an integrated test cycle from system level down to the lowest test level.

2 Each test verifies at least one requirement and each requirement is verified in a test.

3 All the tests can be accomplished with the test software and equipment identified.

4 The tests are performed in a logical sequence, so that maximum use of early test results can be realized in later tests.

5 The tests verify interface compatibility.

6 There are no areas of overtesting or undertesting.

7 All supporting resources are identified.

8 The responsibilities of the test participants are identified.

9 The description of each test is sufficient for correct test conduct.

10 The criteria for success or failure of each test are unambiguously identified.

11 The test inputs and outputs are identified and listed.

12 Sufficient consideration is given to data storage and data reduction.

13 The test schedule is compatible with the design cycle.

14 The actual results of each test are listed and compared with the predicted results.

15 The test results meet the acceptance criteria.

chapter nine

Software Configuration Management

The purpose of software configuration management is to ensure an orderly control of software products produced in the software development process and to provide an effective mechanism for incorporating software changes, both during development and during program operational use. This chapter describes the activities required to achieve these objectives. These activities include: (1) establishing approved baseline configurations for the computer programs (definition); (2) maintaining configuration control over all changes in the baseline computer programs (change control and change processing), and (3) providing traceability of computer program baselines and changes to these baselines (configuration accounting).

Elements of the material in this chapter can be applied to proposals, work statements, and project plans for the development of computer programs. All the procedures and practices described may not be necessary for a particular software development project. The extent to which the detailed configuration management elements are applicable should be identified in the initial Project Plan. This plan should provide the rationale for all waivers to specific configuration control elements and should identify additional elements needed to control the computer program development, such as contractual documentation, particular industry standards, and unique requirements developed specifically for the project.

The major elements of the software configuration management process—*configuration definition, change control, change processing,* and *configuration accounting*— are described in the following sections. In addition, Section 9.5 describes the Computer Program Library, which is an important tool in a successful configuration management program.

9.1 CONFIGURATION DEFINITION

The concept that establishes the basis for a successful software configuration management system is the use of proper configuration definition procedures. Configuration definition utilizes a baseline management concept and provides unique identifiers for each product related to the software subsystem. This includes programs, listings, documentation, and related data base information. The identification and marking procedures described below are required by the control and accounting elements of the configuration management process described in later sections.

9.1.1 Baseline Management

The baseline management concept is used for configuration control both during computer program development and after release to the Configuration Control Board (CCB). The CCB is the key control and approval group in the configuration management process. In addition, the CCB often can provide a forum in which all interested parties can exchange information. During development, the CCB is chaired by the project manager or his designee. Members typically include software supervisors, test representatives, project office representatives, quality assurance personnel, and customer representatives if required. After software acceptance, the software CCB is chaired by the customer.

Technical control points, or "baselines," are established for the computer programs to support systematic evaluation, coordination, and disposition of all proposed changes. Throughout the life of a computer program there are three types of baselines: the *development baselines, test baselines,* and *product baselines.* Figure 9.1 identifies the basic configuration management steps required to establish and maintain the three types of baselines. Each baseline is described in the following paragraphs.

Development Baseline

The development baseline is established at the beginning of the computer program preliminary design by customer approval of the Software Requirements Specification, which contains the performance, design and

114

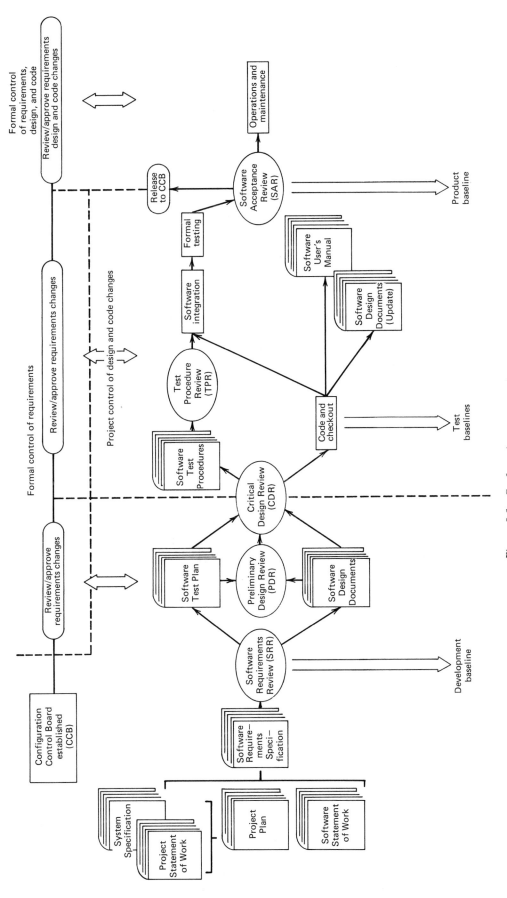

Figure 9.1 Configuration management sequence.

115

qualification requirements. Once established, the Software Requirements Specification becomes the controlling document for the software design and testing activities. Any change or addition to it must be submitted as a design requirements change and must be formally approved and scheduled, as specified in the Project Plan. All approved changes to the development baseline must be reflected in the Design Specification and in the resulting computer program.

The Project Plan describes the techniques for establishing the development baseline and for controlling changes in that baseline. The plan also describes the level of control applied to the Software Requirements Specification upon customer approval, the mechanism by which changes are initiated and implemented, and the allocation of responsibility for document maintenance and for processing the change requests defined in the plan. The basic steps in establishing the development baseline are described below.

The design constraints and practices to be followed during computer program development and the requirements for qualification are documented in the initial Software Requirements Specification. The development baseline is established on the basis of applicable sections of the Project Statement of Work (SOW), Project Plan, Software SOW and System Specification, as indicated in Figure 9.1. Additional requirements analysis is performed to allocate and detail the computer program requirements.

After project manager approval, the Software Requirements Specification is designated as the principal element of the development baseline. It is then placed under internal project configuration control. Formal change control and accounting are initiated after customer approval.

The Software Requirements Specification now serves as the baseline against which the impact of proposed performance and design changes are assessed. The Configuration Control Board (CCB) is established by the project manager to review and approve changes in the development baseline.

Test Baselines

Test baselines are established during the software development cycle to correspond to major milestones in the development process in terms of program capabilities. These milestones usually coincide with major function tests during Module Integration Testing, as described in Chapter 8. The design documentation (including the Unit Development Folders), the Test Plan and test milestone schedules, and developmental versions of the computer program document the test baselines.

The logical establishment of test baselines is facilitated by top-down implementation and testing, since checkpoints in the development process are more readily identifiable. A test baseline version of a computer program is certified as having passed all tests up to the given point. Therefore, changes in the test baseline may require rerunning some of the prior tests. Most changes will be additions to the program to support the next major test and test baseline. Typically, test baselines differ from the development baseline and the product baselines in that design and code change control, although rigorous and formal, is performed within the project, rather than through the external CCB. The basic steps in establishing test baselines are given below.

During early software development and Program Unit Testing, the software is maintained by the individual programmers until sufficient code has been developed to establish the first test baseline. This typically occurs near the time of the first Module Integration Test. Subsequent test baselines are established as the integration tests proceed, based on the Module Integration Test schedule. Each test baseline represents a frozen software system certified to have passed all the previous applicable integration tests.

Control mechanisms must be established so that programmers can have access to the baseline software and are able to create their own working versions without disturbing the baseline software or other programmers' working versions.

Some of the Module Integration Tests may be run from working versions of the software. However, when a major integration test is to be run, a new preliminary test baseline must be formally established. The new baseline should verify all the capabilities added since the last test baseline. If some capabilities cannot be verified by the test, a portion of the integration tests may be rerun on the preliminary test baseline. At the successful conclusion of the tests, the preliminary test baseline becomes the new test baseline version of the software.

When errors are discovered in test baseline code, a mechanism must be available to reestablish the test baseline by rerunning any tests affected by the required changes.

Product Baseline

The product baseline is established when the computer program has been completely coded, successfully tested, and certified as ready for release to the user or for integration with other system elements. At this time, the design documents are audited to determine if they correctly describe the computer program. The Functional and Detailed Design Documents and the released version of the computer program then document the product baseline. From this point on, all changes in the product baseline, including the design documents and the computer program code, must undergo formal configuration control and accounting, as described in Sections 9.2 and 9.3.

The steps in establishing the product baseline are as follows:

1 A preliminary product baseline is established when validated components of the computer program are ready for Verification Testing. Configuration control of the preliminary baseline is maintained within the project, with changes implemented with project manager's approval.
2 The final product baseline is established when the project manager releases the computer program to the Configuration Control Board after successful Acceptance Testing.
3 After release to the CCB, formal change control is in effect, and the procedures described in Section 9.3 are required.

9.1.2 Configuration Identification

Configuration identification includes designation of Computer Programs (or Computer Program Configuration Items, or CPCIs), documenting the configuration identification, and establishing a numbering system for specification elements. The designation of separable Computer Programs (or CPCIs) is made on the basis of the need for formal control, subject to the following guidelines:

1 All operational programs that directly satisfy project requirements are classified as Computer Programs. In this context, "directly satisfy project requirements" means that the results of program operation are used for monitoring functions, control functions, or to provide computations that meet specific items in the Software Requirements Specification.
2 Certain other programs, such as support and utility programs or data processing programs, are designated as Computer Programs if the status of the program directly affects project schedules, or if changes in the configuration of the program directly affect the configuration of other designated end items.
3 Programs that are used to train personnel in the use of the software system are designated as Computer Programs.
4 Programs used in the maintenance or testing of operational hardware are designated as Computer Programs.

5 Computer programs not normally designated as CPCIs include the following:

(a) Programs used as manufacturing quality control aids.
(b) Programs developed as management tools.
(c) Programs developed for assistance in configuration control or internal software maintenance.
(d) Compilers, assemblers, loaders, and other system support software, unless these programs are developed to meet specific project requirements.
(e) Programs developed for computer-aided design and manufacturing.

Additional guidelines to be followed in designating configuration items include:

1 Computer programs are individually designated as configuration items, separate from associated equipment and hardware configuration items.
2 Capabilities or functions developed or delivered at different times are considered for designation as separate configuration items.
3 Computer programs with potential use in multiple systems are designated as separate configuration items.
4 Highly interrelated computer programs are combined as one configuration item.
5 All computer programs to be designated as separate configuration items are identified at the Preliminary Design Review (PDR). The proposed configuration item designations are reviewed and approved at PDR. Configuration item identification numbers are then assigned, as defined in this section.
6 Consideration should be given to designating portions of some computer programs as separate configuration items. An executive routine, for example, may be independent of the project, while the applications programs it controls may change significantly from project to project. A single specification may thus be adequate for the development of an executive, while a series of specifications may be needed for the applications programs. In such cases, designation of the executive and applications programs as separate configuration items facilitates management control.

The degree to which a program, performing the same general function, can change for different applications or for subsequent projects may vary greatly. It is difficult to establish rigid rules to determine whether a program to be used for a particular project or application should be designated as a new configuration item (i.e., given a new identification number and defined in a new specification) or as a change in or new version of an existing configuration item. The following redesignation guidelines, however, should be followed.

A program should be redesignated for use in succeeding projects if one or more of the following applies:

1 New design reviews are required.
2 Significant new functions are being added.
3 A change in computing equipment causes significant reprogramming effort.
4 A new specification is required to incorporate extensive modifications made over a period of time.
5 Slight changes are required, but the original program will continue to be used or will be used again in the future.

A series of programs that are redesignated for each project may be given similar configuration item numbers (e.g., with changes only in the secondary prefix, described later in this section). Since some part of the program may be similar, it may not be necessary to produce a completely new set of documentation for each project. A specification or document addendum, referenced to previous documentation, may be sufficient for a particular modification.

For each designated configuration item, specifications and documents are produced that define the requirements (design, test plans, test procedures) and describe the released version. The documentation described in previous chapters defines the configuration item and establishes the development baseline. The addition of the computer program and listings establishes the product baseline. Each of these elements is properly related to the computer program physical product through a configuration identification numbering system.

Identification and marking conventions must be used in numbering all documents, specifications, and physical items to achieve configuration traceability during the life cycle of all computer program items. The numbering system used for software configuration management should apply to documents, specifications, computer programs, magnetic tapes, paper tapes, card decks, magnetic disks, and listings.

In a typical identification system, each Computer Program Configuration Item is assigned an identifier consisting of a predefined number of alphanumeric characters. The basic number assignment should be made by the Computer Program Library (see Section 9.6) or the configuration management organization and should relate to the number assigned to the associated Software Requirements Specification. (All programs must

have a Software Requirements Specification. In some cases, this specification will be very brief.) The identifier may have a prefix to identify the form of the information, as in the following examples:

1 CP for machine-readable computer program code, data base definition information, and data base values in the form of card deck, magnetic tape, paper tape, or magnetic disk.
2 CL for computer listings of program code, data base definitions, or data base values.
3 CD for computer program documentation, including the Software Requirements Specifications, design documents, test documents, Operating Instructions, and Version Description Documents.

A secondary prefix may also be included to distinguish between different CPs, CLs, and CDs having the same primary prefix and basic number, but controlling different functions. This prefix is typically used as a mnemonic indicator of the function of the Computer Program, such as CP-TAP-123456 for the code of a Telemetry Acquisition Program (TAP) and CD-TAP-123466 for one of the TAP documents.

The initial statements of the computer program code should include comments that specify the identifiers, the revision, and the revision date. If corrections are incorporated, the associated modification number should also be included.

9.2   CHANGE CONTROL

The second element in a successful software configuration management system is rigorous change control. The change control function provides the disciplined environment and administrative framework to control changes in the configuration baselines. This section defines the change classifications and the change control function as applied to the computer program code, documentation, and data base. Changes in the development and product baselines are controlled by the Configuration Control Board (CCB). Changes in the test baselines are under project control.

9.2.1   Change Classifications

Changes in an established baseline are considered to be one of two change classification types: Class I or Class II. *Class I changes,* because they are critical, require formal customer approval before they can be implemented. Changes are designated as Class I whenever one or more of the following is affected: (1) operational capability, as specified in the baseline Software Requirements Specification, (2) software or system development cost or schedule, and (3) equipment, computer programs, or facilities produced by another agency, to the extent that the agency must accomplish a change to maintain compatibility at the interface.

Class II changes are those that may be implemented without prior approval by the customer and at no additional cost to the customer. These may include (1) changes to correct editorial errors, (2) changes to correct computer program errors, and (3) other changes of a minor nature within categories specifically defined by the customer.

9.2.2 Documentation Change Control

During software development, software documentation can be placed under documentation change control by releasing it through the normal company release system or by putting it under control within the project configuration management system. Once released, any change must be approved not only by the software manager, but also by the project CCB. If release is to the customer, changes may also require customer approval. The documents prepared during the software development process (described in earlier chapters), the nominal points at which they are placed under control, and the level of change control (Class I or Class II) imposed at each point are provided in Figure 2.6 in Chapter 2.

The Project Plan must include procedures for implementing Class II changes in the documentation. These procedures should include, as a minimum, approval by the software manager and distribution of change pages, reissued documents, or update notices to the holders of the modified document.

9.2.3 Code and Listing Change Control

Control of the computer program code and listings, which form the test baselines or product baselines (also called software version control), involves control of the software code contained on computer sensible media, such as disk, magnetic tape, paper tape, and card deck and control of the associated program listings. This control includes identifying and labeling the baselined software, providing for storage of baselined software (sometimes called Certified Masters), preventing unauthorized changes, maintaining records, and reporting the status of software being controlled.

The Computer Program Library (CPL) should have the responsibility for implementing the version control procedures. Change authority for test baselines, should reside with the software manager, and change authority for product baselines should belong to the CCB. The

CPL implements only the changes approved by the appropriate change authority.

Software version control should be maintained by a version and modification control system. Modifications should be approved and implemented as change statements between each approved baseline. New modification identifiers are assigned to each update, and a new version number is assigned when the modifications (change cards, patches, correctors) are officially compiled into the program and a new master is built. Throughout the code development process, the version and modification numbers are included in the associated listings through the use of comment cards or special features provided by the compiler or assembler. This provides the means for the Computer Program Library to control the listings associated with particular versions of the computer program code.

Version control is initiated with the first test baseline at the beginning of Module Integration Testing. The version control procedures apply to the computer program source code, data base definition source code, and data base values in source (input) format. The CPL produces executable Certified Masters (CM) from these controlled source elements, duplicates the CM, and distributes copies. When a complex process is required to produce the executable code (such as compiling on one machine, assembling or linking programs on another, and executing on a third computer), the relocatable object code should also be controlled. Such special configuration control requirements should be defined in the Project Plan. For such cases, the responsibility for producing the relocatable master may be assigned by the CPL to a specific group within the project software organization.

9.2.4 Data Base Change Control

The data base provides one means of communication between software elements and with the external environment. It is therefore important that the data base structure and the contents be well defined and that data base change control procedures be utilized.

The data base structure must be defined early and changes must be controlled to ensure that interfacing elements are designed to the same interface requirements. For interfaces with elements produced by other organizations, separate Interface Control Specifications and Interface Control Documents should be included in the Statement of Work, with the contract defining the control mechanism. However, even if all data base interfaces are within the same organization, the data base structure requires special configuration control actions.

As shown in Figure 2.6, the requirements portion of

the Interface Design Documentation goes under Class I control at the Preliminary Design Review, at the point where detailed design begins. This interface documentation is controlled and changed in accordance with the procedures provided in the Project Plan for control of Class I changes.

When the initial data bases are generated, the structure of the data base must be in accordance with the latest documentation. As updates are made, they are controlled in the same manner as code changes in the software. That is, a Software Problem Report is used to document the requirement for a data base change. When the change is implemented, the version number associated with the data base is updated. All program code deliveries should identify the version of the data with which the code has been verified.

Control of the data base contents or data values associated with elements of the data base becomes important during formal testing and can be an important part of operational use. The applicability of multilevel data base change control within the software should be evaluated at project inception. The requirement for such built-in control will impact the data base structure, data base generation and output routine designs, and operational data base access routine designs. This multilevel change control provides a segmented data base with keys, passwords, or predefined station and terminal access capabilities which might include: (1) data anyone can change, (2) data requiring a specific key, password or terminal identifier to change the value, and/or (3) data that cannot be changed operationally, but require an SPR, CCB approval, and rebuilding the data base.

Whether or not a multilevel data base control scheme is required, the data base values should be put under control at the start of formal testing to ensure test repeatability. The level of control after delivery will normally be defined in the contractual documentation and operational procedures. Varying levels of control will be specified for different applications. However, the Project Plan should define the type of control for data base content, the control procedures, and the timing for implementing the control procedures either directly or by reference to other project documentation.

9.3   CHANGE PROCESSING

The third major ingredient for successful software configuration management is effective change processing. The guidelines for processing software changes must be defined in the Project Plan. Initially, changes

that correct programming errors or deficiencies in the software may be informally initiated by the programmer in conference with his supervisor or the software manager. New versions of the program or change statements may then be submitted for incorporation in the test baseline after verification of the change by the programmer.

The Project Plan defines the successive steps from the initial informal change processing to complete formal control of the code. These steps normally include:

1   Operation from a test baseline, with changes prepared, tested, and delivered informally by the programmer, as described above.
2   Initiation of formal version/modification control. All updates to the Certified Master are made by the designated software manager representative on the basis of changes received from the programmer and approved by the software manager. This typically occurs during the first test baseline.
3   A formal change-processing mechanism for all changes. This normally occurs at some point during Module Integration Testing, prior to the start of Verification Testing. Henceforth, only changes required to close out a Software Problem Report (SPR) are allowed. An SPR is generated when the software fails to perform as required during testing, if a deficiency in the software is discovered by a means other than testing, or if a document change or correction is identified. During this phase, approval of the software manager is required to close SPRs and incorporate the associated changes as modifications to the current Certified Master. SPR initiation, definition, and closure are described in Section 9.4.2.
4   Review and approval of changes by the CCB after release of the software by the software manager.

Figures 9.2 and 9.3 illustrate a typical sequence of events for formal change processing. These event sequences can be used as a baseline to establish simpler processing mechanisms in the intermediate stages of development, before full formal processing is required. Figure 9.2 illustrates change processing to correct errors. Figure 9.3 illustrates change processing for planned modifications to the baseline software.

It should be noted that the following discussion of change processing is structured and formal. For small projects, or very early in large projects, the SPR may be sufficient documentation for closure of changes. Also, CCB action may not be formally required for small changes, essentially correction of "bugs", that

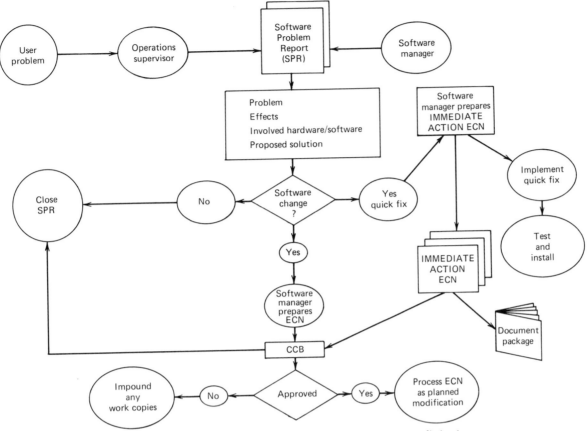

Figure 9.2 Computer program change processing: error deficiency elimination.

occur early in the testing cycle (prior to Verification Testing).

The sequence of actions needed to identify and process changes in computer programs released to the CCB or to the customer are described below.

1 The occurrence of an event (during program execution) that identifies a need for a change to the baselined computer program should be immediately documented as a Software Problem Report (SPR) and communicated to the software manager by the operations supervisor.

2 The operations supervisor is encouraged to recommend changes and alternatives as a proposed solution. These proposals may take the form of quick fixes or work-arounds that could be implemented immediately if concurrence is obtained from the software manager. The software manager, in conjunction with the supervisor, will:

(a) Investigate the problem and its effects.

(b) Determine the involved software and hardware.

(c) Evaluate the proposed solutions.

(d) Decide upon a course of action to resolve the problem.

3 If there is sufficient need and justification for proposing a computer program change, the software manager will ensure the preparation of the necessary Engineering Change Notices (ECNs). The ECN must include the following:

(a) A statement of requirements for testing the computer program change. The ECN must specify test requirements. If no test is required, this should be indicated in the ECN, along with a summary of the facts that led to this decision.

(b) An indication of all related computer programs (including higher-level programs) affected by the described change.

4 The software manager may direct "on site" immediate implementation of modifications to software. All such implementation directions should be in the form of an "IMMEDIATE ACTION–

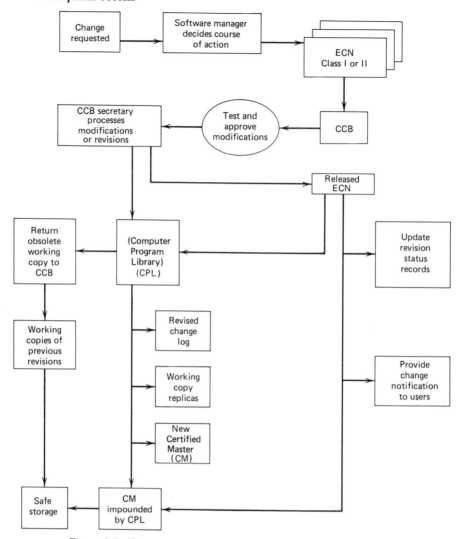

Figure 9.3   Computer program change processing: planned modification.

TEMPORARY CHANGE AUTHORIZATION"
ECN and should be presented to the CCB as soon
as possible. The ECN must identify the specific
medium that will be immediately modified to incorporate the described change. The official product baseline will not be modified to incorporate
the immediate action change until CCB approval
is given for the modification.

5   A copy of the "IMMEDIATE ACTION–TEM-
PORARY   CHANGE   AUTHORIZATION"
ECN should be placed in the documentation
package as the authorizing document. The operations supervisor is responsible for implementing the ECN directions. The software manager
is responsible for presenting the ECN to the
CCB.

6   All CCB-approved changes require either release
of program and/or data base modifications or release of a new version of the program and/or
data base. A new version in the form of a new
Certified Master (CM) should be released if a
number of modifications have been previously
implemented or the current modification incorporates substantial changes. The CCB directs
the release of a new version with implementation
of the current modification. The software manager, the operations supervisor, or the Computer
Program Library may recommend that the CCB
direct a new version release instead of a modification release.

7   The CCB secretary processes the modification or
revision, as described in item No. 9 below.

8   The approved ECN is not released until the following actions have been completed:

(a) Program modifications or a new revision of the CM is provided by the CPL.

(b) Necessary revised Working Copy (WC) replicas have been provided by the CPL.

(c) A revised computer program listing (CL) or the revised portion of the CL is available.

9 The ECN release must include the following actions, performed by the CCB secretary:

(a) Delivery of the signed ECN, with modification or revision identification, to the CPL.

(b) Updating revision status records.

(c) Directing the CPL to impound the old CM.

(d) If a computer program copy has been delivered to an external activity (customer, other contractor, remote-site operator, etc), ensuring that change notification is provided to the user (through contract-defined channels) and making arrangements for the transmittal of the new revision to the user.

10 There may be a need to retain one or more WCs of a previous revision to be used under special conditions. When retention of these WCs is directed by the CCB, they should be marked "OBSOLETED REVISION–AUTHORIZED USE ONLY" without obliterating the previous markings. Such WCs are placed in safe storage, to be released only by the project configuration management function in response to specific needs approved by the CCB.

9.4 CONFIGURATION ACCOUNTING

Configuration accounting is the final major element of the software configuration management process. Records of change actions must be maintained by the CCB, and the CPL must maintain records of baseline documentation, software releases, approved revisions and modifications, and problem reports. The CPL records provide information necessary to trace the evolution of the current revision from the initial released configuration.

9.4.1 Change Log

When the first Software Problem Report (Section 9.4.2) or Engineering Change Notice (Section 9.4.4) is written for a computer program, a change log should be established. The CCB secretary should maintain a current record of all proposed and implemented changes. Entries to the log should be made chronologically and should include, as a minimum, the following information:

1 Log item number (assigned in sequence, as entered).

2 Title or short description of change.

3 Nature of the change, such as a document (editorial or design) and/or code change to correct a certain problem.

4 Date of log entry.

5 Documentation affected, including:

(a) Location of change in affected document, such as paragraph, page, and line number.

(b) Status, such as "red-lined pending release of update pages" or ". . . pending reissue of document, revision C."

6 Software routines affected, including:

(a) Type of change required for each routine.

(b) Status, such as "modification/correctors released pending release of new version."

7 Disposition, such as "closed with CPL Transmittal Form (CTF) No. 42."

Red-lining should be used to revise the document master to reflect a change authorized through an SPR prior to release of update pages or revisions to a document. Before a red-line entry can be made, the software manager (prior to release of the program) or the CCB (after release) must authorize the change, and an entry must be made in the change log. By this process, each change in the released documentation is traceable to the source that authorized it.

Red-lining may be applied to all formally released documentation, except approved specifications. One copy of the released computer program document should be retained by the CPL as the red-line copy. For each change approved by the CCB, a red-line entry must be made in the affected documentation. Red-line changes reference the change log item number which describes the changes.

Similar to red-lining, modifications or correctors may be used to fix program errors before release of a new version of the program. When these preliminary changes are made to the code, comments should be included indicating the lines changed, the nature of the change, and the name of the individual who made the change. As with the document corrections, the software manager or the CCB authorizes the change to be implemented. The CPL Transmittal Form (CTF), which delivers the corrections to the computer program, references the change log item number.

The Project Plan should provide for periodic audits

to ensure that the change log is maintained complete and current. The audits should check that (1) each entry in the log has a corresponding change in the code through a CTF (section 9.4.3) and/or change in a document, (2) each red-lined change in a document has a corresponding entry in the log, and (3) all change paper associated with the computer program, both internal (such as SPRs and CTFs) and external (such as ECNs), is recorded in the log.

9.4.2 Software Problem Report

The Software Problem Report (SPR) should be the primary vehicle for reporting problems from the start of formal software testing through software release. The problems reported on an SPR may be due to any of the following:

1 Coding errors.
2 Test procedure errors.
3 Test plan errors.
4 Design deficiencies.
5 Problems in or incompatibilities with other operational programs.
6 Data naming or addressing errors.
7 Interface incompatibilities.
8 Incompatibilities with or errors in support software, such as test drivers, compilers, assemblers, and link editors.
9 Errors in simulator or emulator programs.
10 Hardware problems in host or target processor.
11 Operating system problems.
12 Display and readout hardware problems.
13 Failures in interfacing hardware.

The SPR form shown in Figure 9.4 is structured to record the problem and track its resolution from SPR initiation through analysis to correction and closure.

Initiation
The originator, usually the person who detects the software problem, completes the "problem" section. Sufficient additional information should be attached to thoroughly document the problem. Attachments may include listings, test data and results, and copies of test cases.

Review
This package of data must be transmitted to the CPL, which will examine the SPR for completeness and accuracy. If information is missing on the SPR, it must be returned to the originator. After review the SPR is assigned a number, logged, and routed as follows: (1) one copy to originator, (2) one copy to the SPR master

file, and (3) the original and one copy with the attached materials to the software design group responsible for problem analysis.

Problem Analysis
After receipt of the SPR by the design group, the design supervisor assigns a programmer to analyze the problem and complete the "analysis" section of the form.

Results of the analysis should indicate an operational software problem, a support software problem, an operational or test procedure problem, or a hardware problem. The analysis results must be reviewed with the supervisor, and the problem should be assigned to the appropriate person or organization for disposition, as discussed below.

Disposition
The method of correction depends on the nature of the problem (i.e., whether in the hardware or the software). If the problem is a result of a hardware deficiency, the SPR should be returned by the analyst for distribution to the appropriate organization for resolution. If the problem is a software deficiency, it may require a change in the operational code, released procedures, and/or support software.

Operational Software. If the required change affects operational software or other contract end item software, the changes should be made and tested to ensure that the problem has been corrected, and the correction section of the SPR must be completed. Test results are then added to the materials accompanying the SPR, and the package is returned to the CPL. The SPR package is reviewed for completeness and verification that the proposed corrections were tested by the programmer. Recommendation should then be made to the CCB to release the change.

Released Procedures. If the required change affects released operating or test procedures, the proposed solution should be written in the correction block of the SPR. The proposed change is then presented to the CCB, and, upon approval, the SPR is entered as a change log item.

Support Software. If the required change affects support software, the support software group is responsible for making the necessary corrections in both code and documentation and for closing the SPR.

Closure
When the proposed correction has been approved and implemented and all follow-up actions have been initiated and documented (or if the SPR has been disap-

SOFTWARE PROBLEM REPORT

SPR No. _____

PROBLEM: (Prepared by User)

Originator _____ Phone No. _____

              (Name)   (Organization)

System, Processor, or   System   Test Case or

Component Failing _____ Computer _____ Version ID _____ Program ID _____

or Project Involved

Description of Problem (Attach additional pages if
necessary – include numbers or other identification
of offending statements or data)

Classification   Enclosures

☐   Minor or Not to Specs   _____   ☐   Program Listings

☐   Major or Missing   _____   ☐   Run Deck

☐   Information   _____   ☐   Run Instructions

☐   Revision Request   _____   ☐   Storage Map Listings

☐   Software Addition   _____   ☐   Data Listings

                  Correction Required By _____   ☐   On-Line Output

                                 (Date)

Authorizing Signature _____ Date _____ Time ____

                    (Name)   (Organization)

ANALYSIS: (Prepared by organization responsible for software)

Received Date _____ Time _____ Charge Number _____

☐   Software in Error   Explanation: _____   Analysis Time Expended:

☐   Software Not in Error   _____   Man Hours _____
     Explain and Return to
     Originator   _____   Computer Hours _____

☐   Insufficient Information   _____   Computer _____
     for Analysis. See
     Explanation   _____   Estimated Cost of Solutions:

☐   Error Previously   _____   Man Hours _____
     Reported on SPR No.
                    _____   Computer Hours _____

☐   Others, Explain   _____   Planned _____

☐   Not Approved   Correction Date

☐   Approved for Correction
     or Change

Signature _____ Date _____ Time ____

              (Name)   (Organization)

CORRECTION: (Brief description of work performed, including test cases used to confirm correction)

Solution: _____   Modules Changed _____

_____   _____

_____

_____   Correction Time Expended:

_____   Man Hours _____

_____   Computer Hours _____

_____   Submitted to _____

Work Performed by (Signature) _____ Date _____ Time _____

CONFIRMATION: Corrections Verified by CCB/CPL

Signature _____ Date _____ Time ____

CTF No(s) _____

Available in (Version ID) _____ Date Returned to Originator _____ Time _____

Figure 9.4   Sample Software Problem Report form.

proved), the SPR must be closed. The problem disposition and change paper are indicated on the SPR. When a problem in the operational code affects released hardware, the SPR must be submitted to the CCB for disposition, as discussed in Section 9.4.1. Changes to controlled code are processed as described in Section 9.3. Change board action may result in initiating an Engineering Change Notice (ECN) (Section 9.4.4). The SPR can be formally closed after the ECN or other change paper has been approved, the change has been implemented, and the applicable CPL Transmittal Form (CTF) has been recorded on the SPR form.

9.4.3   CPL Transmittal Form

The basic medium for submitting code and data base information to the CPL is the CPL Transmittal Form (CTF). A sample form is shown in Figure 9.5. Data are entered in one of two categories: initial entry or change data. The CTF is used both for submitting data for the first time (an initial entry) and for submitting changes to data that have already been entered (change data). If the data are not currently in the CPL under a specific version identifier (name) and do not have a predecessor with that identifier, then they are an initial entry. Whenever data are entered into the CPL with a new name, even though they have a predecessor, they are still considered initial data.

Configuration control for computer programs is normally submitted through the source code. Load modules or applications programs in binary form normally should not be submitted to the library; the load modules should be generated from the source code residing in the CPL.

The computer-sensible media used for data submittals to the CPL are dependent on the type of data involved and whether the entry constitutes a change in an existing data record or is a new entry. Punched cards, magnetic tape, or disk transfer may be used as the medium for computer code submittals to the library. Whenever possible, the CPL should standardize one format to simplify processing and storage.

Initial Entry
Data initially entered in the CPL normally consist of data on computer-sensible media and the supporting data listed in Section 9.5.1. Each initial-entry submittal package is accompanied by a CPL Transmittal Form. The form identifies the data and constitutes a historical file for the entry. The following list describes typical packages for various types of data:

1   Application programs and software (tested).

   (a)   Source code on computer-sensible media.

   (b)   Computer listing of the source code, unless generated by the CPL.

   (c)   Results of program tests.

   (d)   Required changes in the design documents.

2   Test software.

   (a)   Completed program—usually both source and object code on computer-sensible media.

   (b)   Complete documentation of the computer program, including operating instructions and listings.

   (c)   Results of tests conducted on the computer program.

3   Data base items.

   (a)   Data base items on computer-sensible media.

   (b)   Listing of the items submitted.

4   Test input data.

   (a)   Test data on computer-sensible media.

   (b)   Listing of the test data.

   (c)   Documentation indicating how the data are to be used.

5   Other supporting data—usually submitted intact and in the form of documentation.

Change Data
Specific authorization must be obtained to make program or data changes in controlled library files. When a load module change is to be implemented, a source change should be used to generate the modified object code.

During the course of conducting software Verification Tests, changes may be required in any of the data contained on computer-sensible media. Like initial-entry data, change data is accompanied by a CTF. Only changes in the library version should be submitted, not a completely new version. If the CPL does not have the facility for incorporating the changes directly into the library version, a new version should be submitted.

All change data must be accompanied by new listings and text material needed to identify and describe the change. Prior to submittal, all changes should be fully tested to ensure functional and interface compatibility. Changes made directly in object code, not generated by source code modifications, should be avoided, but may be allowed in the CPL controlled files between version updates. These changes require the same authorization as version updates.

COMPUTER PROGRAM LIBRARY TRANSMITTAL FORM (CTF)

☐ Program Element   Base Version _____

       or

☐ Document   Element Name:

       or   _____

☐ Test Case   _____

ATTACHMENTS: SPRs Resolved:

☐ New Source   _____

☐ Update Cards   _____
  & Listing

☐ Compiler/Assembly
  Listing

☐ Test Output

☐ Test Case(s)   (List) _____

☐ New Test(s)   (Include Card Decks, Listings, and Test Output)

For CCB/CPL Use Only

CTF No. _ _ _ _ _ _ _

Date: _ _ _ _ _ _ _ _

New Version: _ _ _ _ _

Description of Changes for Version Description Document:

_____
_____
_____
_____

Dependencies (Specify any actions/modules which may be needed prior to integration and/or testing):

_____
_____
_____
_____
_____

Documentation Changes (Attach edited pages for Design Documents/Specify changes required in other manuals and specs):

_____
_____
_____
_____
_____

Submitted By: _____ Date: _____

Approved By: _____ Development Date: _____

Approved By: _____ CCB/CPL   Date: _____

Figure 9.5 Sample Computer Program Library Transmittal Form.

9.4.4 Engineering Change Notice

The Engineering Change Notice (ECN) provides the official documentation for proposed software and documentation changes. The use of the ECN in the software change process is described in Section 9.3. The ECN provides the following:

1 A description of the proposed change, including test requirements and an indication of all affected software and documentation.
2 An authorizing document for immediate temporary changes.
3 Documentation for presentation to the CCB for change approval and the authorizing document for approved changes.
4 Documentation to describe revision for the CPL.

An ECN is generated when an SPR requires changes in the software or when a significant change to the software or documentation is requested. The ECN form shown in Figure 9.6 is structured to record the

ENGINEERING CHANGE NOTICE

ECN No. ______

Proposed change: (Prepared by Software Manager)

Originator ______ (Name) ______ (Organization) Phone No. ______

Computer program ______ System version ID ______

Change type ______ SPR(s) ______

Change description ______ (Title)

Software affected ______ Documentation affected ______

Change design ______

Operational effect ______

Test requirements ______

Computer program compatibility ______ Approval needed by: ______

Immediate action authorized ______

Authorized signature ______ Date ______ Time ______

CCB Actions: (Prepared by CCB) CCB meeting No. ______ Date ______

Approval ______

Authorized signature(s) ______ Date ______ Time ______

Confirmation: (Prepared by CCB/CPL)

Authorized signature ______ Date ______ Time ______

Compatibility ECN No(s) ______ CTF No(s) ______

Available in version ______ Date returned to originator ______

Figure 9.6 Sample Engineering Change Notice form.

proposed change and track the approval and implementation of the change in all related software and documentation.

Initiation

The originator, usually the software manager of the affected Computer Program, completes the "proposed change" section. He specifies whether the change is required to correct an error (the related SPR(s) is listed) or to improve the software operation (a planned modification).

Change Description

The proposed change must be described in sufficient detail for the CCB to evaluate the impact on all aspects of the project and for each responsible organization to implement the change. The software and documentation affected by the change must be listed, along with program design information that can be understood by another programmer. When needed, additional pages and attachments should be used to clarify the changes. The operational impact (in terms that can be understood by user personnel) and the tests required to verify the change are also included in the change description portion of the form. If the proposed change requires modifications in other Computer Programs within the software subsystem to maintain compatibility, these programs should be listed. This facilitates the generation of ECNs for these programs upon approval of the proposed changes by the CCB.

Approval

The software manager can authorize immediate changes in the affected software and documentation, if the changes are required to maintain the smooth operation of the system. However, all ECNs are submitted to the CCB for final approval. The CCB must evaluate the desirability of the proposed change and its impact on related Computer Programs and the entire software subsystem.

Closure

The ECN is not closed until ECNs are generated and approved for other programs requiring changes to maintain overall compatibility. The related ECN numbers are entered on the ECN form, CPL Transmittal Forms are submitted and approved for all software and documentation changes, and the CTF numbers are entered on the ECN form. This implies that all required changes in the software subsystem are completed, tested, and under configuration control.

9.5 THE COMPUTER PROGRAM LIBRARY (CPL)

The Computer Program Library (CPL) is a key element in a successful software configuration management system. The CPL serves as a central repository for storing and maintaining control over the computer program code, the controlled data base, test software, test data, other information used to conduct the tests, and all other project data requiring control. All software code and data to be controlled must be stored on master copies or in mass storage in a controlled library. The library must provide the necessary environmental conditions for cleanliness, security, and so on, as well as control over the integrity of the data and code. In addition, the CPL provides for the reporting and accountability of library contents.

The data under CPL control are entered and changed only with proper software manager or Configuration Control Board (CCB) authorization; unauthorized changes must be prevented. All controlled data should be accounted for, and periodic reports should be issued showing a complete inventory of library contents, including additions, deletions, and modifications. These reports are placed on file to form a historical record of all data under CPL control. Thus the CPL can (1) identify all software versions, (2) maintain control over currently approved software versions, and (3) disseminate approved software versions to users. The CPL also permits users to reconstruct or retrieve software versions that have been superseded, but that may be required as backup to the current version for traceability, regression tests, and so on.

The major responsibilities of the CPL are entering and storing data submitted from an external source, controlling and accounting, preparing reports, and disseminating data to users. These activities are described in the following subsections.

9.5.1 Data Content in the CPL

Data stored and placed under control in the CPL may be generated by the CPL or originated externally. Data originated externally consist primarily of software code, documentation, and supporting data. Data generated within the CPL consist primarily of duplications of controlled code and data, and records, reports, and forms required by the CPL for maintaining control over the externally generated data. Data may be identified either as (1) data residing on computer-sensible media (such as punched cards, magnetic tape, punched tape, disk packs, and cassettes) or (2) directly readable data (such as documents, listings, and reports). Typical CPL data contents are:

1   Computer-sensible data, consisting of the following:

   (a)   Source code and object code to be tested and delivered as the product-related computer program.
   (b)   Data base items, such as constants and tables, or display formats essential for the testing and operation of the deliverable software.
   (c)   Support software essential for formal software verification.
   (d)   Test software required for formal verification.
   (e)   Test data used as input for formal testing.

2   Supporting data, consisting of the following:

   (a)   Test data resulting from formal testing.
   (b)   Unreleased software documentation and listings.
   (c)   Released software documentation and listings.
   (d)   Version description records.
   (e)   CPL inventories and reports.
   (f)   Software Problem Report (SPR) files.
   (g)   CPL Transmittal Forms (CTF).
   (h)   Test status reports.

9.5.2   Data Entry to the CPL

Entering data to the CPL requires both submittal by the originator and acceptance by the CPL personnel. The responsibilities for submittal and acceptance are as follows:

1   *Data Submittal.*   Data are submitted to the CPL with CPL Transmittal Forms (CTFs), as described in Section 9.4.3.
2   *Data Acceptance.*   Before accepting data for storage, responsible CPL personnel should check for the following:

   (a)   That the data are properly identified.
   (b)   That the submittal package is complete.
   (c)   That the CTF is filled out properly.
   (d)   For change entries, that the requirement for change has been documented on a Software Problem Report (SPR), that the change has been approved, and that the change log entry is complete.
   (e)   That the CTF has been approved by the proper authorities.

If these criteria have been met, the CTF can be approved by the CPL, and the data can be logged and accepted for storage, as described below.

9.5.3   Data Storage in the CPL

Computer code and data may be stored on many different types of storage media. The medium used will depend upon the kind of computing equipment available for use by the CPL. (Note that the library need not be maintained on the project target computer; a general-purpose computer is often more suitable for the CPL.) Regardless of the storage medium used, the following criteria apply:

1   Master copies must be maintained, unaltered, until they become obsolete through the development and verification of a new version.
2   Each master copy must be uniquely identified to distinguish it from all other data and from all other versions of the same data.
3   Sufficient backup data must be maintained to allow reconstruction of a new master copy in the event that the original is destroyed or lost.
4   The library should be organized to permit rapid retrieval of all library items.
5   Records and reports should be such that the library contents, version status, and test status are readily available and easily prepared.

CPL storage and retrieval methods may be either automatic or manual, depending on the computer and facility resources available to the library. Although an automated file-maintenance system requires a large amount of mass storage and a software system for maintaining the files, it is still the perferred method of maintaining files of software code and data during software development. Such a system allows both source and object code to be stored in mass storage, provides automatic generation of reports showing file contents, and contains the facility for changing files by the simple insertion of change instructions to add, modify, or delete information. The master files should be kept on disk pack or other media that can be disconnected from the computer to prevent unwanted modification of their contents. When software and mass storage devices required for automatic file maintenance are not available, master copies must be maintained on another appropriate input medium, such as punched cards, punched tape, or magnetic tape. In all cases a master and a backup copy must be maintained for each approved version of the computer data being stored.

Proper organization of the stored data is a key element of a successful CPL. Computer code and data should be filed in a manner that facilitates the generation of reports. Separate reports are likely to be required for each of the following categories: (1) test input data, (2) deliverable software source code, (3) test software source code, and (4) data base parameters.

9.5.4 Accounting and Reporting of the CPL

The Computer Program Library is responsible for records accounting and reporting for all the CPL activities. Specific types of records should be maintained for the CPL. Each of the forms discussed below should be designed so that the information required for reporting may be entered directly into the computer to enable the use of a computer for report generation.

CTF Logs and Files

As noted in Section 9.4.3, each entry to the CPL is accompanied by a CTF. When a CTF is accepted by the CPL, entries are made in a CTF log. Typical information includes:

1. Date of the CTF
2. Number of the CTF (assigned by the library).
3. Name of the person making the submittal.
4. Type of data submitted.
5. Name and number of data submitted.
6. Related SPRs and change log item numbers, if applicable.

This log also serves as an index to the CTFs that have been filed and provides the capability to correlate with each of the various kinds of data entered, with software changes, and so on. When the CTF log entries have been completed, the data that accompanied the CTF are filed, and the CTF is filed by CTF number.

Test Status Log

A test status log is required in order to maintain visibility over the test progress. Typical test status log entries contain the following information:

1. Test identification.
2. Data base to be used.
3. Other tests on which this test depends.
4. Date test was completed.
5. Version number of the software on which the test is expected to be executed successfully.
6. Version number of the software on which the test was executed successfully.

SPR Logs and Files

The CPL should serve as the repository for the Software Problem Report (SPR) logs. Each SPR should be logged in chronological sequence. A typical entry in the SPR log should include:

1. SPR number.
2. Originator's Name.
3. Name of software unit.
4. Version identifier.
5. Test exposing the problem.
6. Responsible programmer.
7. Closure information.

The SPR log serves as an index to the SPRs on file and may be used for preparation of reports on SPR status.

Version Description Record

Version description records are maintained to describe each new version of the computer programs released for tests. Typical version description records include the following:

1. Version identifications.
2. CTFs included in current versions.
3. SPRs closed against current versions.
4. Changes installed in current versions by change log item number.
5. New capabilities of current versions.
6. Regression tests run against current versions.

In addition to the record keeping activities defined above, the CPL should issue the following reports periodically or by request:

1. *Computer Program Library Inventory Report.* These reports should include the following information:

    (a) Documents on file and pertinent descriptive material (e.g., number, title, author, date, version number, and abstract).

    (b) Listings of software and data on computer-sensible media, identifying each unit of software, its name, identification, and version number, as appropriate.

2. *Test Status Report.* Test status reports are derived from the test status log. They may be simply a copy of the test status log or brief reports for specific purposes. They may include the following information:

(a) The number and names of tests completed.

(b) The number of tests remaining.

(c) The number of tests behind schedule.

(d) The number of tests delayed due to hardware or other external problems.

(e) The number of tests delayed due to module tests behind schedule.

3 *Software Problem Status Report.*   Software problem status reports are derived from the SPR log. They may be simply copies of that log or, like test status logs, may contain brief information, such as the following:

(a) Number of outstanding SPRs against each module.

(b) Total number of outstanding SPRs.

(c) Number of SPRs closed since the last report.

4 *Change Status Report.*   Change status reports are derived from the change log maintained by the CCB. They may be simply copies of the log or may contain brief information for each software unit; for example:

(a) Number of outstanding changes and descriptions of each change.

(b) Total number of changes.

(c) Number of changes processed since the last report.

(d) Number and description of design changes in process.

(e) Number of documentation changes in process.

9.5.5   Data Dissemination from the CPL

Data are disseminated by the Computer Program Library by authorized requests. The data consist of all of the reports summarized in Section 9.5.4, as well as copies of documents and controlled code and data. The following criteria should be applied to data dissemination:

1 Master copies of code and data and their backup should never be disseminated, but should be maintained under control of the CPL.

2 All copies of code and data should be made under surveillance of CPL personnel.

3 Data should be disseminated to authorized personnel only.

4 Classified data should be copied and distributed only in accordance with approved project security procedures.

9.5.6   Version Integrity within the CPL System

The primary purpose of the Computer Program Library, as stated earlier, is to maintain integrity of the computer programs and associated data undergoing testing. This entails ensuring that the actual computer program code to be delivered is the same code that was tested and verified and that it faithfully represents the design described in the released design documents. Version integrity is maintained by controlling the progressive construction of the computer program versions by the CPL personnel and by conducting integrity checks over the code.

Version Construction

Version construction is the process of building a computer program version from its parts. This involves such things as compiling or assembling source programs, linking, and generating executable code (load modules) to make up the computer program. Each time a change is made to the code, a new version is generated from the source data, and the executable element is identified by a unique version identifier, as specified by the project conventions. Consequently, a new computer program version identifier is required when one or more of its executable elements are changed. When approved modifications or correctors are added to the master without building a new version, a new modification identifier is required.

The version construction process should always be performed by CPL personnel. New versions are generated by making approved modifications to the approved source code. Regression tests are performed on the newly generated (modified) versions before they can be used for formal verification. The master copy of each software version is maintained in the CPL. Test masters and other copies are distributed by the CPL personnel as required.

Integrity Checks

Integrity checks on constructed versions of computer programs are performed by the CPL for two reasons: (1) to provide assurance that the version has remained unchanged from the time it was tested and certified as an authorized version and (2) to demonstrate a continuous record of version development. Three types of integrity checks are discussed below: data checks, regression tests, and development traceability.

Data Checks

Data checks provide the lowest level of version integrity checking. Computer program code and data base files stored on computer-sensible media to be controlled should use at least one of the following data checking methods to ensure that the code has not changed since it was placed in storage. The checking methods are checksum, hashsum, and direct comparison. In many cases, special software is required to provide the checking capabilities.

Checksum. The checksum procedure is a machine-implemented arithmetic summing operation of the contents of all locations in a predefined storage region. The end result is a sum of the numerical representations of the characters or words in the code. The checksum is implemented by a simple binary adder. When used to make comparisons between versions, the result is a highly dependable indication of the presence of changes. The checksum provides a single number that can be recorded and compared whenever the checksum operation is performed.

Hashsum. Hashsumming is performed in a manner similar to checksumming, except that the machine operation used is an exclusive "or" and the result is contained in one computer word. It is approximately as dependable an indicator as the checksum method for detecting changes to code and requires about the same amount of time to execute. Therefore, the decision to implement one or the other is mainly a consideration of which is more suitable to a particular machine architecture.

Comparison Check. A comparison check is a word-by-word check between a version master and a copy. The comparison check is an absolute check and ensures total authenticity. The comparison check program should provide an output that identifies all deviations and a copy of the deviant code.

Regression Testing

Regression testing provides the second level of version integrity checking and is performed on new software versions to verify that previously tested functions are performed correctly after the change. These tests are taken from a set that has been previously performed. Regression testing is not a complete check, but it will expose the more obvious problems in the new (modified) versions.

Version Development Traceability

The third type of integrity checking, after data checks and regression tests, is version development traceability. A continuous record of all the versions generated in the development of a computer program is required to certify that all of the delivered code has been tested successfully. The record should identify all changes implemented and tests performed on each version, as well as the errors found during testing. These records are required to certify the program during formal software audits prior to delivery. Complete historical data can be expected to be a requirement for the satisfaction of the audit.

The capability to physically reconstruct previous versions should be established to provide a backup for current versions, to trace problems to their origin, to adapt earlier versions to new applications, or for other special requirements. The following items provide the minimum data required for a complete history:

1 Version description records.
2 Library accounting records.
3 Change records.
4 Problem report files.
5 CTF files.
6 A CPL master of each version.

Documentation Requirements Correlation

The documentation requirements described in this book are consistent with the needs of both commercial and military software development activities. This appendix provides a correlation between the set of documents described in this book and the content specified in two military standards. Tables A.1 and A.2 correlate the documents described in this book with the documents required by an Air Force standard (MIL-STD-483) and a Navy standard (WS-8506). In some cases the Air Force standard does not explicitly call for test documentation. In these cases, the implied documents are noted and correlated with the appropriate documents from this book.

For reference, a list of applicable military specifications for configuration management is included in Table A.3. The list includes specifications on reviews, audits, and engineering changes, as well as software documentation.

MIL-STD-483* Configuration Management Practices for Systems Equipment, Munitions and Computer Programs 31 December 1970 Notice 1 6/1/71 Notice 2 3/29/79	Document Requirement	Software Requirements Spec.	Functional Design Document	Test Plan	Interface Control Documents	Detailed Design Documents	Test Procedures	Test Report	Operating Instructions	Version Description Document
• Appendix VI, Section 60.5 Part I Specification	E									
— Program Definition		x								
— Interface Requirements		x								
— Functional Requirements		x								
— Adaptation		x								
— Quality Assurance Provisions		x								
• Appendix VI, Section 60.6 Part II Specification	E									
— Functional Allocation			x							
— Functional Description			x							
* — CPC Descriptions					x	x				
— Storage Allocation			x			U				
— Functional Flow * Diagram (CP level)			x							
— Quality Assurance				x						
• Test Procedures	I						x			
• Test Results	I							x		
• Operating Instructions	I									
• Appendix VIII, Section 80.12 Version Description Document	E									x

*Computer Program Component Descriptions

*Diagram (Computer Program level)

*MIL-STD-490 Requirements same as specified with B5 Spec = Part I Spec. and C5 Spec = Part II Spec.

E = Explicit   I = Implied   U = Updated

Table A.1   Air Force (MIL-STD-483) Document Correlation

NAVORD WS-8506 (Rev. 1) — Requirements for Digital Computer Program Documentation — November 1971	Document Requirement	Software Requirements Spec.	Functional Design Document	Test Plan	Interface Control Documents	Detailed Design Documents	Test Procedures	Test Results	Operating Instructions	Version Description Document
• Computer Program Performance Specification	E	x			x^a					
• Computer Program Design Specification	E		x		x^b					
• Computer Program Test Plan	E			x						
• Computer Subprogram Design Document	E					x				
• Common Data Base Design Document	E		x		x					
• Computer Program Test Procedures	E						x	I		
• Computer Program Operator's Manual	E								x	
• Computer Program Package	E									x

E = Explicit
I = Implied
x^a = Requirements Portion
x^b = Design Portion

Table A.2 Navy (WS-8506) Document Correlation

Number	Title	Date
MIL-STD-480	Configuration Control - Engineering Changes, Deviations and Waivers	31 October 1968
MIL-STD-481	Configuration Control - Engineering Changes, Deviations and Waivers (Short Form)	30 October 1968
MIL-STD-482	Configuration Status Accounting Data Elements and Related Features	19 September 1968
MIL-STD-483 (USAF)	Configuration Management Practices for Systems, Equipment, Munitions, and Computer Programs	31 December 1970 Notice 1 6/1/71 Notice 2 3/21/79
MIL-STD-490	Specification Practices	30 October 1968
MIL-STD-499	System Engineering Management	17 July 1969
MIL-STD-885A	Procurement Data Package	30 October 1969
NAVORD WS-8506 (Rev. 1)	Requirements for Digital Computer Program Documentation	November 1971
NAVSHIPS 0967-011-0010	Specifications for Digital Computer Program Documentation	March 1966
NAVSHIPS 0967-011-0011	Specifications for Digital Computer Program Documentation	October 1968
AFSCM/AFLCM 375-7	Systems Management: Configuration Management for Systems, Equipment, Munitions, and Computer Programs	31 March 1971

Table A.3 Specifications for Military Software Configuration Management Practices

Document Contents

This appendix provides a description of the contents of each of the documents written during the software development process.

B.1 SOFTWARE REQUIREMENTS SPECIFICATION

The following paragraphs describe the contents of the Software Requirements Specification as discussed in Section 5.2.1

SOFTWARE REQUIREMENTS SPECIFICATION:
CONTENTS

Section 1   Introduction

1.1   Identification
1.2   Scope
1.3   Functional Summary
1.4   Assumptions and Constraints

Section 2   Applicable Documents

2.1   Customer Documents
2.2   Other Documents

Section 3   Requirements

3.1   Interface Requirements
3.2   Functional Requirements
3.3   Special Requirements
3.4   Data Base Requirements
3.5   Identification and Marking Requirements
3.6   Requirements Traceability

Section 4   Quality Assurance Provisions

4.1   General Requirements
4.1.1   Definitions
4.1.2   Software Version Integrity
4.1.3   Software Test Procedures
4.1.4   Test Software Validation
4.2   Verification Requirements

Section 5   Preparation for Delivery

Section 6   Notes

Appendix A   Acronyms and Abbreviations

Appendix B   Definitions and Nomenclature

Section 1   Introduction
The *Introduction* provides a brief general discussion of the overall system, which includes the software subsystem and computer program. The *Identification* subsection provides the nomenclature used in discussing the computer program and defines a computer program *Name* used in the remainder of the requirements specification. The *Scope* subsection describes the relationship of the computer program to the software subsystem, the basic goal of the program, and briefly, the interface of the program with its external operational environment. The *Functional Summary* subsection defines the primary functions to be implemented by the software subsystem. Each function is identified by name, and the purpose and use of the function are described. Also included is a functional block diagram, along with the necessary text to clearly identify each interface between the given function and other functions. These are system functional interfaces, and are not intended to identify the detailed interfaces. The functions to be performed by the computer program within the subsystem are clearly identified. The *Assumptions* upon which this computer program design and use are based and the *Constraints* imposed upon its design or use are also identified. These assumptions and constraints are limited to factors not controlled within the scope of this document. Assumptions and constraints include such items as capabilities of interfacing systems, input data rates, and required programs to be supplied.

Section 2   Applicable Documents
This section should emphasize that the documents listed form *a part of this specification.* If conflicts exist between the requirements in this specification and the applicable documents, this specification supersedes, unless specifically stated otherwise.

Section 3 Requirements

The *Interface Requirements* subsection defines the relationship of external and internal interfaces of the subsystem. Graphics are provided at a sufficient level of detail to identify all *external physical, functional, and operational interfaces* of the computer program. Interfaces may be with external systems, subsystems, equipment, computer programs, operating systems, or operational users. Requirements imposed by each interfacing element are listed. *Internal Interfaces* controlled by requirements in this or higher-level specifications are identified. The interface characteristics are defined in sufficient detail to ensure compatibility of the system elements as allocated in this specification.

The *Functional Requirements* subsection provides the allocation of higher-level requirements to software functions within the computer program. This section includes functional flow diagrams of the computer program at a level below the *Functional Summary* in Section 1. That is, each major functional area to be satisfied by this program is identified in Section 1 and forms a subparagraph of this section. Each subparagraph describes the performance characteristics, physical characteristics, special requirements, and interface requirements assigned to the functional area. Functional flow diagrams, system schematic diagrams, interface diagrams, and so on are provided as required to adequately define the functional area characteristics for system-level control.

In allocating requirements to the functional areas, it must be recognized that verification must be accomplished following the development of the functional area. The functional relationship may be such that verification of requirements specified for a functional area can only be accomplished when the items that comprise the functional area are assembled into the system.

The *Special Requirements* subsection defines system-level or software development requirements not directly allocatable to software functional areas. Examples of such requirements are overall system performance characteristics, backup and recovery requirements, security requirements, reliability requirements, maintainability standards, training requirements, simulation specifications, automatic fault detection, and human engineering requirements.

The *Data Base Requirements* subsection defines the allocation of specific system-level requirements for data content, access, storage, and organization of the software data base.

The *Identification and Marking* requirements subsection defines requirements for software element naming or configuration control marking conventions necessary for compatibility with other components of the system.

The *Requirements Traceability* subsection provides a tabular allocation of higher-order requirements to specific functions within this document.

Section 4 Quality Assurance Provisions

The *General Requirements* subsection of the Quality Assurance Provisions begins with *Definitions* of the verification process. This section defines the levels of testing and verification to be performed and the general methods of verification to be employed. *Software Version Integrity* defines the requirements for control of separable, testable versions of the software and constraints placed on the production of new versions. *Software Test Procedures* defines the overall approach to testing and verification of system-level requirements allocated to software functions. *Test Software Validation* discusses the testing process for software specifically developed to support testing of the software subsystem, such as input generators or simulators.

The *Verification Requirements* subsection outlines the Section 3 requirements to be verified and tested at each testing level by each method of verification defined above. Requirements for each function defined in Section 3 should be considered.

The next two sections define the requirements for *Delivery of the Computer Program* and provide *Notes* with useful information for understanding the specification, but which are not officially a part of the requirements definition.

B.2   FUNCTIONAL DESIGN DOCUMENT

The following paragraphs describe the contents of the Functional Design Document as discussed in Section 5.2.2.

FUNCTIONAL DESIGN DOCUMENT: CONTENTS

Section 1   Introduction

The introductory section defines the *Purpose* of the computer program—to satisfy the set of requirements specified in the corresponding Software Requirements Specification. It also relates the computer program to the rest of the software subsystem. The *Scope* subsection defines what is presented in the document, what is not presented if there is likely to be confusion, and the limitations and spirit of the document in describing the functional (not detailed) design of the software. The *Design Overview* subsection presents the overall design concept, including a description of the primary and backup hardware configurations and a top-level diagram of the overall software subsystem. This section shows how the computer program described in the document fits into the software subsystem.

Section 2   Related Documents

This document provides a stand-alone description of the functional design of the computer program. However, this section should state that the requirements specified in the higher-level specifications are superseding. Other development documents, such as Interface Control Documents and Functional Design Documents for other computer programs should be referenced.

Section 3   Design Description

The *Design Description* section provides the overall functional design information for the computer program. The *Computer Program Description* subsection provides the breakdown of the computer program to the level below the *Design Overview* in Section 1 and shows where each module, described in Section 4, fits into the program. A narrative describing the design approach to satisfying the computer program requirements is provided. The *Computer Program External Interfaces* subsection provides an overview of all the interfaces external to the computer program. Any interfaces not delegated to a software subsystem Interface Control Document (ICD) are defined to the level developed in the preliminary design. ICD-controlled interfaces are shown at the functional level, and the ICD is referenced for more detail. External interfaces include those with the human users of the system. The *Computer Program Internal Interfaces* subsection describes the interfaces between the computer program modules defined in Section 4.

The *Computer Program Operational Concept* subsection describes the overall operating environment and scenario. Included in this discussion is *Operational Configurations,* which describes each separable combination of primary and backup hardware and software which is required to satisfy the computer program requirements. Each of these configurations is analyzed in terms of resource utilization to show that it is within the budgets of memory, storage, and device utilization. *Operational Modes* documents the various externally controlled operation sequences performing different functions within the computer program. *Operational Control* describes automatic or user interaction with the computer program that determines its configuration, modes, and execution characteristics. An overview of required operator actions and options is provided. *Operational Timelines* takes each operational mode in each configuration and traces the program sequence of operation. Included are timing estimates for each processing step (if applicable) and an analysis showing that time resource budgets are met by the computer program.

The *Data Flow* subsection provides an overview of the organization of the computer program in terms of data flow and internal data interfaces, as opposed to the functional block diagrams presented in Section 3.1. Each data path is described, including paths to and from hardware, users, and software. The *Data Base Design* subsection presents the preliminary design of the data base. The available information should include the overall data base structure and design, potential access methods, sizing, and the component definitions down to the generic element type. Names should be given to individual data base items.

Section 4   Module Descriptions

Each *Computer Program Module* identified in the preliminary design is described in a separate subparagraph in this section. For each module, its *Purpose* is stated and related, if possible, to the allocated requirements from the Software Requirements Specification. The *Functional Description* subsection provides an overview diagram of the module to the level of detail that the design has progressed. For some modules, this may be only a brief statement of the module function. For more critical modules, a low-level design may be available. The functional description should also provide an overview of the major functional interfaces of the module with other modules and any primary external interfaces for which the module is responsible. The *Inputs and Outputs* subsection describes each input source, each control source, and each output medium in terms of data rate, data content, and data characteristics. The *Limitations* subsection summarizes any known or anticipated constraints in the development or operation of the module, including timing and accuracy requirements, limits on input and output data, error detection and correction, and operating speed. The categories and types of *Messages* to be produced by the module are listed, along with specific message formats if available. The *Method and Processing Sequence* subsection presents a preliminary description of how the module will perform its task from input to output. Equations, algorithms, and logic flows, if available for this module, are presented. The *Sizing and Timing Estimates* subsection presents the memory and external storage requirements imposed by the module, along with estimates of execution time.

Section 5   Development Conventions

All design and coding conventions to be utilized in the software development process are outlined in this section, including memory conventions, flow diagram standards, and language standards.

B.3 INTERFACE CONTROL DOCUMENT

The following paragraphs describe the contents of the Interface Control Document as discussed in Section 5.2.3.

INTERFACE CONTROL DOCUMENT: CONTENTS

Section 1   Introduction

The introductory section states the *Purpose* of the Interface Control Document—to provide a binding agreement for the structure and characteristics of the specific interfaces defined herein. The *Scope* subsection specifies which portions of the interface(s) will be defined, which will not be defined if there is likely to be confusion, and the extent to which the defined interface will be finalized or subject to change. The *Summary* subsection presents the system-level requirements for the interface and describes the function of the interfacing components and the interface.

Section 2   Applicable Documents

The *Applicable Documents* section includes all hardware and software design documents that describe the interfacing elements, as well as the System Requirements Specifications for the interface. Since derived requirements for the specific details of the interface are presented in this document, higher-level specifications prevail in the event of conflict.

Section 3   Interface Requirements and Design

The *Interface Requirements and Design* section provides the detailed definition of the interface, beginning with the *Interface Block Diagram,* which presents a one-page overview of the interfacing elements and a functional annotation of the data flow across the interface. One side of the interface is the software subsystem or one of its components. The other side may be software, hardware, or system users. The allocated *Interface Requirements* for each component of the interfacing elements are based on analysis of the software requirements. Any *Data Base Requirements* necessary to support the interface must be defined, including control parameters, descriptive parameters, or entire data base files. Any *Special Requirements* for the interface must be spelled out in detail, including timing restrictions, reliability of the interface, alternate paths for the interface, data rates, interface stability, and human engineering restrictions. The *Requirements Traceability* subsection provides a path to the higher-level requirements specifications from the derived requirements in Section 3.2 of the ICD.

The interface design that supports the requirements defined above must include sufficient detail for software or hardware developers to build their side of the interface without regard (conceptually at least) to the development process taking place on the other side of the interface. (Exercise caution in the real world and plan for as many checkpoints as possible to check the integrity of the interface before it is too late). The *Interface Data Definition* must document the content and structure of the data flowing across the interface to the lowest level of detail. The *Interface Design* must include the complete protocol definition, interface servicing techniques, and all functions to be performed on each side of the interface. The *Data Base Design* subsection presents the details of the interaction required with the data base and the contents of the data base necessary to support the requirements of Section 3.3.

Section 4 Quality Assurance Provisions

The *Quality Assurance Provisions* section provides requirements for test and verification of the interface similar to those documented for the software in Section 4 of the Software Requirements Specification. A key difference is that since the interface is with an external element, the verification process may require extra coordination and special techniques. A section is added to the QA provisions for interfaces to include the *Acceptance Test Requirements* for the interface. (These requirements are included in test documentation for software acceptance.) These requirements specify what has to be done to ensure that both interfacing elements are compatible at the interface and that the interface satisfies system-level requirements.

B.4   DETAILED DESIGN DOCUMENT

The following paragraphs describe the contents of the Detailed Design Document as discussed in Section 6.2.3.

DETAILED DESIGN DOCUMENT: CONTENTS

Section 1   Introduction

1.1	Purpose
1.2	Scope
1.3	Design Overview

Section 2   Related Documents

2.1	Applicable References
2.2	Development Documents

Section 3   [Module Name] Design

3.1	Purpose of Module [Module Name]
3.2	Functional Description
3.3	Program Units
3.3.1	[Program Unit Name "1"]
3.3.1.1	Identification
3.3.1.2	Functional Description
3.3.1.3	Usage
3.3.1.4	Subroutines Required
3.3.1.5	Inputs
3.3.1.6	Outputs
3.3.1.7	Processing Method
3.3.1.8	Limitations
3.3.1.9	Sizing and Timing Estimates
3.3.1.10	Subroutine Descriptions
3.3.2	[Program Unit Name "2"]

. . .

3.3.P	[Program Unit Name "P"]

. . .

3.4	Utility Subroutines

Section 4   [Module Name] Design

4.1	Purpose of Module [Module Name]

. . .

Section N [Module Name] Design

N.1	Purpose of Module [Module Name]

. . .

Section N + 1   Data Base

Section N + 2   System Resource Allocation

Section N + 3   Functional Flow

Section N + 4   Formats

Section N + 5   Utilities

Section N + 6   Notes

Appendix A   Acronyms and Abbreviations

Appendix B   Definitions and Nomenclature

Appendix C   Computer Program Listings

Section 1   Introduction

The introductory section defines the *Purpose* of this document—to present the details of the computer program design presented in the Functional Design Document. The *Scope* subsection defines the computer program described in the document, references any relevant detailed information documented elsewhere, and presents the document as the baseline for approval to begin coding. The *Design Overview* subsection presents the same overall description of the design concept and top-level diagram as the Functional Design Document.

Section 2   Related Documents

This document, together with the Functional Design Document, provides a stand-alone design of the computer program. However, this section should state that requirements specified in the higher-level specifications are superseding. Other related documents, such as ICDs and the Operating Instructions Document, should be referenced.

Section 3 Through Section N   [Module Name] Design

Separate *Design Sections* are prepared for each *Module* of the computer program. Within each section, the *Purpose of the Module* subsection provides the name, configuration control identifiers (see Chapter 9), and a brief abstract of the functions of the module, the language(s) in which it is written, and its major functional interfaces. The *Functional Description* subsection provides the organizational structure of the program units within the module; presents the data flow, control, and internal interfaces within the module; and shows the external elements and other interfacing modules within the software subsystem. Each of the *Program Units* within the module are then documented in separate subparagraphs.

For each program unit, the *Name* and configuration control *Identification* are given. The *Functional Description* provides the top-level organizational diagram of the program unit and states the basic function to be performed. The *Usage* defines how the unit is to be invoked within the module, including the calling parameter definitions, start-up, and termination mechanisms. This section also lists all other routines or units that invoke the program unit in the system. Any *Subroutines Required* that are outside the program unit are listed by name, with a reference to the section number in the document that details their design. The *Inputs* and *Outputs* are defined in detail, including the exact format, content, source, and destination of all data. All data must be included, including files, tables, memory buffers, constants, control registers, printed output, error and warning messages, and display pages. The *Processing Method* graphically portrays the operations performed by the program unit. The sequence of operations, major decision points, algorithms, equations, logic flow, and data flow should be included. All local data items and tables with their definitions are also presented here. Any known or anticipated *Limitations* of the program unit are summarized in this section. A listing of all restrictions and constraints that apply to the unit is provided, including timing and accuracy requirements, limitation of algorithms and formulas used, limits of input and output data, associated error correction sensing, and the error checks programmed into the routines. A detailed explanation of error conditions is provided, along with the accuracy and limitation requirements for both input and output parameters. The *Sizing and Timing* characteristics of the program unit must be specified, including estimated execution time, critical timing constraints, and memory and external storage requirements for data and code. Small subroutines may not warrant a complete subparagraph; they may be completely defined under *Subroutine Descriptions*. The *Utility Subroutines* subsection identifies those utility subroutines used by more than one program unit. The detailed design of these utility subroutines is defined in a later section of the document.

Section N+1   Data Base

The *Data Base* section includes a detailed definition of the content and storage location of each file, table, and item within each table that is incorporated in the data base. The file descriptions include a descriptive title for each file, length of file, format, and so on. The table descriptions include a descriptive title for each table, the method of indexing the table, the block format for items in the table, and so on. The item descriptions include a descriptive title, most significant bit, number of bits, coding type, scaling factor and, if appropriate, units and item value. The relationship of the specified items to the tables and of the tables to the files should be graphically portrayed by diagrams or equivalent representation. The graphic portrayal of each table should be sufficiently detailed to identify words per block, bits per item, number of blocks, type of table construction, and so on. A definition of the relationship of the items, tables, and files contained within the data base to the computer program modules and program units described earlier should be included.

Section N+2   System Resource Allocation

The *System Resource Allocation* section defines in detail the memory layout of all operational configurations of the computer program and the detailed storage utilization, organization, and structure of data base and temporary files on external storage media (disk/tape). In addition, a detailed timing analysis of each operational sequence of the software is included. Use of external limited resources, such as printer speed and display update rate, must also be considered and included in the detailed design.

Section N+3   Functional Flow

The *Functional Flow* section shows the general system flow of both data and control. The section graphically portrays the operations performed by the software, depicting the processing performed, the sequence of operations, and decision points. A top-level diagram should be used to depict in a single figure the overall information flow of the software. This diagram should reference lower-level flows included in this section, as appropriate, to provide more detailed information. The lowest-level flows are those which identify as functional entities the computer program modules described in the sections above. This description of functional flow may reference the Functional Design Document, unless a greater level of detail is required to provide transition to the lower-level flows.

Section N+4   Formats

The *Formats* section is optional, but may be used as a convenient place to consolidate the detailed tables that may be required to define print formats, display page formats, or error messages.

Section N+5   Utilities

The *Utilities* section describes two types of subroutines: (1) small functions or routines developed for this computer program, which are used by several modules and are of a general-utility nature; and (2) externally supplied utility routines, such as matrix manipulation routines or scientific calculation routines (SIN, COS).

Section N+6   Notes

The *Notes* section provides additional information that is not part of the basic program design and is not contractually binding (for example: equation derivations and numerical analyses, rejected alternative designs, rationale for selected designs, reference material, and suggestions for future design changes to the computer program).

B.5 OPERATING INSTRUCTIONS DOCUMENT

The following paragraphs describe the contents of the Operating Instructions Document as discussed in Section 7.2.1.

. . .

Section 1   Introduction
The introductory section states the *Purpose* of the document, namely to present all the information required to (1) operate the equipment and initialize and support the software in an operational state, and (2) use the software to perform its intended functions. The *Scope* subsection defines the software described in the document and states its relationship to other system elements. It clearly defines the operating information provided in the major sections of the document. The information presented should allow the reader to easily determine whether this is the manual he wants and which section of the manual serves his purpose. The *Operational Overview* subsection provides a concise description of the use of the hardware and software and the relationship of the hardware and software to other system elements.

Section 2   Related Documents
The Operating Instructions Document should be as complete as is practical and should minimize reference to other documents for material required to operate the software. Typically however, it is impractical to reproduce the material provided in manuals supplied by the computer manufacturer for his equipment and software operating system. These documents are listed as *Applicable References*. The *Development Documents* subsection lists the documents that describe the design of the software.

Section 3   Computer Program Operations
The *Computer Program Operations* section provides all the information required for a computer operator to configure the hardware and software for operational use. First, the *System Components* are described, including the hardware and software. This description includes a block diagram of the hardware environment and a complete equipment list. Since the software description in this section is for the computer operator, it is usually at a very high level. The software block diagram partitions the software components to the level at which the operator must interface and control the software operation. The *System Configurations* subsection describes for the operator all the variations in equipment and software setup for executing the re-

quired functions. These include hardware configuration changes, such as switching terminals between computers or placing equipment on-line or off-line, and software configurations, such as loading specific sets of software for certain functions. Any special configurations required when hardware components fail are described in this subsection. The *Equipment Setup* subsection provides all the information required to configure the environment to the point of software initialization. This includes a description of powering each hardware component, setting any switchable components to their proper positions for system operation (e.g., tape drive density, terminal on-line, etc.), any diagnostic checks required before system operation, requirements for setup of input/output media (e.g., tapes, disks), and loading and initiation of an operating system.

The *Computer Operator Interaction* subsection describes each of the major equipment and software segments with which the computer operator must interface. Interactions with the *operating system* are described, with specific references to vendor-supplied documents when necessary. All the major functions of the operating system to be used by the operator should be addressed, leaving only the details of the interactive process for the reference material. The ways in which the operator must interact with *External Interfaces* must be described, including functional block diagrams of data flow to and from the external interfaces and any operator interactions required to support the interfaces. Reference should be made to the appropriate Interface Control Documents for the details of the interface design. The required computer operator interactions with the *Software* are described, including general input and output message formats, tape or disk mounting requirements, error condition handling, the handling of specific directives from the software system, tasking control, and queue control. The general operating concept of the software is described in this section, with details of specific actions and responses defined in Section 3.4.4 and specific operational procedures defined in Section 3.5. The *Operator Messages* subsection lists each input directive that the operator may make to the software, including its precise form and content, and describes the expected result of that directive. In addition, it lists each message from the software to the operator and defines the complete meaning of the message.

The *Operating Procedures* subsection defines the required step-by-step process of operator actions during each stage of system operation. *Initialization* describes the software start-up procedure for each software configuration, beginning with the completion of equipment

setup, defined in Section 3.3, and proceeding until an operational state is reached. During the operational use of the software, the operator typically performs a *Monitoring* function. The procedures for responding to each message, defined in Section 3.4.4, are presented here, in addition to any other hardware or operating system monitoring functions the operator is required to support (e.g., light-panel indicators, available memory for task initiation, disk space availability, etc.). Procedures for *Shutdown* under any expected conditions (normal or emergency) are presented, as well as procedures for *Standby Operations,* if applicable. For example, standby operations might require the operator to perform certain system maintenance functions, such as disk cleanup, while maintaining the software in a state ready for immediate operational use. Standby operations also cover procedures for operating in a "hot backup" mode in support of a primary system. Operational procedures for *backup* include the definition of data base backup, executable software backup, and periodic memory or transient file checkpoints if required. *Recovery* describes the procedures for restarting software operation after a failure. The restart procedures may be required for restart on the primary configuration, backup configuration, or a degraded configuration, as defined in Section 3.2. *Special Procedures* required by the operator may include configuring for degraded operation using less memory, which might be functionally transparent to the user but have slower response times, or performing a periodic software function for data base cleanup and maintenance, which is defined as an operator function not under control of the users.

All *Parameters* of interest to the computer operator must be explicitly defined in the Operating Instructions Document. These include information parameters, such as memory requirements, disk allocations, and required time for tasks, as well as specific data base items that the operator is required to monitor, set, or use for the diagnosis of error conditions. Special requirements for *Analysis of Error Conditions,* which cannot be covered by the standard procedures defined in Section 3.5.2, are presented in the final subsection.

Section 4   Major Function Operations
Section 4 provides the information required for a system user to control the *Major Function Operations* of the computer program.

Each subsection provides an identification and description of a particular *Major Function* performed by the computer program. Examples of major functions from the user's point of view include log-on/log-off, option control, sending messages to other users, file management functions, data base control functions, and, of course, the major functions that the computer program was built to perform. The *Purpose* describes clearly what the function does, including an overview of the information required for the function and the expected results of using the function. The *Operational Description* subsection provides the step-by-step procedures required to initiate and execute the function. *Program Options* provides a description of user options that may be exercised during the function, including lower-level functions that may be nested in the main function. The *Operations Request Formats* provides detailed descriptions of the formats for all user interactions during function processing.

All *Inputs* used by the function are described, including the basic data to be processed by the function and control inputs that specify the processing alternatives and options. The input information provided includes:

1   Title and description.
2   Purpose and use.
3   Input media.
4   Limitations and restrictions.
5   Format and content.

6   Order of inputs.
7   Expected results.

The definition of the expected *Outputs* of the function operation should include a cross-reference list between the output and the input described above. This definition includes:

1   Description of the output.
2   Form in which the outputs will appear.
3   Output format and content.
4   Instruction on the use of the output.
5   Limitations and restrictions of outputs.
6   Relationship of outputs to inputs.

Error/Recovery Procedures defines each error that may occur during function operation and the appropriate response to the error. *Limitations* describes bounds on input, accuracy of output, and other limitations that may produce errors or undesirable results during function operation. Data base items that affect function operation and system-level variables or conditions that must be set or may be modified for function operation are documented as *Special Parameters*.

B.6 UNIT DEVELOPMENT FOLDER

The following paragraphs describe the contents of the Unit Development Folder as discussed in Section 7.2.2.

UNIT DEVELOPMENT FOLDER: CONTENTS

Section   1   Unit Status

Section   2   Requirements Specification

Section   3   Detailed Design

Section   4   Operating Instructions

Section   5   Code

Section   6   Unit Test Plan and Procedures

Section   7   Test Results

Section   8   Software Problem Report Changes

Section   9   Audits and Reviews

Section 10   Notes

Section 1   Unit Status

This section includes the identification of the unit, the project schedule related to the unit, and an activity log of all important project activities that involve the unit. The unit is first identified within the related computer program and module. Any project schedules and procedure networks that relate to this unit are then included and are kept up to date with scheduled and actual dates. The activity log is an event-oriented log listing the pertinent activities that describe the status of the unit within the development and testing phases. The activity log should describe the activities which relate to the unit, so that an exact status can always be ascertained.

Section 2   Requirements Specification

This section contains a copy of (or provides a reference to) the portions of the Requirements Specification section pertinent to the unit. Any other documentation related to the unit and not included in the Detailed Design Document or Operating Instructions Document should be included in this section.

Section 3   Detailed Design

This section contains a copy of the portions of the detailed design documentation related to the unit. This documentation is updated to reflect the final design and implementation of the unit. This section of the Unit Development Folders will be relied on heavily when producing the "as-built" computer program documentation.

The information in this section should include the following:

1 *Position.*   Position of unit within the system hierarchy, including the call sequence and the required parameters.
2 *Interfaces.*   Data flow in and out of the unit and interfaces with other software units and the external environment (hardware interfaces).
3 *Processing.*   Description of the processing performed by the unit (control flow).
4 *Limitations.*   Special conditions or limitations.

Section 4   Operating Instructions

This section contains a copy of the portions of the Operating Instructions Document (if any) related to the unit. This documentation is updated to reflect the actual user interface with the software subsystem. The wording of user prompts and error messages, as well as the description of the circumstances under which the messages are output, should be updated.

Section 5   Code

This section contains a listing of the developed code, along with any computer-generated cross-reference listings or maps. An explanation of the procedure required to run the code, including code and file identifiers, should also be included, along with the information and/or files required to submit the unit to configuration control for testing.

Section 6   Unit Test Plan and Procedures

The test plans and procedures for unit testing are written by the programmers responsible for the unit and should be included in the Unit Development Folder. These test plans and procedures are informal, but will serve as the basis for accepting the unit for configuration control and higher levels of testing. The test plan and procedures should test the unit exhaustively and specify the acceptance criteria.

Section 7   Test Results

All results of Program Unit Testing should be recorded in the Unit Development Folder by the programmers. Included in the test results should be the test configuration used, the date, and the version of the tested unit. If the unit failed, this should also be recorded, and the tests should be rerun after the unit is corrected.

Section 8   Software Problem Report Changes

A log of the SPRs against the unit should be maintained by the programmer in the Unit Development Folder, as well as an explanation of the resolution of each SPR.

Section 9   Audits and Reviews

This section contains a copy of all review and audit reports applicable to the UDF. Whenever a review of the UDF is performed, the review comments and the associated checklist for verification that corrections have been completed are placed in this section. Comments pertaining to the unit generated in design reviews should also be included.

Section 10   Notes

This section contains the following items:

1   All memoranda and design notes related to the unit.

2   A version description log containing an explanation of the capabilities of each version of the unit, as well as SPRs closed by the versions.

3   Any additional notes the programmer wishes to include to use at a later date or to help the maintenance programmer to better understand the unit.

B.7   VERSION DESCRIPTION DOCUMENT

The following paragraphs describe the contents of the Version Description Document as described in Section 7.2.4.

VERSION DESCRIPTION DOCUMENT: CONTENTS

Section 1   Introduction
The *Identification* of the contents, configuration, and related management information is provided in the introductory section of this document. The configuration management identifiers for each changed software element and for the delivery media are included. The *Scope* subsection defines the intended use of the version and clearly identifies prior, superseded versions and those still in use. The *Summary of Differences* subsection documents which elements of the software have been changed and describes the general changes that were made.

Section 2   Related Documents
Related reference and development documents listed in this section, including the earlier Version Description Documents, are identified as to whether they are obsolete.

Section 3   Version Descriptions
The subsections of Section 3 identify the versions of each controllable element included in this release of the software system. Although a subsection should exist for each element (both software elements and data base elements), the subsection need only reference configuration control identifiers if no changes have been made since the prior version.

For those elements that have changed, the *Change Summary* subsection summarizes the reasons for the modifications and provides a prose and diagrammatical summary of the changes. *Limitations* on software operation imposed by the changes or discovered prior to making the changes are defined. Any changes in hardware configuration, operating procedures, or system usage necessary to adapt the new system to the operational environment are described under *Adaptation Information*. Any changes required to other elements of the system or to external functions necessary to maintain the integrity of the interfaces are specifically described under *Interface Compatibility*. Required *changes* are defined, including *change pages* to system documentation, *program listings* of the new version, change code listings to a prior version, or reference to configuration-controlled hard copy of the software code. Official direction and procedures for installing the software in the operational environment are provided under *Installation Instructions*.

B.8 TEST PLAN

The following paragraphs describe the contents of the Test Plan as discussed in Section 8.2.1.

TEST PLAN DOCUMENT: CONTENTS

Section 1   Introduction

1.1   Purpose
1.2   Scope
1.3   Summary

Section 2   Related Documents

2.1   Applicable References
2.2   Development Documents

Section 3   Test Concepts

3.1   Test Philosophy
3.2   Verification Methods
3.3   Test Levels
3.3.1   Program Unit Testing
3.3.2   Module Integration Testing
3.3.3   Verification Testing
3.3.4   Acceptance Testing
3.4   Organizational Roles
3.4.1   Software Development
3.4.2   Product Assurance
3.4.3   Product Control
3.4.4   Verification and Certification
3.4.5   Integration and Test
3.4.6   Human Engineering
3.5   Test Control
3.5.1   Quality Assurance
3.5.2   Test Procedures
3.5.3   Test Monitor
3.5.4   Test Configuration Control

Section 4   Verification Requirements and Criteria

4.1   Test 1
4.1.1   Test Description
4.1.2   Test Inputs
4.1.3   Test Actions
4.1.4   Expected Results

. . .

4.*n*   Test *n*
4.*n*.1   Test Description
4.*n*.2   Test Inputs
4.*n*.3   Test Actions
4.*n*.4   Expected Results

Section 5   Requirement and Test Phase Summary

Section 6   Module Integration Testing

6.1   Introduction
6.2   Location and Schedule
6.3   Limitations and General Comments
6.4   Preparation of Inputs
6.5   Test Conduct
6.6   Analysis of Results
6.7   Test Environment
6.8   Personnel Requirements

Section 7   Verification Testing

7.1   Introduction
7.2   Location and Schedule
7.3   Limitations and General Comments
7.4   Preparation of Inputs
7.5   Conduct of Test
7.6   Analysis of Results
7.7   Test Environment
7.8   Personnel Requirements

Section 8   Acceptance Testing

8.1   Introduction
8.2   Location and Schedule
8.3   Limitations and General Comments
8.4   Preparation of Inputs
8.5   Conduct of Test
8.6   Analysis of Results
8.7   Test Environment
8.8   Personnel Requirements

Section 9   Control and Reporting Procedures

9.1   Control of Test Program
9.2   Documentation of Test Procedures
9.3   Documentation of Test Reports

Section 1   Introduction
This section identifies the software to be tested, states the purpose of the Test Plan, and presents the test schedule, including all deliverables. It also identifies the software requirements (if any) that will not be verified using this Test Plan and tells why.

Section 2   Related Documents
This section includes a list of documents used as references for writing the Test Plan, as well as related development documents.

Section 3   Test Concepts
This section contains an explanation of the testing philosophy and all explanations or definitions necessary to understand and evaluate the Test Plan. It also delineates the roles and responsibilities of the organizations involved and explains the procedures for controlling the testing. (Top-down development and testing are usually preferred, since system-level design errors are identified early in the testing process.)

Section 4   Verification Requirements and Criteria

This section describes the formal tests needed to verify that all software requirements are met. The *Test Description* subsection briefly describes the test objectives in terms of the software requirements. The test level and verification method are also included in this subsection. The *Test Inputs* subsection describes the inputs associated with the test actions to produce the desired outputs. If it is impossible or tedious to precisely define the test inputs, the method for their generation can be provided. The *Test Actions* subsection describes the actions required to produce the desired results. The *Expected Results* subsection specifies the results to be obtained from the test actions. It should be indicated whether the test totally or only partially verifies the requirement described in the *Test Description* subsection.

Section 5   Requirements and Test Phase Summary

This section identifies the software requirements to be satisfied by (1) Program Unit Testing, (2) Module Integration Testing, (3) Verification Testing, and (4) Acceptance Testing. The best way to present these data is to provide a five-column table with the following headings:

1   Requirement specification paragraph.
2   Verification method.
3   Test level where verified.
4   Test number (test plan).
5   Comments.

An entry should be made for each requirement in the Software Requirements Specification (by paragraph number).

Section 6   Module Integration Testing

The Module Integration Testing implementation is described in this section. The *Location and Schedule* subsection contains a detailed schedule of all the tests, including test location. The *Limitations and General comments* subsection lists any limitations of the testing process. The *Preparation of Inputs* subsection describes the general methods used to prepare the test input data. The general procedures for conducting the tests, including briefings and debriefings, test direction, equipment and system operations, and observations are described in the *Test Conduct* subsection. General procedures for analysis of test results are described in the *Analysis of Results* subsection. This subsection also (1) identifies any computer programs used for data reduction and analysis, (2) identifies any requirements and responsibilities levied on external agencies, and (3) establishes fault isolation procedures for operator, hardware, or software errors and the rules for test continuation/abort and retest when errors are discovered.

The test *Environment* subsection lists the requirements for support software, hardware, test software, and test data during the testing process. For each organization involved, the *Personnel Requirements* subsection lists the organizational responsibilities and authorities during testing.

Section 7   Verification Testing

The information presented in this section is the same as that in Section 6 for *Module Integration Testing*.

Section 8   Acceptance Testing

This section contains the same information for *Acceptance Testing* as Section 7 contains for *Verification Testing*.

Section 9   Control and Reporting Procedures

This section outlines other test documents and procedures describing how the test documentation controls the testing process.

B.9 TEST PROCEDURES

The following paragraphs describe the contents of the Test Procedures Document as described in Section 8.2.2.

TEST PROCEDURES DOCUMENT: CONTENTS

Section 1   Introduction
The *Introduction* identifies the software to be tested and the location and schedule for the briefings, testing, data reduction, and analysis.

Section 2   Related Documents
This section includes a list of the reference documents used for writing the Test Procedures. This list should include the Test Plan, Operating Instructions Document, Detailed Design Document for the software, and user's manuals for test and support computer programs and equipment.

Section 3   Test Objectives
This section contains detailed test objectives, brief functional descriptions of the tests, and references to the applicable sections of the Test Plan. The functional capabilities of the tested software are identified, along with general information about the structure and content of each test.

Section 4   Manning and Responsibilities
This section lists the requirements and responsibilities for console operators, test directors, technical consultants, data analysts, and other essential test personnel.

The organizations or companies that must supply the test personnel, as well as any special knowledge or skill required, are stated. Requirements identical to those stated in the Test Plan are specified by reference.

Section 5 Equipment and Computer Program Requirements

This section specifies the requirements for computer programs other than those being tested and the equipment necessary to support the test, including software drivers, data reduction programs, compilers and assemblers, simulators, and test equipment.

Section 6 Test Operating Procedures

This section specifies how to operate the computer programs under test. This information is further expanded in the description of the conduct of each test. The section gives an overview of the whole system being tested. Normally such specifications are made by references to the Operating Instructions Documents specified in Section 2 of the Test Procedures. Procedures to initiate system operation are provided; these specify how to enter the programs into the system, establish the required mode of operation, initially set the required parameters, provide for required inputs and outputs, and begin operation of the computer program. Input materials required to accomplish these procedures are listed.

Procedures to maintain system operation are included when operator intervention is required, as for example, to maintain data flow and replenish tape supplies. Procedures to terminate and restart system operation for normal and unscheduled termination of program operation are specified to ensure that the necessary output data will be obtained for evaluation.

Section 7 Detailed Test Procedures: Module Integration Testing

Sections 7, 8, and 9 describe the tests to be performed in detail. Test objectives that satisfy requirements stated in the Software Requirements Specification are referenced. Test events are described in the order in which they are planned; the interdependence of events is indicated. Interdependence of operating positions with respect to specific events is also described. Any input required to perform the tests should be attached to these sections of the Test Procedures or referenced here and included as an appendix.

The *Module Description* subsection describes each module in the Detailed Design Document to be tested. The *Test Description* subsection briefly describes the objective of the test and its relation to preceding tests. This subsection should also include a precedence net-

work stating which programs should be tested and integrated first. The *Test Inputs* subsection describes the inputs—whether manual or automatic—for the test, including all external inputs to the system. A step-by-step procedure for execution of the test is included in the *Test Conduct* subsection. This includes all computer operator inputs described in detail for each user function in the Operating Instructions Document. The expected results of the test conduct are described in the *Expected Results* subsection. For observable results, the device and the output should be specified. For recorded results, the values of the items of interest should be specified. For observable results, a description of what will occur should be given. A form that can easily be filled out by the test operator should also be provided for each test to record the results. These test forms will be collected and published as part of the Test Reports.

When data reduction is employed to provide test data, this section should contain the expected results of the data reduction pass(es) in a form easily reconcilable with the data reduction output. A cross-reference to the requirements verified by the test is also contained in this subsection.

Section 8 Detailed Test Procedures: Verification Testing

This section contains detailed instructions for Verification Testing. A cross-reference of the requirements from the Software Requirements Specification is given for each test. The *Test Description* subsection describes the new software capabilities to be verified and the test to be performed. The *Test Inputs, Test Conduct* and *Expected Results* subsections contain the same type of information for Verification Tests as the corresponding subsections in Section 7 did for Module Integration Tests.

Section 9 Detailed Test Procedures: Acceptance Testing

Any software requirements not verified during module integration or verification testing must be tested during acceptance testing. This section contains a detailed description of the acceptance tests; it has the same format as Sections 7 and 8. The cross-reference table listing where each requirement in the Software Requirements Specification is verified should be completed in this section. Verification tests to be rerun during acceptance testing are included by reference.

Section 10 Data Reduction and Analysis

This section contains general procedures for recording, reduction, and analysis of test data. Specific test information is provided in descriptions of individual test conduct and expected results. The procedures should be specified in a manner that will clearly show whether the test objectives have been met. The *Recording and Reduction* requirements subsection specifies the data that must be recorded, the reduction procedures, and the data format and content resulting from the data-reduction process. The methods for recording the data, the inputs to the data reduction process (which may be a computer program), and the qualifications of the data reduction process are also contained in this section. The *Data Reduction and Analysis Procedures* subsection contains the procedures to be employed in reducing and analyzing test data. Reduction and analysis to be accomplished manually or by computer program are identified, and procedures are established for their accomplishment. This subsection also contains proce-

dures for operating data reduction computer programs, including:

1   Initiating computer operations.
2   Establishing the required mode of operation.
3   Setting required parameters.
4   Providing for required inputs and outputs.
5   Beginning computer program operations.
6   Maintaining computer program operations when operator input is required.
7   Terminating and restarting the computer program.
8   Collecting output data and making them available for evaluation.

Listings of data reduction computer programs or inputs required for testing and data analysis are included in appendixes to this document.

B.10 TEST REPORT

The following paragraphs describe the contents of the Test Report Document as described in Section 8.2.3.

TEST REPORT DOCUMENT: CONTENTS

Section 1 Introduction

This section identifies the software being tested and the tests to be performed by referencing the Test Procedures Document.

Section 2 Related Documents

This section lists the documents used as reference for writing and compiling the test reports. In most cases, these documents will be the same as those listed in the Test Procedures Document.

Section 3 Test Objectives and Results

This section provides an overview of the test objectives and how they are satisfied by the testing process. The details of the actual test results are included in Sections 4 through 6. This section provides a cross-reference matrix for each test objective or requirement, including the following contingencies:

1 The expected test results were identical to the actual test results or within specified limits. In this case, the user can be assured that the software satisfies the requirements specified.

2 The actual test results differed from the expected results beyond the specified limits. In this case, the user should consult the test results to determine the reason for the discrepancy. The appropriate documents should be modified in the *Recommendations* section of this document to attain consistency.

3 The actual results were not attained. In this case, the reasons for not fulfilling the test objectives are stated and the user should consult the *Recommendations* section.

Section 4 Test Reports: Module Integration Testing

This section contains the actual test results obtained by performing the tests in each test level. If the test results are too voluminous, they should be provided in an appendix or separate annex to this document, but a summary should be provided here. The format of this section is almost identical to Section 7 of the Test Procedures Document. For each test, verification is provided that the test inputs and test conduct were followed, and a comparison of the expected results with the actual results is given. All Software Problem Reports (SPRs) generated during a test level are included in this section, along with the status of all SPRs and the disposition of the test outputs of the final successful test execution. A log of all test activity and deviations from the scheduled testing should be included in this section or in an appendix.

Section 5   Test Reports: Verification Testing
This section contains the same type of information for verification testing as contained in Section 4 for module integration testing.

Section 6   Test Reports: Acceptance Testing
This section contains the same type of information for acceptance testing as contained in Section 4 for module integration testing.

Section 7   Recommendations
Recommendations for subsequent action are contained in this section. The *Document Revision* subsection contains change pages for system documentation that should be changed as a result of the testing activity. If a required software response is unobtainable or not worth the cost of implementation, change pages should be included for the Software Requirements Specification, as well as a *Waiver Request.* The Software Requirements Specification should also be changed whenever the test results disclose ambiguity or conflicting requirements. Change pages for the Detailed Design Document should be included whenever the computer program design is modified to meet requirements that were not fulfilled by the software design presented at CDR. If operator error (or similar-type errors) during

testing causes the abortion of critical functions or seriously impacts operations, recommendations for changes to the design and/or Operating Instructions Document should be made and change pages provided. The Test Procedures Document should be revised by red-lining if major deviations are required to fully test the software.

The *Additional Testing* subsection includes recommendations for conducting additional tests to fulfill objectives not met by the test results. A list of the software portions that should be accepted by the user as a result of the testing process is given in the *Qualification and Acceptance* subsection.

Section 8   Attachments to the Test Report
Since there are usually multiple attachments, this section contains a list of the additional information provided with the Test Reports. This information includes the following:

1   Test log.
2   Test briefing minutes.
3   Test debriefing minutes.
4   Data reduction output.
5   Hard-copy output collected during testing.
6   Reports supporting recommendations.

appendix C

Tear-Out Charts

T he following charts are full-size versions of the major graphics in the text. They are useful for quick reference or presentation material.

Title	Text Figure Reference
Project Plan Objectives	3.4
System Hierarchy	2.1
Software Subsystem Hierarchy	2.2
Software Development Phases	2.3
Development Documentation and Review Summary	II.2
Software Development Products	2.4
Software Development Reviews	2.5
Software Development Documentation	2.6
Preliminary Design Phase Activities and Products	5.1
Detailed Design Phase Activities and Products	6.1
Implementation and Operation Phase Activities and Products	7.1
The Testing Process Activities and Products	8.1
Software Test Levels	8.3
Configuration Management Sequence	9.1
Software Requirements Specification Definition	5.2
Functional Design Document Definition	5.4
Interface Control Document Definition	5.6
Detailed Design Document Definition	6.3
Test Documentation Definition	8.4
Unit Development Folder Definition	7.4
Operating Instructions Document Definition	7.2
Version Description Document Definition	7.6

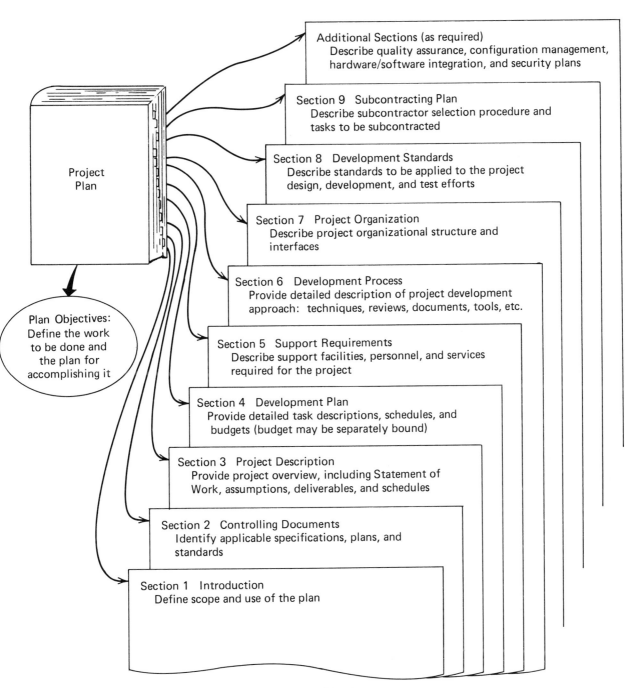

Additional Sections (as required)
Describe quality assurance, configuration management,
hardware/software integration, and security plans

Section 9   Subcontracting Plan
Describe subcontractor selection procedure and
tasks to be subcontracted

Section 8   Development Standards
Describe standards to be applied to the project
design, development, and test efforts

Section 7   Project Organization
Describe project organizational structure and
interfaces

Section 6   Development Process
Provide detailed description of project development
approach: techniques, reviews, documents, tools, etc.

Section 5   Support Requirements
Describe support facilities, personnel, and services
required for the project

Section 4   Development Plan
Provide detailed task descriptions, schedules, and
budgets (budget may be separately bound)

Section 3   Project Description
Provide project overview, including Statement of
Work, assumptions, deliverables, and schedules

Section 2   Controlling Documents
Identify applicable specifications, plans, and
standards

Section 1   Introduction
Define scope and use of the plan

Project
Plan

Plan Objectives:
Define the work
to be done and
the plan for
accomplishing it

Project Plan Objectives.

163

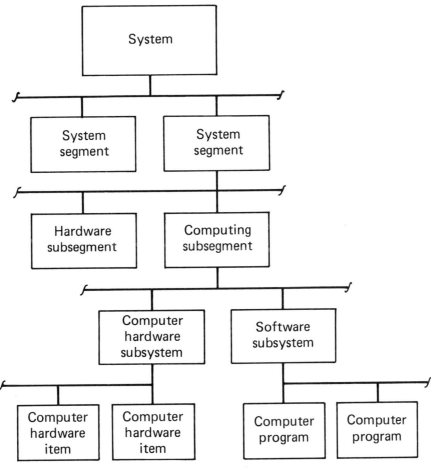

System hierarchy.

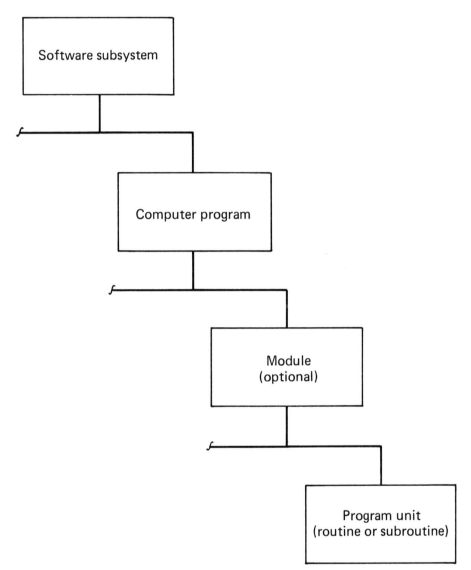

Software subsystem hierarchy.

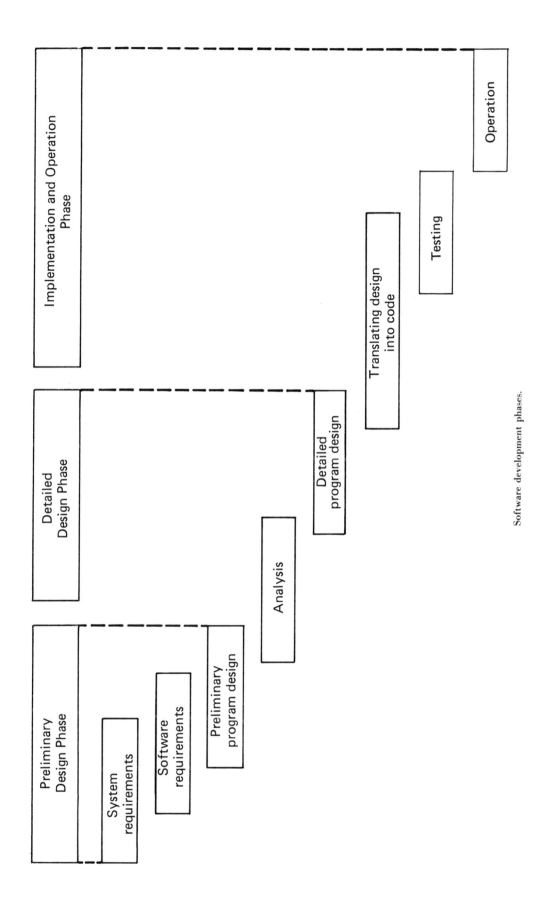

Software development phases.

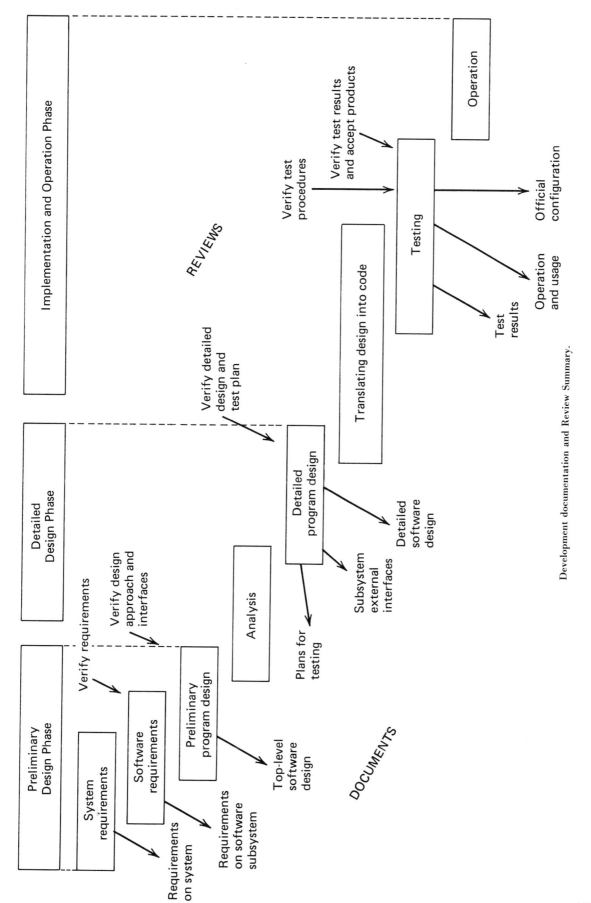

Development documentation and Review Summary.

171

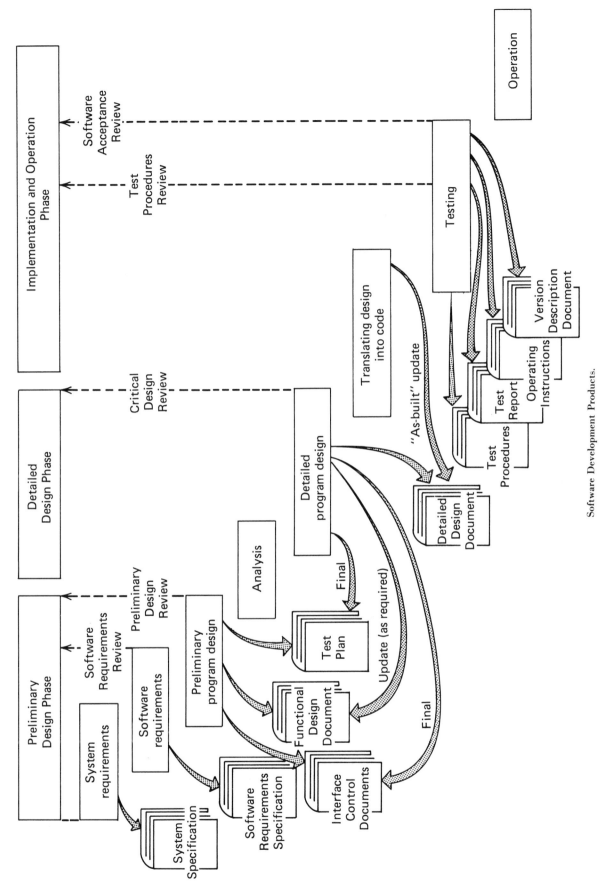

Software Development Products.

173

Name	Purpose	Materials Reviewed
SRR (Software Requirements Review)	Verify software requirements	Software Requirements Specification
PDR (Preliminary Design Review)	Verify design approach and interfaces	Functional Design Document Interface Control Documents (requirements and preliminary design sections) Test Plan (preliminary)
CDR (Critical Design Review)	Verify detailed design and test plan	Detailed Design Document Interface Control Documents (final) Test Plan
TPR (Test Procedures Review)	Verify test procedures	Test Plan Test Procedures
SAR (Software Acceptance Review)	Verify test results and completed product (code and documentation)	Test Procedures Test Report Operating Instructions Version Description Document "As-Built" Updates Functional Design Document Detailed Design Document

Software development reviews.

Document	Purpose	Review	Control[a]	Remarks
Software Requirements Specification	Establish software requirements to provide basis for design	SRR PDR	Class II Class I	
Functional Design Document	Establish a software functional design that satisfies specified requirements	PDR CDR SAR	Class II Class II Class I	"As-built" update
Interface Control Documents	Establish concurrence on interface requirements and design	SRR PDR CDR	Class II Class I/II Class I	I: Requirements II: Design
Test Plan	Establish testing required to verify the software	PDR CDR	Project Class I	
Test Procedures	Establish procedures for test conduct	TPR SAR	Class II Class II	
Test Report	Document the test results	SAR	Class II	
Detailed Design Document	Provide complete software design	CDR SAR	Class II Class I	"As-built" update
Operating Instructions	Describe procedures for operating the software	SAR	Class II	Update as required
Version Description Document	Describe content and capability of delivered software version	SAR	Class II	Update with each version delivery

[a]Class I changes require formal customer approval and Class II changes require project approval (see Chapter 9).

Software development documentation.

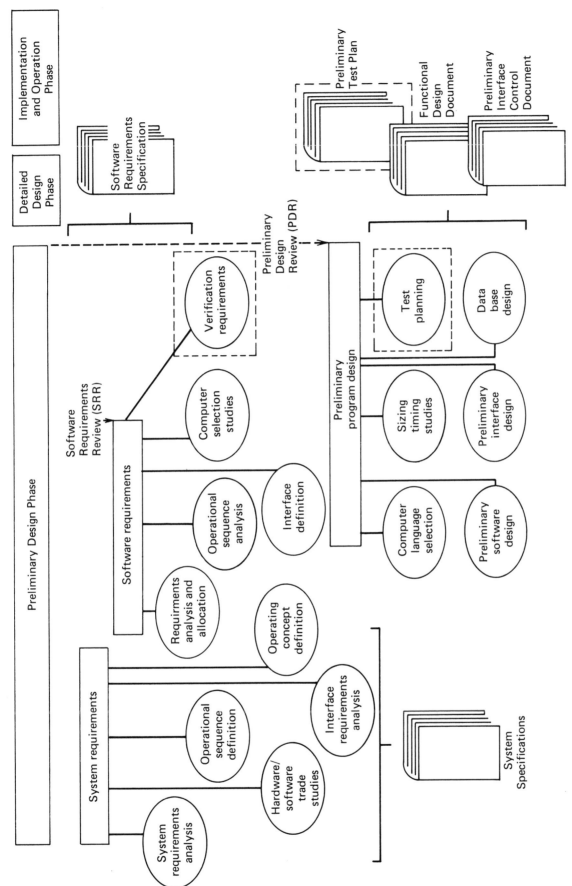

Preliminary Design Phase activities and products.

179

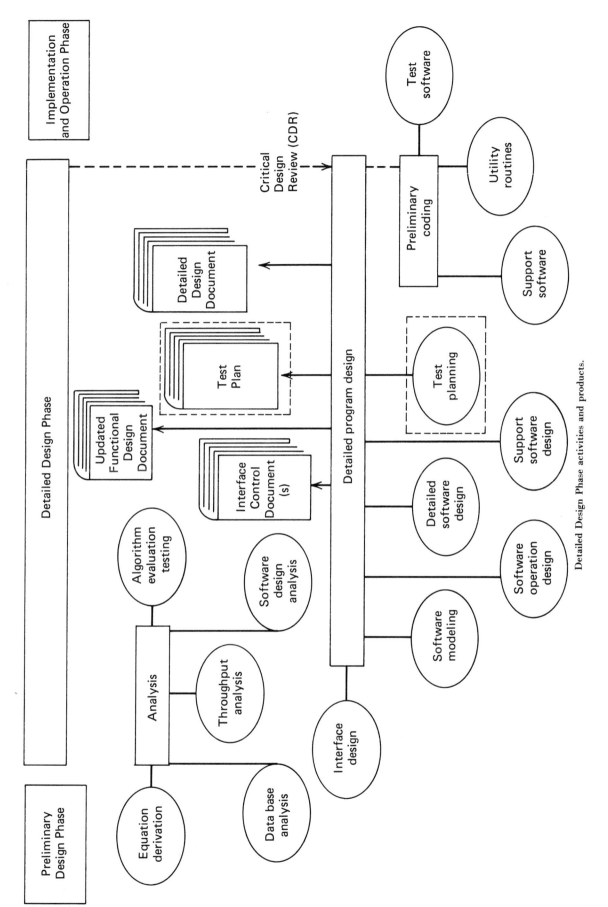

Detailed Design Phase activities and products.

181

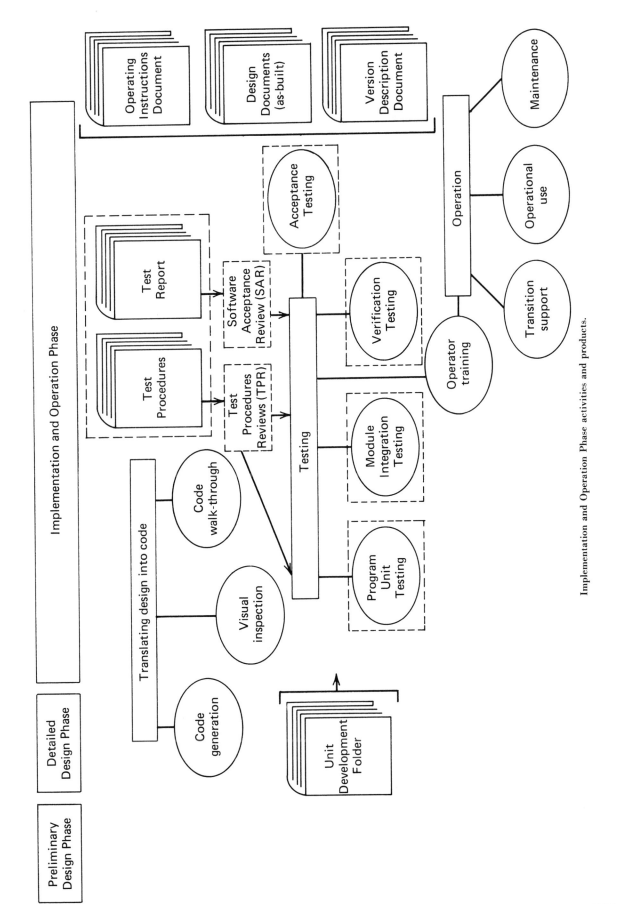

Implementation and Operation Phase activities and products.

183

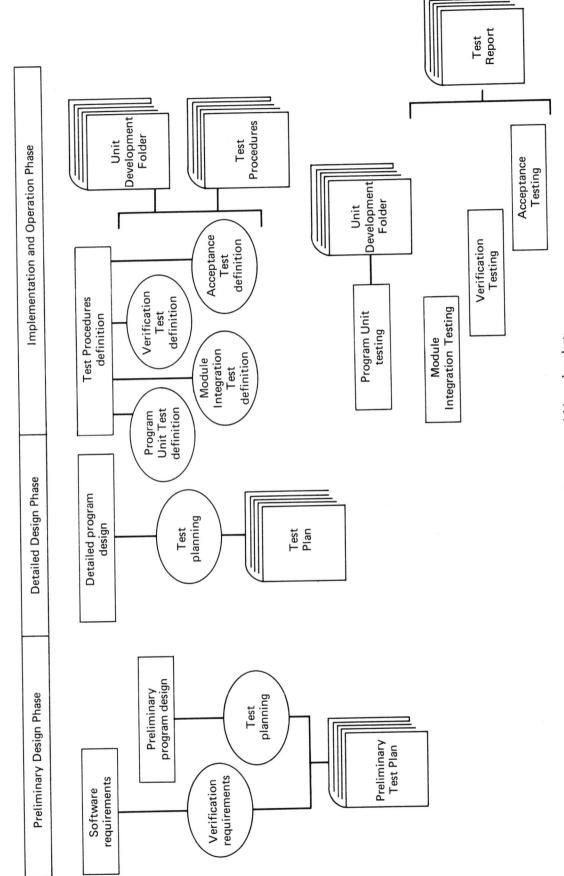

The testing process activities and products.

Test Level	Test Basis	Performed and Controlled By	Purpose
Program Unit Testing	Design	Programmer (informal)	Verify program unit logic Verify computational adequacy Verify data-handling capability Verify interfaces and design extremes Execute and verify every branch
Module Integration Testing	Design requirements Interfaces	Software development organization (formal)	Integrate program units into modules Verify modules through anticipated range of operating conditions Demonstrate that modules meet acceptance criteria Integrate modules into software system Verify software system through anticipated range of operating conditions Turn over test of software to independent test group
Verification Testing	Requirements Interfaces	Quality assurance organization (formal)	Formally verify software performance and interface requirements
Acceptance Testing	Requirements	Quality assurance organization and user (formal)	Test software end-to-end scenario Demonstrate that software satisfies the set of predetermined acceptance criteria

Software test levels.

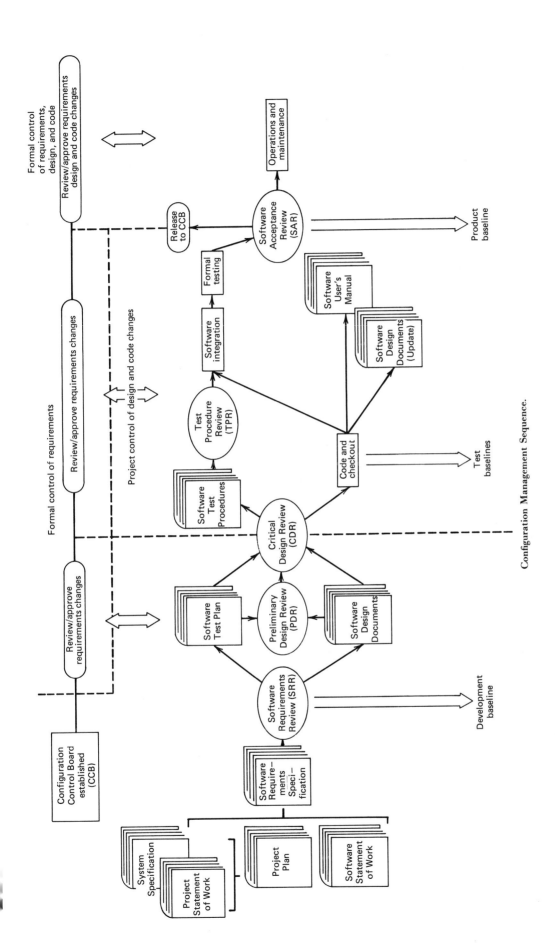

Configuration Management Sequence.

189

PURPOSE: Establish functional, performance, interface, design, and verification requirements
Provide basis for design and development of the software

Review
Software Requirements Review (SRR)

Approval
Customer
Contractor
Software
Systems engineering
Quality assurance

Control
(defined in Chapter 9)
Class II at project start
Class II after SRR
Class I after PDR

Software Requirements Specification

Contents
Interface requirements
Interface block diagram
Functional requirements
Equations (if required)
Human performance requirements
Programming requirements
Growth requirements
Data base requirements
Special test features
Verification requirements

Data Sources
System specifications
Interface specifications
System functional design
Hardware/software trade studies
Software requirements analysis

Software Requirements Specification definition.

191

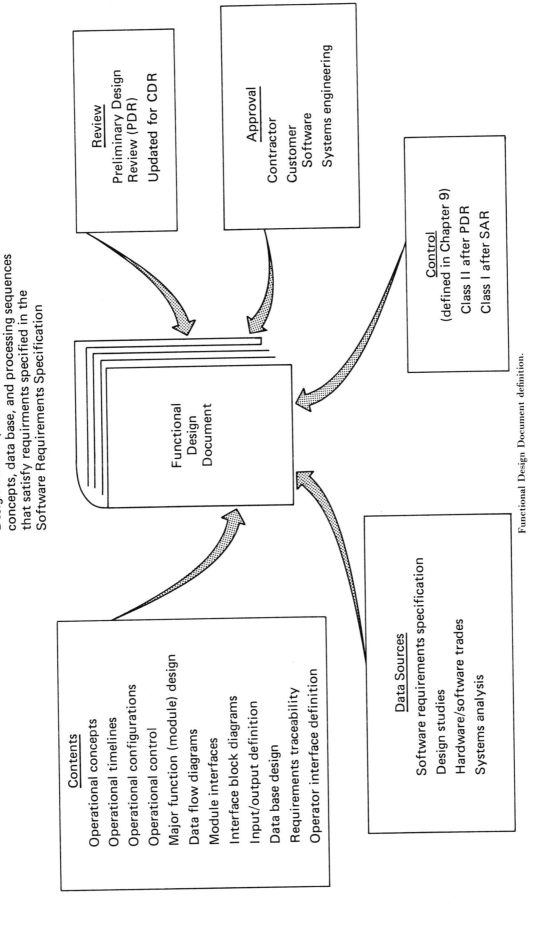

PURPOSE: Establish functional design of the software
          Design modules, interfaces, operational
          concepts, data base, and processing sequences
          that satisfy requirements specified in the
          Software Requirements Specification

Review
Preliminary Design
Review (PDR)
Updated for CDR

Approval
Contractor
Customer
Software
Systems engineering

Control
(defined in Chapter 9)
Class II after PDR
Class I after SAR

Functional
Design
Document

Contents
Operational concepts
Operational timelines
Operational configurations
Operational control
Major function (module) design
Data flow diagrams
Module interfaces
Interface block diagrams
Input/output definition
Data base design
Requirements traceability
Operator interface definition

Data Sources
Software requirements specification
Design studies
Hardware/software trades
Systems analysis

Functional Design Document definition.

193

PURPOSE: Establish concurrence of customer and development organizations on interface requirements and design

Review
Requirements at SRR
Preliminary design at PDR
Design at CDR

Approval
Customer
Interfacing organizations
Contractor
  Software
  Systems engineering
  Quality assurance

Control
(defined in Chapter 9)
Requirements
  Class I after SRR
Design
  Class II after PDR
  Class I after CDR

Interface
Control
Document

Contents
Interface requirements
  Data format
  Data content
  Data rates
  Data protocol
Interface design
  Hardware
  System software
  Applications software
  Data base

Data Sources
System specifications
Hardware specifications
Interface analysis
Interface working groups

Interface Control Document definition.

PURPOSE: Provide complete programming design sufficiently detailed for a programmer to code from with minimum additional direction

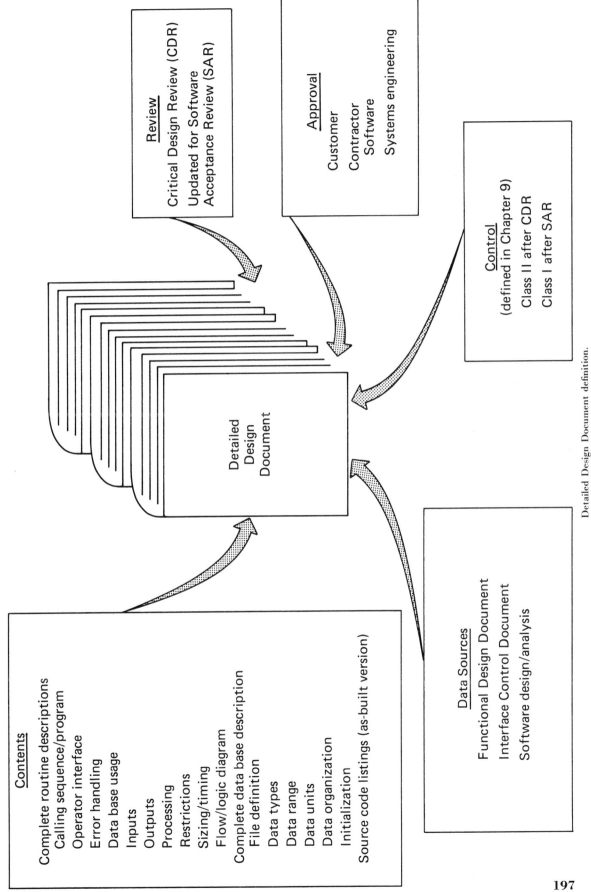

Contents

Complete routine descriptions
Calling sequence/program
Operator interface
Error handling
Data base usage
Inputs
Outputs
Processing
Restrictions
Sizing/timing
Flow/logic diagram
Complete data base description
File definition
Data types
Data range
Data units
Data organization
Initialization
Source code listings (as-built version)

Review

Critical Design Review (CDR)
Updated for Software Acceptance Review (SAR)

Approval

Customer
Contractor
Software
Systems engineering

Control
(defined in Chapter 9)
Class II after CDR
Class I after SAR

Data Sources

Functional Design Document
Interface Control Document
Software design/analysis

Detailed
Design
Document

Detailed Design Document definition.

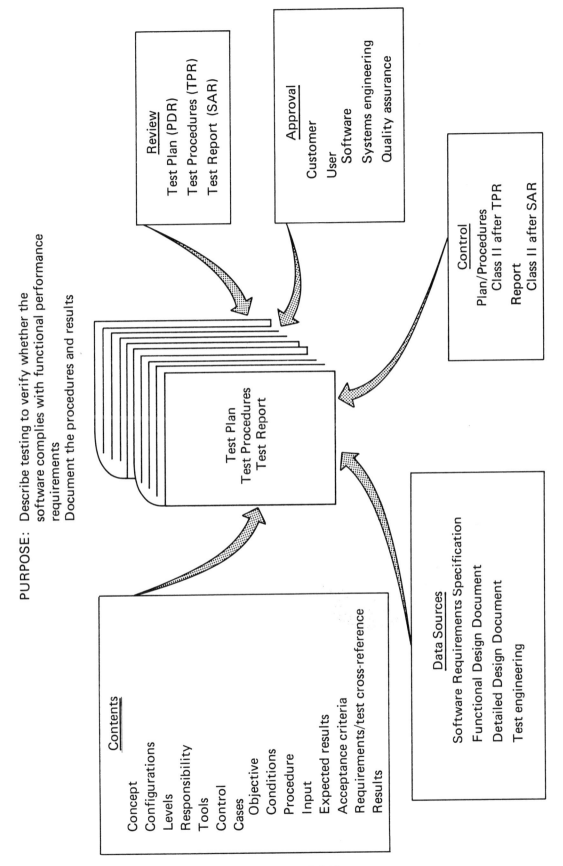

PURPOSE: Describe testing to verify whether the software complies with functional performance requirements

Document the procedures and results

Review
Test Plan (PDR)
Test Procedures (TPR)
Test Report (SAR)

Approval
Customer
User
Software
Systems engineering
Quality assurance

Control
Plan/Procedures
Class II after TPR
Report
Class II after SAR

Test Plan
Test Procedures
Test Report

Contents
Concept
Configurations
Levels
Responsibility
Tools
Control
Cases
Objective
Conditions
Procedure
Input
Expected results
Acceptance criteria
Requirements/test cross-reference
Results

Data Sources
Software Requirements Specification
Functional Design Document
Detailed Design Document
Test engineering

Test Documentation definition.

199

PURPOSE: Record software development activities
associated with a program unit
Provide basis for final as-built documentation

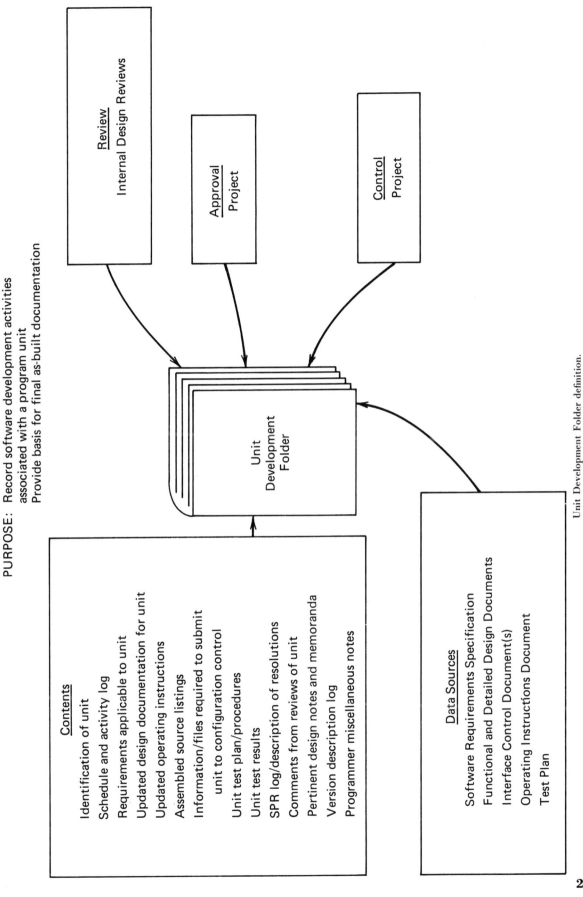

Review
Internal Design Reviews

Approval
Project

Control
Project

Unit
Development
Folder

Contents

Identification of unit
Schedule and activity log
Requirements applicable to unit
Updated design documentation for unit
Updated operating instructions
Assembled source listings
Information/files required to submit
unit to configuration control
Unit test plan/procedures
Unit test results
SPR log/description of resolutions
Comments from reviews of unit
Pertinent design notes and memoranda
Version description log
Programmer miscellaneous notes

Data Sources

Software Requirements Specification
Functional and Detailed Design Documents
Interface Control Document(s)
Operating Instructions Document
Test Plan

Unit Development Folder definition.

201

PURPOSE: Describe the computer program operating procedures

Review
Software Acceptance Review (SAR)

Approval
Customer/user
Contractor
Software
Systems engineering
Quality assurance

Control
(defined in Chapter 9)
Class II after SAR

Operating Instructions Document

Contents
Computer program operation
Equipment requirements
Supporting documents
Operator interaction
Equipment setup
Initialization
Recovery
System monitoring
Special parameters
Major functions operation
(for each function)
Purpose
Operational description
Options
Control input formats
Inputs
Outputs
Halts and recovery procedures
Limitations
Special parameters

Data Sources
Functional Design Document
Detailed Design Document
Hardware operations documents
Operations engineering

Operating Instructions Document definition.

PURPOSE: Describe the content and capability of each delivered version of a computer program

Review

Software Acceptance Review (SAR)

Each version delivery

Approval

Customer/user
Contractor
Software
Systems engineering
Quality assurance

Control
(defined in Chapter 9)

Class II after SAR

Version
Description
Document

Contents

For each version
Content
Limitations
Adaptation data
Interface compatibility
Changes
Class I
Class II
Other
Installation instructions
Program loading
Hardware configuration

Data Sources

Detailed Design Document
Listings
Configuration management records
Data base listings

Version Description Document definition.

Index

210 Index